AFRICA IN TRANSITION

AFRICA IN TRANSITION

The Journey from Traditional to Modern in Africa

George Coulter

Book Guild Publishing
Sussex, England

First published in Great Britain in 2011 by
The Book Guild Ltd
Pavilion View
19 New Road
Brighton, BN1 1UF

Typesetting in Garamond by
YHT Ltd, London

Printed in Great Britain by
CPI Group (UK) Ltd, Croydon, CR0 4YY

A catalogue record for this book is available from
The British Library.

ISBN 978 1 84624 632 6

Dedication

To many people I have lived and worked with in Africa. Though too numerous to mention individually, I remember with gratitude their ready help, long patience and good humour.

Contents

# *Acknowledgements*

I wish to thank my family for their encouragement, in particular my daughter, Dianne, for comments on the manuscript at different stages, and my grandson, Ralph, for scanning and advice on the photographs.

Every effort has been made to trace the copyright holders of all images reproduced in this book. The publishers would be pleased to hear from any we have been unable to reach in order to give full credit in any future editions.

Thanks go to the International Africa Institute for permission to reproduce as Figure 1 the map by Lawson (1972) of the lower Volta River; and to the Royal Society of South Africa for permission to reproduce as Figure 4 the map of the area covered by the Joint Fisheries Research Organisation (from Jackson 2000). I thank the family of Dr C.K. Bertram for permission to use two photographs taken in the Bangweulu Swamps in 1936-37. The rest of the photos are my own.

Special acknowledgement is given to the Northern Rhodesia Journal for valuable historical material. This journal ceased publication with Volume VI in 1965, but fortunately all issues are available in full on the internet.

Lastly, I wish to express sincere appreciation to Book Guild Publishing, for their extremely helpful assistance through the processes of publication, and for editorial criticism which has improved the text.

Introduction

This book is about changes in human culture and circumstances in Africa over the past half-century. Some of it is based on personal experience in research and development projects in West Africa (Ghana) and also the region of the Great Lakes in East and Central Africa, in particular Lake Tanganyika. Thus it has regional bias, but discussion is also extended to other parts of Africa south of the Sahara (SSA), except for the Republic of South Africa, which is a special case.

There are three parts to the book. Part I covers six projects. Part II gives a historic perspective of Central and East Africa by focusing on certain phases of history. Part III concerns the social and economic evolution of people on the move from traditional to modern lifestyles.

Part I

The projects are outlined chronologically, with the purpose of presenting circumstances and people as they appeared at the time. Development paradigms in Africa changed a lot during the period, which of course influenced personal viewpoints. The approach is not autobiographical, but rather attempts to give a picture from inside each project, reflecting working environments, mistakes and successes.

Three tribal peoples discussed were still largely traditional in lifestyle in the 1950s and 60s. They were fisherfolk who also farmed, and they are described in some detail to define their livelihood strategies and traditional mindsets. Accounts of what happened to them in later years are added.

The first project was in the Gold Coast, West Africa, 1955 – still colonial times. It was shortly to become Ghana, the second British territory in Africa to reach independence. Preparations to build a large dam on the Volta River for hydroelectric power were in train. The dam would disrupt the traditional fishery and way of life of the Tongu people living downstream, and the author was employed to make a survey of likely effects. It was found the new flow regime of the river would fundamentally alter both fishing and farming livelihoods.

A second project dealt with introducing mechanised boats, and exploring their fishing potential along part of the Ghana sea coast. The Fante people there have long fishing traditions, and it was intended to assist their transition to mechanised and commercial methods. A fishing boom followed with huge foreign aid inputs. Motorised boats multiplied, but problems arose largely from business management. A complex history followed in which the diesel-powered small boats declined, but traditional canoes improved their methods and prospered. It is a story of the growth and persistence of a near-shore artisanal fishery that, among other difficulties, has had to bear competition from modern offshore fishing fleets.

The scene shifts to Northern Rhodesia (Zambia) in 1959 and the remote Bangweulu Swamps. The specialised swamp-dwelling Unga people went about their traditional fishery in ways little different from those described by David Livingstone in 1872–73 (he died there). The author participated in an ongoing study of the fish, and of a society which gains its living in an extreme environment.

The next project was in the Zambian sector of Lake Tanganyika – the south end. This beautiful and ancient lake possesses the most diverse aquatic fauna in Africa, and its fishery is an important one. Research activities studying fish and lake dynamics are described, working with the Lunga people.

From the 1960s, foreign scientists supported by international aid agencies began working alongside those remaining from colonial times, and with African professionals as they became qualified. There was also a shift from a system in which individual researchers worked in isolation to a more centralised institutional approach. In Zambia this meant uniting the work of a UN-FAO project with that of the government fisheries department to cover all the major lakes and rivers. Various research undertakings over five years are described, including surveys and activities such as the aerial transfer of sardines from Lake Tanganyika to the new Kariba Dam on the Zambezi River.

Lastly, another UN-FAO project with government inputs is described in Burundi, at the north of Lake Tanganyika. Its five-year life (1970–75) was divided into two epochs, before and after a terrible genocide between Tutsi and Hutu peoples. Long-lasting political repercussions extended to Rwanda and the Congo. Problems for development posed by irruptions of violence are discussed in general.

These projects all concerned research and development, subjects related to the theme of this book – the transition from traditional subsistence to modern ways of life. Emergency humanitarian relief operations are distinctly different from ongoing development undertakings, although poverty, of course, figures largely in both.

Part II

Part II covers a sequence of historic phases in the Great Lakes region, especially around Lake Tanganyika; the phases characterised by exploration, slave trading, Christian evangelism, early colonialism, the first Great War and later colonial times. The author had the benefit of knowing the region well, and being acquainted with certain old inhabitants whose memories went far back. Some of these recollections are drawn upon, including ones of a distinguished African who as a boy remembered Livingstone.

Well-known names in exploration were closely associated with the lakes region in the search for the sources of the Nile. The pathways of exploration largely followed river and lake systems. Modern data throw new light on some of the hydrological problems. Lakes Tanganyika and Nyasa/Malawi were centres of the slave trade in East Africa; caravan routes to the coast passing between and across both lakes. Missionaries used Tanganyika as a highway for their work around its 1,800 km coastline. As early as 1886 they built a steamship at the shore from parts head-loaded up from the distant coast. It is a romantic, little-known story of heroic efforts defeated in the end by malaria and the tsetse fly. The lake played an important strategic role in the part of the first Great War fought in German East Africa. The Cape-to-Cairo railway was routed to pass Lake Tanganyika but never reached it, although the associated overland telegraph line did. In the 1960s, personal memories of the remarkable story of Northern Rhodesia were still accessible, from its beginnings at the turn of the twentieth century until it became Zambia.

Part III

Part III concerns the social and economic evolution of African people in the move from traditional to modern ways of life. Step-by-step development within tradition changed to the ideal of rapid modernisation, and now emphasis is placed on poverty relief. The Burundi project discussed earlier is evaluated. Although it recovered from violent interruption and achieved its material aims, and the fishery intensified, it did not succeed in establishing the mindset necessary for replacing traditional subsistence priorities with modern economic ones.

Traditional African social characteristics and implied mindsets are compared with modern ('western') attitudes by contrasting a series of ideal types. Characteristics of the three tribal subsistence peoples described in Part I are included in the comparison.

Africa has changed unevenly and in complex ways over the past half-century. Unfortunately, subsistence lifestyles of the rural majorities in sub-Saharan countries remain economically static. A significant proportion of rural people, mostly young men, have migrated to towns and cities, with urbanisation rising at a startling 5% to 7% per year. This has led to uncontrolled growth of peripheral slums. Both urban and rural development alternatives have turned out to be economic cul-de-sacs, in which standards of living for the great majority remain poor. Three salient facts hit the eye: soaring populations, stagnating agriculture and burgeoning cities without industrial growth.

Conditions of poverty in the agrarian countryside differ from those of the city, so separate chapters are devoted to rural and urban poverty. The former is examined under various headings: poverty definitions, situations where agricultural land is scarce, historic shifts in poverty type, the growing food crisis, and agricultural involution. The Millennium Villages approach of the Millennium 2000 Development Programme is outlined. General parallels are suggested, with lessons from fisheries development programmes.

Urban poverty is examined under headings of the growth of African cities, employment in them, and possible futures. According to the UN-HABITAT Programme (2008): 'During the next two decades, Africa will have to find ways of facilitating urban housing, services and livelihoods for more than twice as many urban dwellers than today. Urban conditions will crucially determine transition to modern.'

A final chapter sums up various views on the social transformation of Sub-Saharan Africa (SSA). Administrative restructuring of government functions in the 1980s and 90s ('structural adjustment'), was an initiative of international lending bodies with policies determined by the so-called Washington Consensus. It affected ordinary lives deeply. Since then, certain countries have simply not grown economically, and foreign aid to them has served merely as a holding operation. Of the 'bottom billion' of the world's population, those living on less than 1 US$ per day, 70% are in Sub-Saharan Africa. Economists stress the importance of poverty traps in retarding progress; another opinion is that Africa chiefly suffers from chronic lack of human, societal and institutional capital.

A theme of this book is that gaps in cultural mindsets have presented fundamental barriers to modernisation. In subsistence societies development is chiefly about social and cultural change. Persistence of tradition raises concrete issues retarding reform. Assimilating modern understanding probably means changing cultural foundations, and this is the most difficult element in development.

Social economics have an important role to play in understanding traditions centred around community welfare and survival, and in helping to change them – probably more important than econometrics. A principal question is whether transformation is to be into the competitive individualistic materialism of the market world, or to a way of life that permits retaining the human-centred character of traditional Africa with its concern for harmony within community. Related to this are the questions of whether foreign aid can help cities, where most Africans will live within two decades, to become economically productive, or should foreign aid rather be concentrated on helping to build viable local communities in a rural background.

PART I
Sundry Projects

1

The Volta River

Prelude

There was still an Empire in 1954 when I first enquired at the Colonial Office for a job. To my young mind The Empire was a permanent institution, like the Bank of England. I assumed it would continue to offer opportunities. I was a biology graduate with an interest in aquatic organisms, preferring field to office work and with a desire to see the world – Africa in particular. The interview in London was reassuring on the whole, but I came away from Great Smith Street rather daunted by the great reach of the organisation to uttermost parts of the earth. My experience did not seem relevant. When there was no sequel – not even a 'Dear Sir, Thank you for coming' letter, it was not unexpected. But the idea remained.

I took a teaching post as biology master in a grammar school. For two terms I entered school life with as much enthusiasm as I could drum up – which unfortunately grew less and less. On the very last day of the school year, when everyone was packing up for summer holidays, a small OHMS envelope arrived from London. It asked for a quick decision on the offer of a fisheries officer post in the Gold Coast in West Africa – two contracts covering three years. This was neither a steady prospect nor the part of Africa I wanted. But it was enough. I telegrammed acceptance, and then had to face the headmaster with rudely short notice. It was not a happy parting Colleagues were nicer, though some could not help murmuring about 'the white man's grave', which was probably how many thought of West Africa then.

Was it wise to take one's wife on first appointment? Sun-stroke was not so much feared – pith helmets had become obsolete – but a list of nasty things were mentioned in a Colonial Office pamphlet sent with their letter. It gave the impression they were part of tropical life: malaria (daily prophylactics and mosquito boots), bilharzia, onchocerciasis, elephantiasis, blackwater fever, etc. A snake bite outfit was to be carried (razor, tourniquet and potassium permanganate). Rather ominously, conditions required a 'tour of duty' to be only eighteen months, then leave of four months in a temperate climate was obligatory. Basic house accommodation would be provided, but it might be isolated and one should expect to be away from home often (folding safari bed recommended).

Decisive choices on one's future are not always arrived at rationally when one is young. Deeper motives must be at work to overcome common sense and the incentive to survive by sticking to well-known ways. Perhaps a deep orientation in the sub-conscious mind may push one to take an eccentric plunge. Which I did.

The lower Volta

The house looked over sloping bush to a wide turgid river. Hundreds of miles to the north its tributaries began at the fringe of the great desert. Gathering strength through the rain forest of Ashanti, it descended through gorges and then came quietly over the last 100 kilometres to the sea. In front of me a canoe moved slowly near shore against the current of the river in flood.

I'd rather expected a house of mud walls and thatch, but this was modern and newly built. It stood alone with no sight of other habitations, surrounded by long grass and bush. I knew the house of the District Commissioner (DC) was not far off, and somewhere near was the small village of Sogankope. The wide-eaved asbestos roof of my house drained to a reservoir tank beneath the verandah – the domestic rainwater supply. Glass louvre windows were dimmed by mosquito gauze. The rooms were bare except for basic, government-issue furniture. Inside, the sticky October heat was about the same as outside in the shade.

And all around was still. Yet it was a silence full of sounds that formed a constant background; sounds made by permanent inhabitants. Cicadas stridulated harshly, loudest when the day was hottest. Late afternoon was full of hoopoe calls, staccato cries declining in pitch to drawn-out, melancholy notes that were shortly taken up by a distant mate. As evening came, rhythmic drumming began, and human voices shouting and singing. Hesitant at first with slow beats, the drums settled to a steady rumble that went on late into the night. Along with the whine of insects, a cacophony of frogs and muted calls of night birds, they were background sounds as regular as the crickets by day. I realised these were conversations, species talking to species in their own languages. Life throbbed with incessant communication at all times. But I was a stranger to the discourse and had none of my own kind to talk to. By day I was busy, but at night recent events leading to this point had time to sink in.

My boss in the capital, Accra, Chief Fisheries Officer F.R. Johnson (FRJ) seemed an austere man, not given to trivial conversation. In fact he proved sensitive and considerate. He was quite single-mindedly dedicated to his work, and had served in Accra over twenty years, which showed in a complexion tinged yellow from malarial pills. On my arrival he put me up at his house for a week, during which it became clear this was less for job instruction than to give me a short course in Expected Behaviour – the dos and don'ts of living in a British Colony, the Gold Coast 1955.

Clearly, I had much to learn. There were at least two cultures to come to grips with: the bewildering teeming one in Accra containing various regional tribes and languages, and the hardly less unfamiliar European one with its own attitudes, dress and behaviour. FRJ indicated I should not be seen riding a bicycle; he would get me a repayable loan for a car. I learned much in a short time, including how to interpret FRJ's expressive ways of saying 'Oh' in different pitches that went with changing altitudes of his eyebrows. It could mean surprise, pleasure, distaste, sadness and sarcasm – setting the tone of our conversation

Few work details had been given me in London, other than that the job was concerned with the lower Volta River where a great dam was proposed for the near future. The notion of harnessing the Volta for power and industrial development had long been in the mind of the colonial authorities. As part of the preparations, the Gold Coast Fisheries Department was asked to survey the lower river and its seasonal floodplains, as the way of life of the river people, the Tongu, might be changed drastically by the dam. In a nutshell, my small part in the great project was to investigate the fishery and lifestyle of the river people, in order to predict likely consequences of changing the river flow.

Sounds straightforward enough, but in fact little knowledge existed on the biology of the river, the fishery, or the economy of the Tongu on the Lower Volta.[1] An economic study was being done by the university, and knowledge of the district had been accumulated for years by the administration, but not of the kind needed to predict a big change in the river environment. FRJ said, 'First, get to know the area. You have about 50 miles [80 km] of river to cover, but mostly you'll be moving around the floodplains on foot or by canoe. Spend as much time as possible in the villages and with the fishermen. For the river, there will be a boat and outboard engine. You'll have a senior Fish Scout and two men.' Thus, lots of personal contact and little technology. So I set off in my new car east towards Togoland, crossing the

Sundown on the Volta River at Sogankope

The Volta at low level in the dry season

Volta ferry at Sogankope where I was to live. The DC and his wife were the only other Europeans there.

It is worth glancing at the interesting history of the Volta River. Its story has parallels with many other parts of the coast of Africa. The notorious West African slave trade involving various European countries and their New World colonies had gone on for about 350 years. The Volta with its extensive tributaries to the Muslim north was doubtless a major slave route. Long before that, the upper Volta reaches were linked to the ancient trans-

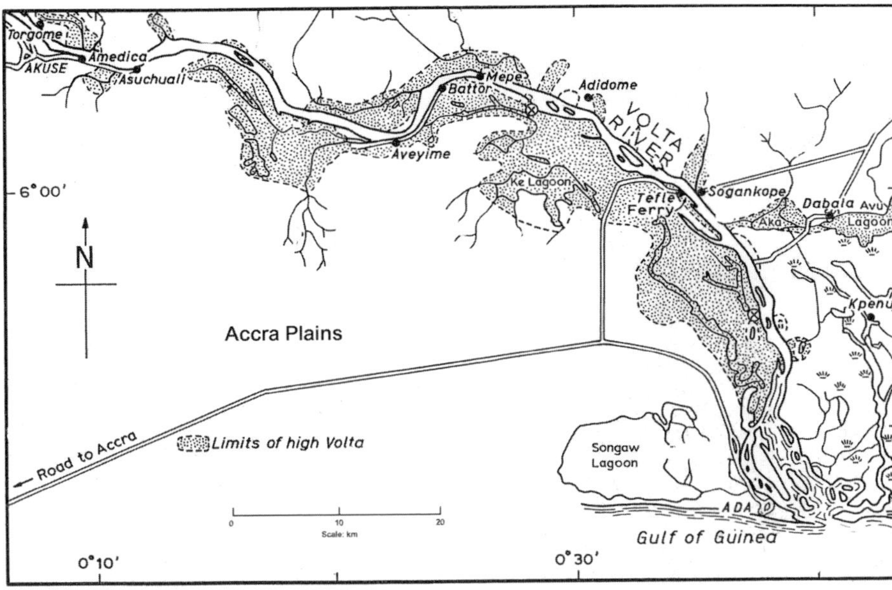

Figure 1. The Lower Volta River downstream from the Volta Dam site in 1956. From Lawson (1972)

Sahara slave trade (which Herodotus reports was established by the fifth century BC). And as part of that trade, salt from evaporation pans near Ada at the Volta mouth (Figure 1) was perhaps transported north (it still was in the nineteenth and early twentieth centuries).

Slavery preoccupied the minds of Victorians when they thought of Africa; most saw it as the main obstacle to extending European civilisation. The immediate difficulty for explorers, missionaries and traders was to find ways of penetrating inland. River and lake slave routes were the most feasible means – as Livingstone found with the Zambezi and Shire Rivers, Lakes Malawi and Tanganyika, and Stanley with Lakes Victoria, Tanganyika and the Congo River. Early in the nineteenth century the travels of Mungo Park had shown the potential of West African rivers as routes inland.

The earliest British commercial interests were confined to a coastal strip less than 100 km wide, but in the nineteenth century expansion by the warlike Ashanti tribe in the interior began to threaten these interests. A series of wars with the Ashanti took place until the 1870s, when Britain established the coastal region as a crown colony with Accra as its capital. But it took until 1902 for the Ashanti kingdom to be fully pacified. It was annexed along with country beyond, the so-called Northern Territories (NTs), to form the Gold Coast (now Ghana).

The first steam launch on the Volta, the *Eyo* of 250 tons, passed over the formidable bar at the river mouth in 1868. Soon after, four British steam warships went up to Akuse, near the first great rapids (see Figure 1) to transport troops for an intended flanking attack on the Ashanti capital, Kumasi. Interestingly the largest of these, a 250-ton former pleasure steamer from Lough Erne in Ireland named *The Lady of the Lake*, brought the explorer H.M. Stanley who was on a short visit to West Africa, some 40 km upstream. So, if I had been standing at Sogankope in 1873 I might have glimpsed the great man.

A trading era began on the Volta in the late nineteenth century. Many of the traders were unscrupulous toughs (nicknamed POR for Palm Oil Ruffians), representing a generation between the wholesale slavers of earlier days and more respectable twentieth-century merchants. River trading centred on Ada, and new steam launches were introduced. Demand for Ada salt extended hundreds of miles upriver. Some trading companies survived well into the middle of the twentieth century. One of the more distinguished of these was the Dumas family, founded by the grandson of the author of *The Three Musketeers*. With the Volta River Transport Scheme in 1901 the river was busy for the first 100 km up to Akuse, but there the great rapids at Kpong and Senchi meant that goods had to be taken onwards by canoe or portage.

Ironically these turbulent rapids flowing through a narrow gorge, the chief obstacle for river steamers, were to become the focal point of the next era on the river. In 1915 the potential of the gorge as a dam site caught the eye of a geologist surveying the river by canoe, Albert (later Sir Albert) Kitson. By 1925 he had developed the idea into a hydro-power proposal, linked to processing local deposits of bauxite into aluminium. The project was taken up in 1939 by men with a financial base in South African mining. However, it was a firm of British engineers (Halcrows) who produced the report 'The Volta River Project' in 1951. The British government was willing to meet the majority of the cost – the rest was to come from the government of the Gold Coast and aluminium companies – and they appointed a final Preparatory Commission to study all aspects, including human and environmental factors. It reported back in 1954 with an estimated cost over 40% higher. About this time I became a humble cog in the planning machine, recruited to fulfil one of the studies recommended by the Commission.

'Get to know the area'

It being the dry season, I covered nearby bits of floodplain by car, cautiously bumping along foot tracks and avoiding boggy patches by intuition – something like the thin-ice instinct Scandinavians are said to have. Mostly I went on foot with my assistants: middle-aged Kansu and the two helpers togged out in khaki uniform and solar helmets. I never really got to know Kansu in the year spent working with him. Though informative about local customs and behaviour, he remained reserved and watchful. FRJ said he'd been a businessman (and in later political times he became rich.) None of them liked long walks, so until I learned where villages and fishing activities were concentrated, I was taken pretty well where they pleased.

A visit to a village usually went as follows: approaching by footpath through trees one first encountered children, whose shouts of *yevoo* (white man) brought hordes of others. People in the first huts often went back in shyly, while others stared curiously. Whites were rare except for routine visits of the administration or of a missionary father. First to the chief, slowly preceded by Kansu who took care to call greetings to all and sundry, which were responded to with interest. I was led to a chair or box under a tree or in a porch, while Kansu found the chief, giving him time to wrap up in his colourful kente cloth. My two juniors kept off the growing crowd, the size of which varied depending on how many were out cultivating or fishing. Then the chief and some elders approached formally, and there was handshaking and a welcoming ritual.

A slow conversation took place, Kansu interpreting, on fishing, the crops, the weather, sickness, etc. A pause, and I would say my piece. If it was the first visit, I'd introduce talk about the Volta Dam. Few questions came. What I'd said would sink in and be discussed among themselves; later visits brought up lots of questions. There must be no hurry to leave, but when pauses in our talk became longer I stood up. Customary farewells and smiles followed, the hum of the crowd increased, and we went our way at the head of a trail of children. If I had given notice of the visit, there were usually plenty of people present. The elders were polite and reserved. One sensed they were friendly and felt keenly their curiosity and isolation.

At one large and well-kept village I accompanied the DC on his routine visit. Having little time to talk myself, I arranged to come back, and asked if I might bring a camera. They took me seriously, because when I returned at a set time the chief and elders were dressed and ready for the photograph. They made a colourful group in traditional garb beneath the ceremonial umbrella, the chief seated on his stool of office holding a short ceremonial sword – it seemed an ancient piece – while his ebony staff of office was in the hand of the 'fishing master'. The group included the religious adviser ('ju-ju man'). They listened quietly to the account of my study and the proposed dam, but obviously could not imagine a man-made phenomenon great enough to transform their river.

Village chief and elders

Certain fundamental questions were growing in my mind. I was clearly not going to cover the area like this. Most river villages on my stretch up to the dam site (see Figures 1 & 2) were out of reach unless I made walks of several days. Hiring paddlers and a canoe on the swift river had been futile. A speedy boat was vital, and a floating dock to cope with rises and falls of the river.

Patterns of life in the villages were dictated by fishing and farming seasons. People took their tempo from the river. It was rather like the Nile story – the annual rise covered extensive floodplains; water released organic matter lying on the ground and it deposited mud. When it receded the refreshed land was cultivated or grazed by cattle. Most fishing took place as the floods receded. In the low-water season when the plains dried out, other kinds of fishing continued in the river itself, including diving for clams. Keeping in touch with all this was going to be a big job.

Another problem: how could one explain to the Tongu people what was going to happen to the river? Should I even try? In tribal memory the river had always flowed with more or less the same inevitable annual cycle. It must have seemed, as I told my story, that to question this perpetual regime and say it would be interrupted and controlled in some way, was madness (the story of King Canute came to mind). Indeed, their faces showed obvious incredulity. They could hardly be blamed. This was the first big hydro-dam in Africa, so there were no precedents to mention or pictures to show.

A third problem was getting close enough to comprehend village life when I did not speak Ewe (pronounced eh-weh). Some village youths had fluent simple English from elementary school, and a minority of these wrote it passably well. Could I perhaps recruit a dozen or two intelligent youngsters, post them round the villages, and get weekly reports of what was

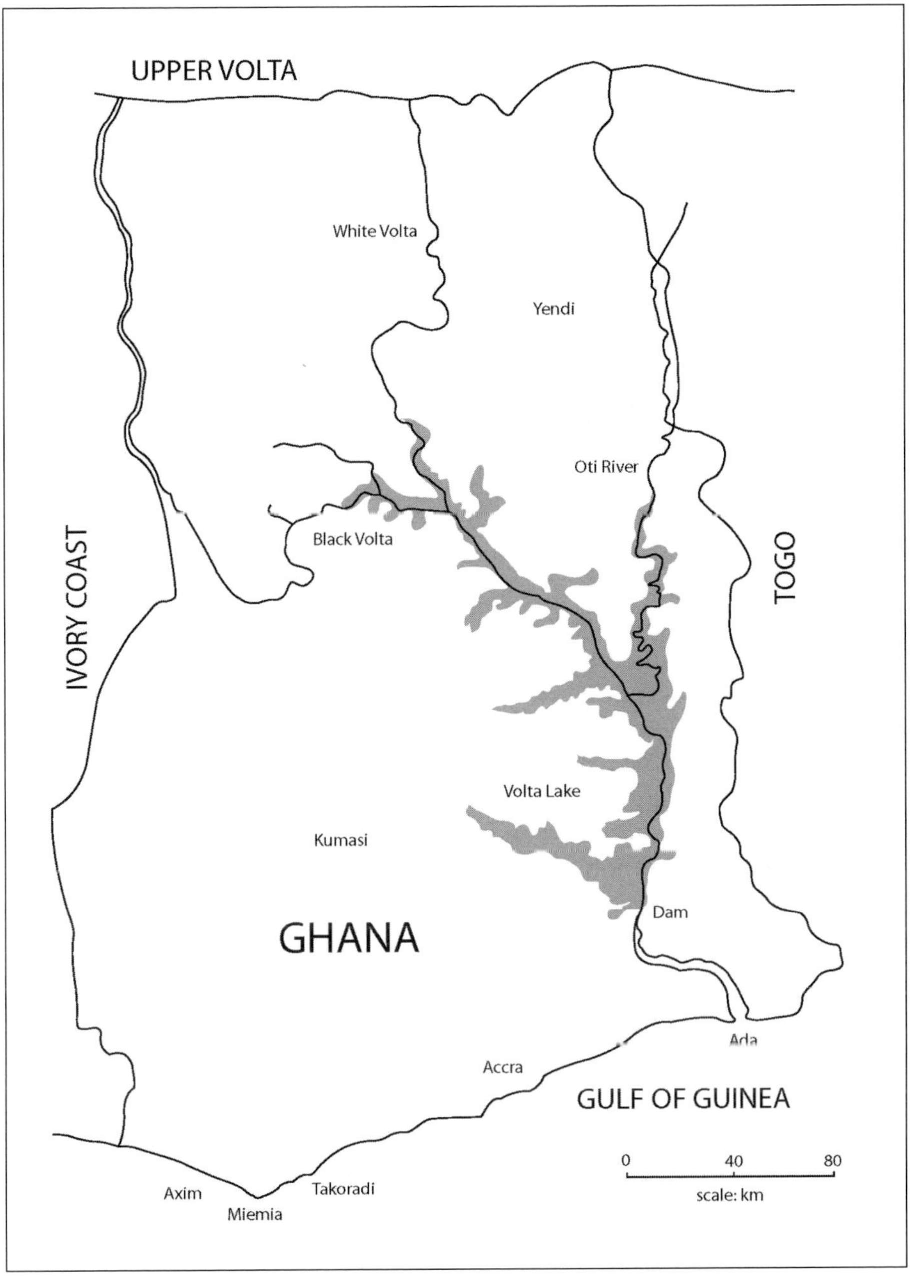

Figure 2. Ghana, showing Volta River and Volta Lake (shaded area).

happening? They would be my eyes and ears. Did such potential exist? Kansu said yes, an abundance of jobless 'Standard-6' youths had been produced by schools in the past decade or two who would jump at the chance. About this time I met Maurice Hewson, an experienced DC, who'd been engaged by the Commission to advise on social matters pertaining to the dam. He supported my idea with FRJ, who agreed to find wages, 'provided, Coulter, you get round to check them often, or you'll have only fairy stories to show'.

Home on the river

Now, at the end of the first month, my new wife was to arrive in Accra. One could actually meet the plane on the tarmac in those days. Margaret descended in a smart buttoned-up Donegal-tweed suit, and gasped at the heat. Only six weeks had gone by since our marriage, but I felt I already had one foot in another world – and I hoped very much she'd like it. At Nellie Johnson's home we had a very English tea and cakes. Margaret said, 'But it's just like home.' She was in for a shock.

Had we ever set up home in Ireland, even briefly, there might have been backward glances and regrets for comforts left behind. As it was, we had to start with what existed at Sogankope, and Margaret did her best. We possessed no pictures or ornaments, and never even got around to fitting window curtains. Furniture was serviceable basic issue, but at least new and clean. Margaret insisted from the beginning on cooking herself, despite lack of experience. Our cook/house-help, Kwaku, kept a fiercely hot wood stove in an out-kitchen, where he boiled things and washed up. There was no electricity, but we had a tabletop kerosene cooker and pressure lamps. Fortunately, our constitutions were strong, and stomach upsets came from unfortunate choices of local resources rather than Margaret's lack of skill.

Kwaku and Margaret started a garden, the only reward from which came in the rains. Pineapples flourished briefly, but monkeys raided them as they ripened. Though we could not know it, this unpromising patch was to be the first of many gardens Margaret would create over the next 50 years, some of them lovely. Gardens are of course a special grace, but perhaps particularly important to have in Africa. Margaret adopted a pet monkey, 'Murphy', of which she grew fond. He had freedom of the house, and would perch on her shoulder, but at night he was chained to a perch outside and there met a sad end. I had regarded the bees in the roof as just bees and ignored them. But the African wild bee is a formidable animal. When swarming they attack, and multiple stings can be fatal.

In his place we got a Siamese cat; distinguished by having its own mind and a tendency to climb. For FRJ's first visit, Margaret had prepared carefully. All dishes were laid, and she pushed the roast chicken through a small serving hatch to the dining room. While occupied with the salad, the cat fed on the roast chicken at the other side of the hatch. In panic, Margaret salvaged some slices of chicken and served it with a straight face. A trivial incident perhaps, but important to us because we wanted to give our first visitor a good impression, and show we had successfully settled in.

Life became a little more difficult when Margaret became pregnant and morning sickness and hormonal moods set in. But we were fully occupied and Africa became ever more absorbing. October had been a good point in the natural cycle to start work. The river rose to 'bankful' in September–October, then overflowed into watercourses and then on to the surrounding plains. When levels started to decline, intensive fishing and farming would begin – the busiest time of year. To avoid leaving Margaret alone at night, we did some trips upriver together. She'd been a nurse, but quickly saw more naked people than ever in her life, for men lined the river bank in the evening to soap and splash their well-developed bodies. In a canoe one had to be prepared that someone might relieve himself over the side.

Most of the lower Volta region then was remote to a degree now difficult to imagine. The road to Accra, 120 km away, was largely unsurfaced, and corrugated. Transport to the city for local people was on open trucks and they were not many. Villages were connected by footpaths, which in the rains and months of flood were difficult. Paddling a canoe upriver in the flood was laborious, but a few big trading canoes were assisted by sail. Motor-driven boats were just the DC's launch, a little mission boat (which I envied for its speed) and my own skiff; the only public transport was a slow barge of the United Africa Company that went up and down river on alternate days. Inhabitants seemed to live local lives on just this short stretch of river, rarely travelling far inland.

On trips, we stayed for overnight stops in government 'rest-houses' of whitewashed mud brick, each with a caretaker who gave some help in the house. One such man was asked to 'please drain these dishes', and next day they were found neatly lined up in the smelly drain outside. Our senses of humour in exasperating conditions could differ. For instance, one rest-house had a four-poster bed with mosquito net hung from the posts. The place smelled sordidly of bats (one of the worst smells in Africa, and the reason no one spends long under mango trees where they roost). Tired on arrival, we

A trading canoe under sail on the Volta River

extinguished the lamp and got into the bed which immediately collapsed, bringing down not only mosquito net and bedposts but loads of accumulated bat manure. Margaret was amused.

My motor boat in a floating dock

On monthly shopping trips we stayed in the Accra Club, then a venerable institution with rules and traditions. It was a friendly place with polo field, tennis courts, cricket pitch, the sea nearby. The original wooden building was said to have been imported from India. Nearby stood Christiansborg Castle, a Danish fort from slaving times and now the seat of the Governor. Friendly, but formal. Dress for dinner, and at weekends the police band would play Gilbert and Sullivan tunes or military airs and marches. The dining room had the atmosphere of a distinguished, long-established restaurant. Waiters in white waistcoats, pantaloons and red cummerbunds, wearing tasselled fezzes, bustled around widely spaced tables. Occasionally one of the diners would pop up as his particular regimental march was played. Unfortunately Monday began for us at dawn, despite strong temptation to overstay, an early start being necessary to avoid queuing for the Sogankope ferry in the roasting sun.

I was glad to have glimpsed the old Club more or less as it had been for a long era. Europeans were then a pretty homogeneous lot, mostly civil service with some police and medical types. There were some Indians and Syrians in business, not many Africans – a predictable and settled, apparently congenial, society where rank and race counted. Soon it would be replaced by the multi-racial assemblages now the norm in Africa, with few expats, most transient, and a majority of Africans. I suppose no one at the club – even those in the mainstream of affairs at Government House – anticipated so complete a transformation.

Security

We lived peacefully and I believe safely. However, one night drumming suddenly ceased and next day there was a palpable feeling of trouble in the air. No one turned up for work and few people were to be seen about. FRJ phoned to ask if all was well with us, and I told him the silence was making us a little uneasy. He mentioned he thought police were on the way. Another quiet night, and in the morning I set off up the river to look around and shortly came upon a large canoe near the shore, paddled by a single man. It contained bodies. I returned home.

There was nothing more. We occupied ourselves around the house, and within a week drumming started up again. Kansu and the others said little, but gradually revealed that a fishing expedition to the north had unexpectedly returned to exact retribution on certain persons who had moved into their possessions. Kansu said 'wife palaver'. Vengeance must have been swift, for the parties had vanished again.

This brief episode of violence seemed completely out of keeping with the quiet assured surroundings, the friendliness of the villages and general order of things. When alone, I had not even locked the house door. One was too vulnerable to hope to put up any effective physical defence. There were no local police. The DC and his wife in their house were in the same position. I saw we lived trusting in established peacefulness. But what underlay such an assumption of law and order?

The absence of official force was normal and intentional. Government had to be by consensus; it was the way the system worked. In the event of serious non-cooperation or rebellion, squads of police or army could be called upon, but that was the last resort and rarely used. Obviously much depended on the good sense and integrity of the locals, as well as the character and judgement of the District Officer. Out of a system of this kind (I refer only to English-speaking dependencies, the French and Portuguese had their own variations) arose the mystique of imperialism – which obviously helped things along. Far away was a Governor and beyond him an imperial government, and the Queen ruled over all.

At local level the DC was the Queen's man. Though we did not see much of each other, I felt familiar with his type. He fitted the category of ex-service students I'd known at university. Separated by less than a decade from the other students, they were far older in experience and maturity. The DC's job in the district was administration of justice and of a small bureaucracy devoted to improving facilities – roads, schools, health clinics and so on – in a step-by-step process of consultation and improvement. Essentially the 'pax Britannica' worked by progress within the local tradition, and on a small budget; a pragmatic system that enabled millions in such colonies to live out their lives in conditions better than previously.

When we came into the picture there had been over 70 years of colonial rule, at least near the coast. There were very few European 'settlers' in West Africa of the kind found in South and East Africa; rather foreigners tended to have been traders or import–export agents, some of whom stayed for life. The first half of the twentieth century had seen a *modus vivendi* established under nationwide laws, the modalities of which consisted of indirect rule through traditional chiefs and their counsellors (the 'dual mandate' system). Provinces and Districts were fixed taking ethnic entities into account as far as possible. In the Gold Coast there were at least seven major tribes and languages. Courts were held around each District, sometimes in the open air, presided over by a District Officer assisted by local advisors and assessors. Uniform law was dispensed, but it had to be in terms understandable by the people and flexible enough where possible to take into account local customs and circumstances. Cases would be heard in public, judgement given, and the opinions of local advisers and assessors taken as to punishment. The case was recorded, and the court moved on.

Where did newcomers like us fit in? Well, assistance by technical specialists in government departments (medicine, agriculture, forestry, fisheries, etc.) dated mostly from the late 1940s or the 50s. Until then DCs were kingpins in all fields, and even afterwards often behaved as though they still were, causing a certain friction thereby. Christian missions of numerous persuasions did social work – schools and health care. One can see now that while individual administrators and missionaries were mostly of high personal quality, the system itself was becoming outdated. Mass education, radios, and other paraphernalia of modern times were inconsistent with isolation and tribal tradition. We had entered near the end of the old regime, and were privileged to have seen it working.

Nevertheless, the brief incident of violence made us aware one did not live in a utopia where order could be taken for granted. In my enquiries it helped that I was obviously confused with the administration and regarded in a familiar light. As traditional fishing had always been self-regulated in customary ways, I was not associated with any management measures.

Fishing

The 'recorders'

Kansu duly produced his Standard-6 'recorders', as we decided to call them. All were capable of writing me a report on lined foolscap each week. We held the first basic classes under a tree, and then they were posted out around the villages. Some turned out to be unsuitable, some could not settle and had to be moved to a different village, but before long we had a routine going and the 'fairy stories' started to come in.

I wish I had kept those untidy, revealing sheets. My instructions were to take notice of anything significant going on the villages, especially what pertained to fishing. But village life is very dull, so I received a mishmash of events – ceremonies, funerals, visitors, scandal and gossip, plus personal flights of imagination. Among all this was indeed relevant information on current fishing and farming activity. So now my visits to villages took on a different character. In each I spent time with my young recorder, discussing his latest report and events for the next one. I went with them to sites of fishing and farming, and met many villagers. So it was possible to follow the recorders' stories with my own eyes, and a picture of activities in the annual cycle began to emerge.

Similar annual floodplain fisheries have now been described from many parts of the continent. Tropical floodplains are among the most productive waters on earth. For a few months there is a great burst of productivity as fertilising nutrients are released from dried vegetation and animal dung, boosting plankton and water weeds. Fish move out over the floodplain and spawn, and the young grow quickly in the cover of aquatic vegetation. When the waters recede, fish predators reap their harvest of young-of-the-year prey concentrated in shallows.

This is also the time that humans take their toll. On the Volta floodplains the main fishing method was to move fences of bamboo or papyrus to concentrate fish. Mounds of tree branches had been heaped up in the water beforehand and fish took cover in these. Each mound was surrounded by a

Men moving bamboo fencing to concentrate fish in traps

The *atidza* method – fish being scooped out of the trap

fence and men moved in, threw out the branches, and scooped out the densely packed fish with nets and baskets. It was called *atidza* fishing. It required a party of people working together in a communal food-gathering operation. The Tongu made all the gear themselves. Supplementing *atidzas* were many other traditional methods – basket traps, hook-and-line and fishing spears.

After the floodplains had drained, the river continued to fall, and from January sandbanks started to emerge and the water became clearer. Finally the river was a slow, but still wide flow between high, eroded banks. Then two kinds of fishing continued, seine-netting and diving for clams.

Groups of men could be seen wading waist-deep hauling ropes. Nets were pulled to shore, with catches mostly of catfish bearing sharp spines. I soon got to know the different groups. One man, Siame, with shoulders and arms strongly muscled, occasionally swam over to my boat for a chat and I introduced him to nylon twine. With a smile he looped it in calloused hands and tried to snap it, but only after exerting his great muscles did he succeed. I gave him the roll for patching his net, and in consequence next time had to show him nylon non-slip knots.

In odd shallows the men had circles of stout stakes driven into the river bottom. These were traps for manatees, a seal-like vegetarian mammal, relative of the dugongs of South America. Weed was placed in the middle as bait, and a manatee entering through a funnel-shaped gap had difficulty getting out – just like lobster pots. I never saw the animal, but was advised 'he good for eat if bury him in sand till he stink small'.

Women clam divers on the lower Volta

At this time the lower river was crowded with women. About two thousand dived for clams (*Egeria radiata*), each from her own small dug-out. The natural distribution of these clams was confined to the lower stretch of river between Tefle and Akuse (see Figure 1). Their life cycle depended on

Processing clam shells to make lime

Sorting clams beside the river

increased salinity at this time of year when low river levels permitted sea water to penetrate further upstream. I was the object of teasing curiosity by the divers, but had to keep my distance as, for reasons of modesty, they quickly shifted to the other side of their canoes when I approached.

At the back of my mind I wondered about crocodiles. They were abundant in places further up the Volta. But the women told me there was only one in the lower river, and they knew where he lived. 'In any case,' they said, 'we don't worry, for he will only take someone who has done evil,' I thought, How does the croc know? Perhaps it was wise enough to leave them alone; becoming a fetish enabled it to grow old in peace.

By weighing clam catches at several sandbanks, it appeared a woman could average four and a half tons per season. I also measured growth rings on shells. Growth seemed important when I noticed the women frequently 'transplanted' some of their catch to shallow water near the river shore, marking the clam beds with sticks. Whether clams grew faster in these places, as they said, or were put there merely for convenient storage was uncertain. The women smoked some of their catch, and traded it in markets. Empty clam shells were processed to make lime. Deep strata of shells in some eroded river banks were probably ancient middens – perhaps indicating the clam fishery was historically old.

The women's market

At any rate, it was entirely a woman's business, which is unusual in that men predominate in fishing in Africa though women have roles in processing and trading. Many even migrated from their villages to temporary camps close to the river. Clams formed a significant part of the Tongu domestic economy, as a household food and a source of cash. The women's operations made the river quite a social place between January and June. As mothers dived their children played on the river bank. One was rarely out of sight of

Children on the river bank

groups of canoes or the sound of the diver's chatter across the water.

Woman with head-load of firewood

Far upstream

In the same months many of the men departed on a fishing migration to far tributaries in the Northern Territories (NTs) to earn money for household extras by catching fish for sale. There were possibly many motives such as saving for marriage or to build a house. At home in the villages money was a rarity. As well, the absence of the men meant that a sizable part of the population was maintaining itself elsewhere during a relatively lean time of year.

To follow the activities upstream I travelled by road several hundred kilometres to the Oti River – a branch of the upper Volta (see Figure 2) – crossing the confluence of the Black and White Voltas (up to which point the vast new Volta Dam was expected to extend). It was the season of the *harmattan*, a hot dry wind from the Sahara. With the car windows open to keep cool one gets rapidly desiccated and must drink often. The country is correspondingly dry, much of it low forest or scrub. The people in this part of the NTs are mainly Muslims and even poorer than in the coast regions. They appeared smaller and slighter than the coastal people.

FRJ's briefing was: 'Call on the DC to say hello, then meet the Na (chief) of Damon. He will tell you he wants our support for a better road to the river so more fish traders will come and he can collect tribute from them.' I should pay attention to the welfare of the fish scout posted at the river, and enquire about relations between the migrant Tongu and the local Dagumba and Konkomba people; then spend time on the river with the fishermen.

The house of the Na was of a distinct tradition. Getting accustomed to the dim light inside I saw it was circular and had a skilfully thatched high roof. At one side the floor was raised and covered with carpets and skins. There the Na lived. The other side was occupied by a horse bedded in straw. To have a horse was a sign of status among the northern Muslim people. Our conversation turned exactly on the points FRJ had predicted.

At the fishermen's camp on the Oti River, I stayed in a hut with no windows, but a towel was hung in the door for 'privacy'. The fish scout kindly shared his food with me – boiled fish, cassava, tea and bread from a

A bush bakery

nearby 'bakery'. In return I contributed some canned stores. At night, hippos could be heard snorting in the river. In the early morning the air was cool and sweet; spoor on the river bank gave clues to night visitors, such as antelope.

The versatile Tongu used different fishing methods than on the lower river, and more lightly fished stocks gave them higher catches. The men used cast nets where there were deep pools, and multiple lines set overnight yielded catfish and Nile perch. The size of cast net a man can throw depends on strength and skill, and the Tongu used much larger ones than the local people. Their method of stringing unbaited hooks along a line fixed just above the bottom to foul-hook fish was copied from the Hausa of Nigeria. It was easy to see the advantage of their long migration at this time of year. Traders came and money changed hands – something I'd not seen in the home villages.

Yet everyone grumbled. Money had been borrowed at home for the trip,

Fish foul-hooked in a Hausa line

Tongu man throwing large cast net

NTs boy throwing smaller cast net

and would have to be repaid on returning; and they had to live on goods and drink bought from the traders. Of course there would be a big homecoming party, but then the money saved would all be gone. Here they had no wives ... and so the complaints ran on. A few – perhaps those who could not repay their loans – stayed on at the Oti longer and cultivated a patch of land, virtually as colonists, but for the great majority it was an expedition.

I visited a market at the town of Yendi with some fish traders. It being at an important crossroads, the market was thronged – with foodstuffs in basins, cloths laid out, animals tethered or caged, all on display. People

Yendi market

Ashanti rain forest

bartered and argued vociferously. The women in coloured dress moved through the market chatting, unhindered for once by head loads. Youths beat long narrow drums tucked under an arm. Squeezing on cords that tightened the drum-skin varied the pitch, and their rhythmic drumming and strident yells spread excitement.

The fish scout seemed glad to talk away from the others at the river. He was unhappy and anxious. 'People don't like me here since I'm from a different tribe. I fear what they will do.' In fact a month or two later, in Sogankope, I heard he was dead. Witchcraft was mentioned. One could not know if it was a consequence of being a stranger.

The river at the north had a quite different ambience. In the high forests of Ashanti en route, one was aware of yet another culture.

First national election

Politics reached even the lower Volta in 1956. A historic event was coming, the election to determine national independence – perhaps the first government election in British colonial Africa. A political movement in 1948 attracted a Commission of Enquiry from London, leading in turn to Kwame Nkrumah's Convention People's Party (CPP) participating in the government of the Gold Coast along with senior British officials, under the Governor. The impending election, however, was for an all-African cabinet led by Nkrumah. Of course, it was important for him to have a landslide victory.

It seemed any government officer could be drafted into helping with the election, and to my astonishment I became the Returning Officer for Lower Volta constituency (with detailed procedures to follow). Its population was around 50,000. Adequate polling booths had to be installed through the scattered villages. All adults were encouraged to vote, and the drawing up and checking of lists of voters in each place had to be done – an onerous job causing me to sign my name thousands of times. But the hardest thing was to explain to the voters what the whole thing was about, why an election was taking place, and what its advantages might be. Most difficult, even at repeated meetings, was to get across the notion of voting, making an individual private choice. The procedure itself was simple enough – the closed booth, a box, a paper for you to put a cross next to a symbol (a fish or a cock, etc. since most people were illiterate).

What a battle! Six weeks of frantic activity, but on the day things went surprisingly well. In each of many villages, people queued in orderly lines before a tent or hut, shepherded by two special (temporary) constables. A clerk and witness checked voters' names against a list. I buzzed around the villages from dawn onwards. When polling closed, each box was parcelled in brown paper, the cords sealed with red wax, and taken by the constables to Sogankope (along footpaths, or head-loaded over swamps or canoed along the river). I broke the seals in the schoolroom, and counting was supervised. The DC's office helped greatly in all this, but he himself kept a low profile in the interests of impartiality.

Looking at the lines of people turning out to vote I was struck by the great number of sick and aged individuals, many I certainly hadn't seen before. They must have been at home in the villages all the time. A lot of good-natured laughter took place, but obviously the whole affair was some kind of ceremony contrived by distant authority. Village people were used to rule by consensus under their intimately known elders and chief. Strong traditional sanctions existed against individualism, so the making of a personal and private choice about who was to govern was strange to the point of unbelief. In any case, the 'government' was far away, and they knew not what went on there; so how could they take part in it? Puzzlement was evident in the number of spoiled votes, lost pencils, wide consultations about matters supposed to be private, and loud ribald opinions.

There were three candidates: CPP, Independent and an opposition party. In the run-up it became evident the Independent (call him Mr Mensah) was popular, while the CPP man was not. As in many other parts, notably Ashanti and Northern Territories, the Tongu were suspicious that politics might affect their customary ways and rights, not to mention their taxes. Mensah got his following by proclaiming he belonged to no party, but had listened well and understood their concerns and would represent these concerns to the government. I announced his victory outside the counting room to a crowd. He made a speech, we shook hands, said goodbye. Relieved, I headed home for a drink and a quiet evening.

The phone rang. 'Yes, Mr Mensah?'
He said, 'I have two things to say. One is thanks for the good work.'
'Oh, don't mention it, Mr Mensah,' (the usual polite response in West Coast English). 'Second is, I want to change my party.'
I, unbelieving, said, 'But you have just been elected an Independent.'
'Doesn't matter, I'm going to change to CPP, and it will be all right.'
Words began to fail. I replied, 'Oh, don't mention it.'

Of course it was a put-up job. Seeing no hope of getting in under his true (CPP) label, he had run as an independent then changed, indecently soon. I reflected on the huge waste of time setting up the props and machinery when the outcome was already arranged, at least at party level. It betrayed the people, and did not bode well for a democratic future.

Back to Accra

Six weeks remained to complete an annual cycle on the river, and it was time to draw the data together. Clearly, if the dam reduced the river to a steady low flow, without high floods, the Tongu people would lose their floodplains – their chief resources for agriculture and fisheries. It could be catastrophic. This had to be reported to the Preparatory Commission, making clear the impacts of the dam so that alternative livelihoods could be planned.

It was the hot season in Accra, and I sweated over the task of describing a conservative people whose balanced traditional way of life was to be seriously perturbed or destroyed. They were highly adapted and self-sufficient, but dependent on complex strategies to make a living from their floodplain/river environment. The scope of impending changes meant all aspects of life needed to be taken into account, to help substitute or compensate for their loss. Years later I read an economic study of the same part of the river by the University of Accra about the same time (in 1954); repeated again in 1964–65).[2] My results were in general agreement with that more comprehensive work. Perhaps it is of interest now, some fifty years later, to review the original traditional scene and what followed.

Social and economic aspects of Tongu life

Social structure

The people of the lower river were a homogeneous social entity, sharing the same language (Ewe) and culture. Resident strangers were rare. Lifestyle was much the same in each village. Cultural tradition regulated life through unquestioned acceptance of social institutions.

Any sizable village had a hierarchy, a chief and senior men (councillors). Below them individual prominence was limited; some had special skills such as carpenters and canoe builders. There were small traders possessing a store, and as well itinerant Hausa traders wandering from village to village, their haberdashery carried on the head of a small boy. The great majority of people engaged in fishing and farming within seasonal cycles.

Kinship bonds knitted the society. For example, a man would often be introduced as 'my brother', sometimes adding 'same-father-different-mother' (or vice versa). I wondered if polygamy was common, or did fathers tend to be Casanovas, but in fact 'brother' simply meant a co-lateral of some degree in the same extended family to whom, therefore, obligation was due. The practical result of the kinship web was a security system, which spread any adventitious wealth. Anyone lucky enough to improve their fortunes was instantly plagued by poor relatives to shell out bounty to them. As might be expected, this obligation was often felt as a burden by the fortunate. For example, my 'recorders' were unhappy to be posted to their own villages because they now had a regular source of pay.

Communal bonds of course existed between villages dispersed along or near the river. Communication was reinforced by fishing and agricultural methods requiring cooperation; for example, the floodplain *atidzas*. Again, the river women divers worked in company and cooperated in processing and marketing their clams. In farming, people generally worked in groups especially during planting and harvesting. Mutual assistance could also be recognised in the giving of loans, for example, to the men going upstream to fish seasonally. These were made on an individual or family basis, without interest, to be repaid on return home.

Much of the gossip filling my recorders' reports was concerned with irregular behaviour (startlingly intimate, often funny). It is certain that scandal and gossip within a village was a force restraining individuality and increasing pressure to conform to general custom. Another conspicuous topic was about disagreements over property or alleged injury or some sort of infringement of personal rights. Disputes could be between individuals or families. At any place and time, it seemed, 'cases' were either in process or being aired by gossip. It indicated a very litigious people, with an acute sense of rights and boundaries. Probably most village problems were dealt with within a community, while more serious or persistent ones got as far as the District Court.

Work in the villages was irregular. There seemed plenty of time for social intercourse – chatting, singing to drums at night and visiting friends and family – as well as for ceremonies or celebrations. Fishing and farming cycles were generally launched by a particular ritual. The beginning of *atidza* fishing on the receding flood was ordered by the 'fishing master'. He decided the time and who would participate, and presided over ritual ceremonies. A sacrifice was made, usually a goat or cock, with a libation – the pouring out

Sacrifice of a goat at a fishing ceremony

of palm-wine or gin with the blood. Similarly, the end of an episode of successful fishing was marked by a celebration (harvest festival). Another occasion for parties and sprees was the return each year of migrants from months of fishing upriver. Attendance at family funeral ceremonies was obligatory, with prolonged mourning and socialising. These activities of course reinforced communal bonds.

Despite the presence of a few Christian missions or occasional visits to the villages by a missionary or priest, fetish worship and witchcraft co-existed and seemed important though their significance was not easy for an outsider to comprehend. Most obvious to see were numerous fetish shrines, at which symbolic gifts were left. Witchcraft could be aggressive and used to invoke harm or vengeance, or it could be used for propitiation or protection against harm. Many were the hints and mentions of such things in my recorders' stories, indicating that the unseen world played a significant part in life. Traditional religion no doubt had a functional role for counselling the anxious, sick or bereft.

Economic factors

A village community held common ownership of local resources (with recognised floodplain and land boundaries), and therefore proprietary right to exploit and use, or rent to outsiders. There was common sharing of production. For example, all villagers had a share in *atidza* fishing catches, though not all took part in an operation. Any outsiders taking part came by prior arrangement, paying for the privilege in kind or cash. An exception to general sharing was that women kept the profits from clam diving for their own particular households.

Display of wealth, except by the traditional leaders, was discouraged. In the very open circumstances of a village, attempts to hide anything would be difficult, as indeed would any other personal innovation. Lawson's study suggested an alternative to obvious display (with resulting taxation) would be to invest in cattle. In large herds, ownership of particular animals would be difficult to determine. I often saw herds, totalling perhaps twenty to thirty thousand, on the fringes of floodplains to the north or east of the river. A large investment. These shifted according to grazing needs and were not obviously associated with particular villages. Interestingly, they were in the daily care of Hausa or Fulani rather than Tongu herdsmen.

It has been suggested that consumption in this economy was culturally determined. This was probably broadly true; certainly consumerism in the modern sense of addiction to attractive manufactured goods was absent. Life went in cycles of plenty alternating with intervals of shortage. Food abundance was linked to seasonal availability, because the means to store food were limited to smoke-curing fish, storing groundnuts in baskets or shelters, and leaving cassava roots in the ground during the dry months. 'Management' consisted in fact of close adaptation to seasonal cycles of fish abundance and plant growth, and spreading the risk through alternative food sources. It is important to note that environmental cycles varied widely within and between years. The river went seasonally from floods overspilling the banks to low shallow flow. Flood amplitude varied also between years, determined by regional rainfall far to the north. Local rainfall came at a different time than in the north.

Being a biologist perhaps disposes me to think in terms of natural cycles, and adaptations for survival.[3] The traditional Tongu way of life on the lower Volta seems an excellent demonstration of deliberate strategies, which can be summarised as follows.

After peak high water in November–December, intensive fishing (*atidza*) took place on the floodplains, as well as planting near the receding water's edge. The crops – cassava, maize, sweet potato, ground nuts and peppers – were harvested in February. Then a second crop was planted with the onset of local rains in April–May, and harvested in August. While the second crop was growing, the men went upstream exploiting different stocks of fish. Thus there were two sets of crops, corresponding with flood and local rainy seasons, and two phases of fishing, corresponding with flood (floodplain fishing) and dry season (river fishing). As well, the women gathered clams at low water. This regime tended to make extensive use of resources, and to spread availability of food through the year.

It also made good use of labour. Division of labour between men and women was marked. The men engaged in all kinds of fishing as well as constructing and repairing gear, while the clam industry – diving, processing and trading – was the women's affair. In farming, women did much of the digging and weeding. At harvest times both sexes worked and additional labour was provided by children (most of whom did not go to school) and the elderly. Thus labour was concentrated locally in September to December in floodplain fishing and planting, and dispersed between December and August – clam diving and upstream fishing. Division of labour undoubtedly increased productivity, for example the simultaneous occupation through the dry season of women with clams, and men with upstream fishing. It showed organised interdependence at family level, and it maximised income to the village. Farming tools were simple, hoe and machete; fishing gear and canoes were home-made.

Clearly the Tongu had a set of prudential tactics to manage the risks of shortage or famine.[4] Key environmental risks were variable flood levels (floodplain extent) and fluctuation in local rainfall.

Apart from community well-being and survival in adverse times, it is tempting to speculate whether deliberate relationships existed between rates of exploitation (catches and crops) and ecological sustainability.[5] Could this society be regarded as having attained a stable livelihood, in the sense of balance with environmental limits, through highly adapted exploitation and culturally-determined consumption? Or might it simply have been that margins between exploitation rates and sustainable limits were wide? No effort was made that I could see to control fish catches. Indeed the general idea was to catch as much as possible within the scope of methods and fish abundance. Total catches varied from year to year. Perhaps only the intense natural productivity of the tropical floodplain cycle and the inefficiency of home-made gear (though it seemed to me very little got away), permitted high catch levels to be kept up from year to year.[6]

As to crops, the amount of land planted might have been determined by estimated needs. Naturally irrigated land on the floodplain was preferred because soil moisture content remained higher for longer than in unflooded land. There was no rotation of crops, but perhaps a system existed of rotating land.

In brief, 'management' was self-regulated by each village community and its leadership. Motivation was driven by the need to provide sufficient food for all. Individual profit and the saving of cash were of less importance. It seems likely there was scope to produce more if the population pressure had been greater. Why then was it not greater?

After the dam

I left with uneasy feelings about the gap between my own conviction that the dam would have dire effects, and the apparent lack of appreciation of that by the people themselves. The future Lake Volta's great area, 8,500 square kilometres, and expected high evaporation rate, would largely smooth out fluctuations in river flow – especially if the dam was held at levels best for generating electricity, which seemed likely be the case. Obviously the river would not spill onto its floodplains as before. Also the isolated world of the Tongu downstream would inevitably be ruptured by new roads and dam building, and the traditional way of life could not continue. The dam represented a cut-off point from age-old, self-supporting tradition. Considerable aid finance would be needed to find alternative livelihoods.

As well, the local Volta election experience had left me wondering about the quality of the new government – an unease to be borne out by events. Nkrumah and the CPP party were indeed elected by a landslide in 1957 and remained in power until he was deposed by military coup in 1966. He rapidly became a dictator, with all political opponents in jail or having fled the country. In his short reign, the Volta Dam was built, as well as ancillary projects such as a port and aluminium smelter. Vast irrigation schemes were planned and begun on the Accra plains. It was an era of 'think big' schemes. Nkrumah also had wide political ambitions extending far beyond Ghana. The eyes of the world, and particularly those of the rest of Africa, were on Ghana.[7]

The Nkrumah years were a vast spending spree. At the time of independence, the Gold Coast government had built up national reserves of 250 million pounds sterling (from cocoa exports and prudent savings), but in less than a decade the country had virtually no reserves left and owed around 300 million pounds in foreign debts. These were enormous sums for the time. Not all the spending was visible because those holding power had neither the capacity nor integrity to oversee so much expenditure so quickly. Temptation for corruption was irresistible and private fortunes were made locally and built up overseas – an example followed widely in time by many other developing countries.[8] Hard times followed from the early 1970s despite continued inputs of UN and bilateral assistance. Severe economic decline affected the poorer rural people in particular.[9]

As to the Volta, the Tongu were duly hit by the altered river flow, and their livelihood pattern broke down. However, as the dam filled (1964–66) its fishery proved hugely productive and more than compensated for losses in the downstream region. The Tongu fishermen had only to move a short way upstream to make fishing camps around the lake (see Figure 2). Catches there rose to 63,000 tonnes in 1969, the highest from any man-made lake in the world. The effect of this boost in income was immediate, giving rise to a spate of new building in the villages downstream. Bigger family houses were erected for prestige and investment. There was no need to hide personal savings made from this obvious source.

A temporary rise took place in the clam fishery. As the river dropped very low while the dam filled, the women continued to dive for clams right through 1964–65. It was natural enough to take the opportunity, but initial high yields fell off as clam stocks became exhausted. Moreover, salinity concentrations in the river changed; the altered flow regime allowing sea water to penetrate the river continuously. This crucially affected the clam's life cycle, and in a few years its stock collapsed completely.[10]

Great changes also came about for the lower-river Tongu through prodigious foreign spending on new roads, bridges, markets, clinics, schools, administrative centres and agricultural projects. For example, two fine bridges were put across the Volta, one near the dam by a British company, and one at Sogankope (where we'd so often waited for the ferry) by a German company. These multiple developments were not directly associated with fishing and farming, but initiated from outside. One consequence was a large influx of well-paid strangers, who set examples to the local people of different lifestyles and the use of money, and introduced a variety of unfamiliar commodities. Thus was an almost closed economic and social scene quickly transformed. Interestingly, the villagers did not at first respond by increased 'consumerism', as might have been expected; their priority seemed rather to seek for social security. Perhaps the volatile economic changes were felt to threaten understood ways of life.

Overall, however, the 1960s were boom times. The rising fishery on Lake Volta and exceptional though short-lived clam production brought relative wealth. Then the influx of state capital, overseas financial aid and foreign workers, augmented the local economy. Markets and trade thrived. Among numerous introduced projects were irrigated sugar cane plantations and a sugar refinery, vegetable cropping trials, a tannery, farming of rice and maize. Aid sources included Russia, Poland, Czechoslovakia, Germany, the USA and the UK. Unfortunately, most of these approaches to bring prosperity failed. After the 1966 coup expelling Nkrumah and a change in foreign policy, aid from Russia and Eastern Europe dried up. State funding was much reduced. It was found the various methodologies tried in local projects worked successfully on a small scale, but did not become established. Simply, they did not take root. None had a lasting impact upon local people, who by and large continued to farm and fish in traditional ways.[11,12]

Subsequently, things did not go so well for the Tongu. There was a large demand for fish from Lake Volta throughout Ghana, so the catch was distributed especially to the big towns. Instead of a subsistence fishery providing food for local people, the Lake Volta fishery became an industry with a large commercial network. Fishermen multiplied manyfold, fishing intensified and as a result the catch per man fell drastically. Not only was he still poor, but his way of life had changed. Instead of having a traditional occupation with proprietary rights and shared catches, he became a participant in a commodity business, organised into companies well equipped with gear. Soon some of the gear became mechanically powered and more efficient than manual methods. In the end the fisherman, with only his labour to contribute, of which there was a surplus, secured but a small share of the business.[13,14]

Local leaders in later years tried further measures to alleviate economic hardship. For example, shrimp farming ponds were introduced, to help replace income from the lost floodplain fishery. The methods were demonstrated, and financial capital for stocking shrimps and instruction was not a constraint, but the business did not develop. It appears failure was due to 'the general apathy of the local people towards a progressive attitudinal and behavioural change'.[13] In fact, a lack of will.

A major health problem became associated with the Volta Dam – schistosomiasis (bilharzia). Dense growth of aquatic weed occurred throughout the lake, providing a substrate in which the 'intermediate host' snail multiplied. An explosive outbreak of bilharzia resulted, prevalent among schoolchildren (90%) and fishermen. The problem involved the people of the lower river too. It was much researched and counter measures employed to deal with the weed and treat the disease. But weed, snails and infection return if suppression measures are not kept up. Bilharzia is debilitating and could explain a great deal of the misery and lassitude of populations where it is rife. The problem is still there, requiring, like malaria and various other diseases of the rural tropics, continuous and expensive control.

Thus the story at the villages of the lower Volta is dismal, despite abundant financial aid. Intense poverty, with breakdown of traditional culture and social values has occurred, along with emigration of the young and energetic. The villages are now mostly 'communities of old men and women who live in deplorable conditions'.[13]

What can be said about this transformation of a living community? Could there have been better outcomes? In hindsight, the Tongu were simply caught up in large political trends outside their own local world, and were dealt with along the lines of conventional political and economic wisdom of the time. Nkrumah's political advance was understandable in the context of Britain's desire to pull out of the country.[15] No doubt giving sovereignty was convenient for the British Labour Party at that moment, and it satisfied anti-imperialists at home. It must also be said that Nkrumah's economic theory was consistent with the current worldwide belief among economic planners that industrialisation was the way to transform peasantry into a 'modern' society (see Part III). His 'revolutionary' politics and think-big macro-economic approaches in fact fitted advanced current beliefs. Fitted so nicely, that the doctrine he preached sounded plausible – that 'African Socialism ... could somehow combine modern growth and traditional values'.[16]

However, this doctrine in practice meant more than just a shift from colonial government to self-rule. It meant a fundamental change, a different paradigm. The former step-by-step strategy had altered to a one-stage jump – immediate modernisation. Nkrumah and his party believed that industrialisation in a 'big push' was both necessary for Africa and was possible. After all, the Russians had done it (though with what human cost was not understood until the 1960s; in any case, Russia had been developing its industry from the late nineteenth century). About this time too, Chairman Mao Tse Tung was launching his Great Leap Forward, a crash programme in industrialisation and collective farming – the same big push thinking. As is well known, the disastrous result in China was industrial chaos and sixteen million dead from famine.

Nkrumah was therefore not alone in attempting to engineer a break-through from peasantry to industry. The rationale behind the Volta Dam ran something as follows: 'development is the key to [national] economic independence ... [Electric] surplus energy capacity for production is a precondition for setting off a progressive increase in ... mutually reinforcing cycles of economic growth and further expansions in generating capacity'. [This should result in] 'creation of employment opportunities in the modern sector that enables rural-urban flow. An ever-growing and prospering modern sector will then reach out and, in turn, modernise the traditional sector until the whole nation is developed'.[17]

Thus the Volta Dam was to be used as the major instrument to bring about desired sequences of change in Ghana. Many governments of the Third World have intended, and some still do, to use big development projects and resettlement as means of introducing 'progress'.[18]

The people to be displaced by the rising waters of Lake Volta presented an immediate challenge to the jump theory. The lake would cover 850,000 hectares, and 80,000 people had to be resettled (not including those downstream of the dam). Unfortunately, priority was given to engineering and power production, and the time and money for human and environment adjustments were left short. In the end it was decided to supply mass-produced houses of concrete blocks and aluminium sheeting. So 740 assorted villages of various ethnicities and traditions were to be placed in 52 resettlement towns. The question of what the people were to do for a living was never solved.

The decision from above was based more on hope than on knowledge. Quote: 'the new communities should not revert to traditional subsistence-farming practices. Instead they should grasp this opportunity to move with the times and balance their own staple food crops with crops that they could sell for cash and with scientifically fed livestock. This would mean at least partial mechanisation of the land and the clearing and stumping of vast acreages.'[19]

In the event the houses were generally rejected by the recipients, and not enough land for farming was cleared of trees. Despite US-AID and help from other agencies for the first two years of resettlement, the people were reduced from independent subsistence farmers to landless peasantry dependent on food hand-outs. Within a few years the majority departed, and the houses became a slum with little life left in them.[20,21]

What would the Volta power scheme have been like in colonial hands (remembering that comprehensive planning had already been done)? Typically it would have proceeded in stages – rather as the Volta Dam Preparatory Commission had planned in 1954; i.e., in the step-by-step style with emphasis on human factors.[22] The displaced who lost their land would have had to be resettled, but perhaps more time and money might have enabled them to rebuild in traditional ways and cluster more or less as in former villages. Similarly, the Tongu below the dam would have needed appropriate assistance to adjust to a different lifestyle. But the overall outcome would probably not have been much different, only the worst impacts might have been ameliorated. The dam was bound to bring physical change and an encroaching modern world to disturb old social patterns and livelihoods.

It is now better understood that cultural coherence in tribal societies covers all aspects of daily life, from the religious to the economic, and these 'fit together to form a unified whole'.[23] It is therefore practically impossible to re-construct societies over a short term, as attempted in the Volta case. The universal problem remains how to effect transformation to the modern world while holding on to social integrity and self-reliance.

Poverty is still the lot of most people in Ghana, despite Volta power and vast foreign aid and loans over many years. Of the considerable electrical output (over 1,000 megawatts), most goes to aluminium industry and mines and to providing power for a few cities.[24] Relatively little goes to rural areas – even to the generating area around the lower Volta! Energy production has benefited an urban elite and foreign companies at the expense of the rural majority.[25]

Deforestation has gone on around Lake Volta to get firewood for fish processing. All wood within easy reach has been used, and fishermen rely on women of the Gonja tribe, who have no other work in the farming off-season, to bring them firewood. It is a barter trade – fish for firewood – of tremendous importance to the tribesfolk.[26]

The Volta Dam was certainly a great engineering achievement, but whether it has justified itself economically, commercially and industrially, as was thought in the 1960s, is arguable. Its economic performance has been volatile with less output than hoped for, and with little positive influence on the majority of Ghanaians. Certainly for the people displaced by the dam, and for the Tongu of the lower Volta, the social costs have in the long run outweighed any benefits.

Notes and references

1. Moxon, J. (1969). *Volta: Man's Greatest Lake.* Praeger. New York.
2. Lawson, R. (1972). *The Changing Economy of the Lower Volta (1954–1967).* Oxford University Press.
   Note: Symptoms of economic change among the Tongu people of the Lower Volta during the crucial 1954–1967 period, leading up to the building of the dam and immediately following boom conditions, are here summarised from Lawson:
   Cash earnings from dam fishery spent largely on prestige family housing.
   New pattern of status and prestige; including withdrawal of status from traditional rulers and growing demand for prestigious commodities.
   Class structure beginning to develop based on wealth and ownership.
   Consumption increases above levels of culturally determined subsistence.
   Growth in income much higher than growth in consumption.
   Gradual assimilation of cheaper imported commodities into lifestyle.
   Wage employment in villages; increase in casual and part-time work.
   Higher production from farming leads to increased income flows.
   More land brought under cultivation and improved prices for local foodstuffs.
   Less time for social activities; ceremonials, funerals and visiting.
   With decrease in traditional festivals, more cash for alternative uses.
   Economic relationships between men and women changed.
   More money invested in education of young as a route to higher income.
   More travelling from home to visit markets and urban centres.
   Need for social security as economic changes threaten traditional life.

3. Survival mechanisms: It is an over-simplification to regard behaviour of a human society merely in terms of survival mechanisms. Parallels between human and biotic communities break down because of the strength of influence of human culture, which can determine behaviour profoundly without altering the genome. Biological systems are primarily concerned with renewing themselves, and also 'contain flexible mechanisms which equip them to match the fluctuations and perturbations of the environment' (see Note 6 below). *Homo sapiens* is essentially a generalist and versatile opportunist, exhibiting the usual profligate behaviour of generalists. But culture tends to act conservatively to create an equilibrium organism in the biological sense, meaning one that varies narrowly or specialises. In the case of the Tongu their traditional culture seemed to confer high degrees of specialisation and adaptation, which through risk management made the most of natural conditions on the lower Volta.
4. Sustainability: I do not want to evaluate Tongu traditional life in the 1950s as being qualitatively 'better' or 'worse' than it later became; I merely wish to describe its character and adaptations to natural cycles, also its strategies for survival. It should be said, however, that for all the limitations of this society, such as poor education and lack of medical care, it was self-sustaining, and more integrated with greater social security than after modern development changed it.
5. Catches: I did not try to quantify floodplain catches. The main point for this study was that total catches fluctuated considerably from year to year; the local fishermen affirmed unanimously that this depended on the extent and duration of flooding. Conversely, the clam fishery in the season when the river was low thrived best when river levels were lower than usual.
6. Bruton, M. (1989). The ecological significance of alternative life history styles. In Bruton, [ed.] *Alternative Life History Styles of Animals*; pp.503–553. Kluwer.
7. Yergin, D. & Stanislaw, J. (1998). *Commanding Heights.* Simon & Schuster Inc. New York. See also: Crawley, A. (1988), pp.295–303. *Leap Before You Look: A Memoir.* Collins.
8. Guest, R. (2005). *The Shackled Continent.* Pan, Macmillan, London
9. Report on the Nutrition Situation of Refugees and Displaced Persons, FAO, 1990. Accra, Ghana, stated: 'The severe economic decline which the country went through between the early 1970s and the early 1980s affected poorer socio-economic groups in particular through depressed wage levels and increased unemployment. Also between the late 1970s and the early 1980s, there was a serious decline in national food production and food shortages, which were caused by drought and were exacerbated through the enforced repatriation of over one million Ghanaians in 1983 from Nigeria.'
10. Pople & Ragoyska (1969). The effect of the Volta River hydroelectric project on the salinity of the Lower Volta River. *Ghana Journal of Science, 9*(1): 9–20.
11. Obusu-Mensah, K. (1996). Ghana's Volta Resettlement Scheme. In: Agbemabiese & Byrne – see Note 14 below.
12. Braimah, L.I. (1995). *Recent developments in the fisheries of Volta Lake (Ghana). Status of Fisheries in the Four Largest African Reservoirs.* FAO Publication, Rome.
13. Fobil, J. & Attaquayefio, D. (2003). *Remediation of the environmental impacts of the Akasombo and Kpong dams.* Horizon International, Yale University, USA.
14. Agbemabiese, L. & Byrne, J. (2005). Commodification of Ghana's Volta River: An example of Ellul's Autonomy of technique. *Bulletin of Science & Society, 25*: 17–25.

15. See Crawley (1988) – especially his account of the influence of the USSR in the 1960s and 1970s on ideology and aid politics in Africa.
16. 'African socialism' was a set of ideas much discussed in British universities in the late 1940s and 1950s, influencing some who were to become leaders of newly independent countries. It was socialism of a totalitarian sort. Another example of its dogmatic application was by President Nyerere in Tanzania, where rigid centralisation and the notion of ujamaa villages retarded progress for many years (Yergin & Stanislaw, 1998).
17. Agbemabiese & Byrne (2005) p.18.
18. Goldsmith, E. (1984). Social and cultural destruction. In: Goldsmith, E. & N. Hildyard. *Social & environmental effects of large dams: Overview* (p.15). Wadebridge Ecological Centre, UK. Vol.1.
19. Moxon (1969), p.162.
20. Goldsmith (1984), p.7.
21. Agbemabiese & Byrne (2005), p.23.
22. Moxon (1969), p.160.
23. Goldsmith (1984), p.9.
24. Van de Giesen, M. Andreini, van Edig, A. & Vlek, P. (2001). *Competition for water resources of the Volta basin.* Proceedings Symposium 6th IAHS Scientific Assembly, Maastricht, The Netherlands: IAHS Pub. 268.
25. Agbemabiese & Byrne (2005), p.24.
26. Braimah (1995), p.130. Author Note: My personal image of poverty in Africa is of a woman carrying a heavy load on her head – usually a bundle of wood or a drum of water – a common sight. Such loads are borne in many cases on a slight human frame. Usually it is hoisted up with help and placed on a head pad. The woman then goes forward with rapid steps in a little staggering run. Stopping for rest would involve off- and on-loading, requiring help. So she tends to cover long distances without respite. She generally receives little reward, for it is a menial task. I mention this mental image here in order to point out the paradox of its continuation beside an immense development project producing millions of dollars of energy. It poses challenging questions about development criteria, and 'appropriate aid'.

2

Step by Step

Guinea Coast

It was the best time of day to be sitting on Labadi beach near Accra – before the sun is high and while the breeze comes cool from the sea. Shading coconut palms rustled above, and the big surf rollers made gentle thunder against the sandy shore. Far out, sails were coming into view – white handkerchief-like patches over the horizon. I was turning over in my mind the news that my second project (1957–58) in the Ghana fisheries department was to be concerned with sea fisheries at a place called Axim.

The sails approached and were hauled down into large canoes paddled at speed through the surf. On hitting the sand, men leapt out to beach them. These were *alii* canoes, graceful seagoing dug-outs 12 metres long with swept-up bow and stern, too heavy to drag far up the beach without the help of the tide. The fishermen had sailed offshore with the night wind, and sailed back when it changed in the morning. Women fish traders were approaching along the beach to buy the catch.

One young fisherman, splendidly muscled, came up near us where a group of children had brought down some coconuts. Using the universal long knife of Africa (cutlass/panga/machete) he chopped the end off a nut, threw back his head and drank the milk. The same with another, and then he split both and scooped out the flesh to chew, grinning at us with white teeth. I had never seen a more physically impressive human being. Each muscle defined, his skin shining with salt spray, he was an image of grace and power yet quite unselfconscious. While admiring him, I thought of my assignment with dismay: 'What can I teach such people about fishing the sea?'

On the way to Axim, we called at the port of Takoradi (see Figure 2), where a colleague, Gordon, lived along with several assistants. All hailed from Yorkshire. They had a boatyard and training school in nearby Sekondi. Gordon explained, 'Our job is to help these people mechanise and introduce new fishing boats and gear. They are fine traditional fishermen, and their women manage the business of processing and marketing.' He showed me, for instance, a metal bracket they had recently invented for mounting a long-shaft outboard motor on the side of *alii* canoes. It was already enabling the canoes to move further and follow schooling fish and get bigger catches. Simple stuff, but possibly a big step if the fishermen adopted it in practice. But they needed training to operate the motors and to be introduced to credit schemes to buy them.

As well, Gordon was concerned with inboard-engined vessels. Two 10-metre wooden ones had been imported from Millars of Scotland, each with a 22-hp Kelvin diesel engine and winch, seaworthy and reliable. Replicas of these were being built from local wood, engines fitted, and crews trained to operate a small trawl net (with a mechanic per boat). I was to get one of the Scotch boats (the *Kanfla*) and a trained crew, Gordon's best, for exploratory fishing off Axim. Other private boats and crews would follow in due course and my job, in brief, was to get a number of such outfits running as profitable businesses.

We were thinking like Europeans, of course. Our minds ran simply along the lines of increasing fish landings by improving efficiency and introducing mechanical methods. I suppose we were influenced partly by our two ex-North Sea master fishermen, who thought naturally in terms of diesel engines and trawls, commercial profits and wages for workers. Trials with the prototype motor fishing vessels (MFVs) had been promising and the catches good. Cold storage facilities would be set up, along with a marketing system. The sea off Ghana was not heavily exploited. In short, we could build an improved artisanal industry for the coastal Fante people, based on their already competent fishing communities with long traditions. It seemed reasonable to hope they would adopt the 'improved' methods.

On the other hand, we did not much consider the possible social effects of the new ways on conservative village life – boosting trade and commodifying fish. Nor was there any thought at that time of bigger ships and large commercial companies. Rather it was intended – in retrospect it seems simple-minded – that the fishermen who habitually worked in teams in large canoes would switch smoothly to motorised vessels and new gear. They would make bigger catches, and benefit from more extensive marketing systems. But it would be a gradual process, depending on demand and success – in short, colonial step-by-step.

So I proceeded on to Axim rather more reassured about my role, and grateful for Gordon's experienced counsel and the knowledge he would not be far away. I would also have a trained crew to help me.

Axim

The house for Margaret and me, and our new baby Dianne, was on a hill a little back from the sea, old-fashioned and fairly typical of out-stations. Successive expatriate families had no doubt occupied it over many years. The bedrooms upstairs were cooled by fresh sea winds. My office down a winding dirt road to the beach was a very ordinary wooden construction, but set unexpectedly beside a most remarkable ancient pile, the fort of Santo Antonio de Axim. Portuguese explorers and traders had first erected a trading post on the rock promontory in 1503. It was overrun soon after by the local people, so this large stone fort was built in 1515. Its solid lime-washed walls and quarters had jutted out to the sea through the centuries, serving as a holding place for slaves and trade goods and housing successive garrisons of Portuguese, Dutch and British soldiers and traders. Ancient cannon muzzles stuck out from the battlements. Forts like this stud the coast of Ghana, testaments of a long history of trading and human misery.

From the terrible past one might think these old forts, isolated and anomalous on the shores of Africa, would have an alien atmosphere, brooding on long experience of slaving evils. Certainly the West Coast was regarded by Europeans as one of the most dismal and unhealthy trading spots in the world. These forts still stand, indomitably asserting their presence. One was aware of a numinous aura which somehow made them seem at home in that place, as if embedded and assimilated over ages into the African environment. To me, at least, Santo Antonio did not feel unfriendly. Later I got something of the same feeling at the old Portuguese fort of Mombasa on the other side of the continent.

Approaching from the sea, Santo Antonio is framed by very tall coconut palms close to the walls. There is little shelter for small boats, merely a rough breakwater. However, 8 km further along the coast to the east is a well-protected cove, Miemia, which seemed perfect for mooring a dozen or so motor fishing vessels. My crew would lodge in a village nearby until houses could be built for them. A few facilities, such as a slipway to draw up boats for maintenance, a storeroom and a workshop could be built there. That meant lots of walking to and from Miemia for me – not a hardship on a beach under palms. My impressions of subsequent life at Axim fall under two headings.

A house at Axim

Fort Santo Antonio – the view from the sea

Fishing

Separation between sea and land is more distinct in the tropics than temperate climates. For one thing, on tropic coasts there are scents from inland, particularly at night, and the sound of palm leaves clashing together. Moving seaward you penetrate successive lines of breaking surf, and after the splashing and hissing of water beneath the boat has ceased it becomes very silent. Further out the air is less turbulent, land scents entirely disappear, and at night with no white breakers, lights or smells, one feels isolated, almost suspended in space.[1]

You knew when you'd reached the edge of the continental shelf. At least, the crew knew, and in time I understood the signs too. Heading offshore in the early afternoon we arrived in several hours at a point where the sea surface had a certain slick, and its colour and transparency were different. One felt too by other senses the significant change of depth. Here the slowly sloping bottom fell sharply and steeply from about 100 m to abyssal depths below 1000 m. It was a region of upwelling, where rising currents enriched the water and boosted marine life of all kinds.

We would arrive shortly before dark. The crew of the *Kanfla* cooked their evening meal on a charcoal brazier, and I'd have a flask of coffee and sandwiches. Now was a peaceful interlude before the night's work. The engine had ceased to thump and the sea was heaving us gently on long smooth swells. The sun's slanting rays still penetrated into the clear sea. Land was long out of sight, and the edges of sky and sea merged seamlessly. On the way out, evening had been beautiful with sky colours changing and merging as the sun descended, ending in a blaze that transfigured the firmament as far as the gold lining of clouds in the east. The sea faded from turquoise to pale green with approaching night. In the mood cast by these transitions one became aware of vastness and solitude. At times the surrounding deeps brought a shiver of uneasiness, or maybe it was from some sinister association in my mind with the tropic sea – like Conrad's account of the night disaster struck the pilgrim ship *Patna*.[2] As the last streaks of red sunset dissolved, small fish splashed at the still surface. And with the dark came preparations for work.

Practical reasons had brought us here. I needed to find alternative fishing grounds. Nearshore trawling had given variable catches; perhaps stocks of bottom fish were too sparse for sustained fishing by numbers of boats. If big fish could be found further out which would take bait, that could be another option. Two Tilley pressure lamps were suspended fore and aft over the water. The men busied themselves coiling hand-lines, tying on each a chain trace and a butcher's hook. Baited with the herring *Sardinella aurita*, lines were thrown out by five men equally spaced between bow and stern. Whenever a little breeze drifted the boat, the lines angled out. The lamps hissed in the silence continuously; no insects around them out here. We were an island of light enveloped by darkness, and our attention drawn down into unimaginable depths. The crew kept up a comfortable chatter as we waited.

There is probably no better way of getting to know people than working together in a small boat. Personalities become sharply outlined – showing up strengths, weaknesses and quirks. Roles are accepted and interdependence builds. Humour helps smooth out dissent and raises spirits. Working with a good-natured crew can be very congenial, and I was to be fortunate in similar experiences with African crews in later years. This was one of the best, and I have a photograph of them. Mannah (centre of photo) was quite naturally the leader. Tall, active and quick-witted, he believed in the chain of command and was certainly boss on his boat. The crew called him *bosu* (from the English bosun). He was the only Ewe, the others Fante, all fishermen by upbringing. The core of the crew consisted of Nana (title for a village chief, as I believe he was), Tawia and Duku (known as 'lucky Duku'). The other two were young but willing learners.

Crew of MV *Kanfla*

Duku was the 'card' and clown, and also the strongest. He'd been a policeman, but binges brought his downfall. As a fisherman, he'd done illegal dynamiting – a fairly common practice. At sea, canoes could often be seen paddling frantically after fish schools, with one man standing in the bow. When he threw a charge, the water erupted and then bobbing heads could be seen as men jumped in and gathered stunned fish. I generally kept clear of such manifestations. Not unexpectedly, sharks come around, perhaps associating explosions with prey, and Duku had been taken. A shark grabbed him by the head, but he wriggled free and got back to the canoe. He bore deep scars up the back of his head.

Duku landing a snapper

I had spent the first few months at Axim trawling with them. The method was simple. Net and otter boards were pushed over the stern, and dragged along the bottom at 20 m to 30 m depth. The warps were winched in over pulleys on davits. Since my crew were paid by the Department, I'd been afraid they might not work as hard as the private (commercial) MFVs, which came in due course from Takoradi. No need to worry: Mannah's crew were aware of their status as the model boat. Rivalry ensured they usually landed the best catch. We found the best places to fish were near patches of rocky bottom, but the net often got snagged on rocks and torn. This problem was overcome by Ken, one of the Yorkshire master-fishermen from Takoradi. He mounted rollers ('bobbins'), along the foot-line enabling the net to ride over rocks. I enjoyed hearing Mannah shout orders ('go astern', 'go ahead', 'steady') using Ken's accent. Normally we spoke in West Coast pidgin, which to my surprise came easily.

The first strike of the night raised whoops and yells. One line streaked out while the others were pulled in to avoid tangles – two fish on at once was troublesome. The initial run of a fish was usually its strongest. I had tried leather gloves to haul the line, but it was best just to slow it by pressing the rope on the gunwale with a jute sack. Calloused hands brought the line in, with several runs on the way, until a shark came alongside. A noose slipped around the line was eased over the head at the gill slits. Two men hauled the snout up while another bashed the head with a cudgel until the fish stopped threshing. The trick was to remove the hook while keeping fingers clear of jaw reflexes, particularly avoiding the upper row of triangular teeth. Catches were mostly around two-and-a-half metres length, which fortunately was the most abundant size. They were the 'night shark', *Carcharhinus signatus.*

Sometimes we had a boatload in two or three hours, sometimes only a few fish all night. The average load was worthwhile coming out for. Very occasionally, we'd get into a yellowfin tuna, which exploded on the line and took longer to bring in than shark. Occasionally a line would be simply unstoppable, as if attached to a tractor. Then we'd just take the hint and move away a distance and start again, for it would have been unprofitable to try to land anything bigger. We had only one accident – a hook thrown out of the mouth of a twitching shark that lodged in a man's leg. Normally we turned for shore at 3 am, taking a course to compensate for the east-setting Guinea current.

I had concerns about engine breakdown and unplanned trips to Togo or Nigerian waters. We took spare fresh water, and I carefully checked the engine, but trouble was nearly always a result of dirty fuel. So the golden rule was laid down to filter fuel through a sock of chamois leather within a funnel – a wretchedly slow process. Two men were permanently appointed as 'fillers', and suitably compensated. I tried to get the commercial MFVs to do the same, and as a precaution against breakdown took one of them with us when possible.

The first sight on land was invariably one or more large kente-clad ladies, our very much interested traders. Each fish was hung and weighed under a tripod and gutted (shark give off a strong ammonia smell). Prices were agreed in vociferous haggling and the trader had her own truck and marketing set-up.

Miemia

Ask anyone their vision of heaven on earth, and you will likely hear, 'A tropical bay of golden sand fringed with palms, a gentle breeze and lucid warm water to swim in.' Miemia is, or was, such a dream: a little horse-shoe cove just a few hundred metres across, not far west of Cape Three Points – the most obvious protrusion on the fairly even coast of Ghana (see Figure 2). A low tree-covered hill on one side provided shelter from surf, and the rest was sandy beach. Patches of rocky bottom in the clear water were home for myriad brilliant fishes. It offered a fine safe anchorage for a dozen or more MFVs. While I tried not to clutter its beauty with artefacts, there had to be mooring buoys, and a concrete slipway and winch. A solid gantry of local teakwood enabled engines to be lifted out for servicing, and a workshop and fuel store completed the clutter.

Tinkering with boats, slipway and workshop at Miemia was congenial – except for a notable mistake. I should have begun building the slipway in the sea, the difficult part, but instead made a nice concrete platform sloping to the sea and installed on it the solid winch and gantry. Attempts to build out further resulted only in the concrete being washed away. The entire enterprise was futile, and unfortunately at this point the boss, FRJ, was due from Accra. I tried prematurely to pull up a boat at high tide for his inspection but it stuck, trailer and boat tilted at a terrible angle.

Miemia bay (MFVs at moorings)

This was the sight that met FRJ. I hadn't known how to mention the problem on our walk to Miemia, he seemed burdened enough by headquarters' worries. As we emerged through the trees, he gave vent to one of his ambiguous '*Ohhh*'s. After a grim inspection of the tilted boat and failed slipway, the air grew a little tense. The crew knew, of course, as they always do when things go wrong. Never a talkative man, FRJ was even more silent on the way back. He did observe distinctly that 'one should never attempt to do what one cannot finish', and went away, saying he'd be back in two weeks. It was clear all would not be well unless it ended well.

Tide tables showed spring tides in ten days. Gordon advised by phone that an additive could be purchased in Takoradi to make concrete set quickly. From these two bits of good fortune a plan was made. Trials showed that concrete with the additive set under seawater in about two hours, perhaps enough to beat the rising tide. We would build a wooden box outwards from the slipway at the spring tide low, insert iron reinforcing, mix concrete and hopefully have the extended slip topped off and hard enough in time.

About forty labourers, men and women, plus the crew, were assembled for two dummy runs several days before the spring low. Each time, iron spikes were driven into the shallows and long planks lashed against these. As the box grew and the tide went out, a team of diggers excavated sand from the box, digging frantically to get enough depth for the imaginary slip. Nearby, another team hand-mixed piles of stones and sand (without cement), while others were ready to wheelbarrow and head-load the mix to the box. We estimated volumes and time, and recruited a reserve team to work in shifts. Confidence grew.

On the day, the sea was calm and work began at dawn; the box was built and digging and hand-mixing went ahead as practised. This time I added the magic cement additive. We finished by 08.30, and lay exhausted beside the completed slip. The workers had shouted encouragement and laughed the while. As one fell out another took his place. At last the rising tide slopped over the box and the concrete seemed hard enough to stay. A few days later we hauled up the first boat easily.

FRJ duly came and plodded to Miemia once more without a word beyond polite conversation. My Great Mistake was not mentioned, though uppermost in our minds. In a peculiarly English way the matter was simply not referred to. I would have loved to describe to him the fine plan and vast exertions, but we stiffly remained silent. As we emerged from the trees at Miemia, Mannah's ship *Kanfla* was up on the slip with the crew fussing over it. Miemia had never looked more beautiful. 'Ohhh,' said FRJ, in a different tone. It must have been obvious much sweat had been expended, and that a nice surprise was intended. Faces peered from the trees around the cove to see the effect, and the workers shyly gathered in a small crowd. A melted FRJ made a warm little speech of thanks, in Fante, and good feelings abounded. But he and I never got round to discussing how the job was done.

Fishy business

Our little trawlers landed their catches at Axim in the afternoon, having been out since dawn. Bedlam reigned beside my office, which looked down on the proceedings. Quite often the surf in our practically unprotected beach below the buttresses of Santo Antonio prevented the boats coming in close. So they anchored well out, and boxes of fish had to be brought through the surf by canoe. Some of the splashing and yelling arose from men launching a big canoe into the surf for this purpose. When the canoe was far enough out between breakers, it was left to one strong paddler to propel it to the anchored boats. On the return trip he was helped by crew members coming ashore. They did not like to stay rolling at anchor. They quickly unloaded the 40 kg boxes on the beach, but getting them to my office for weighing, without fish being pinched by the milling crowd, was a problem. Such a system was far from ideal, but it reproduced the open conditions motorised boats would have to contend with along the mostly unprotected Ghana coast.

I used to think of 'Axim-in-the-afternoons' as the business end of my job – checking catches, vessels and gear, and noting fish sales. The profit margins of each MFV had to be tallied to see whether they could meet monthly loan repayments on boat and gear. But the hardest part was getting actual money from each boat company secretary on time ... like blood from a stone. Indeed the entire charade of running a business had to be gone through to prove whether these more capital-intensive methods with MFVs were viable, and the little companies could eventually go independent.

Of course one should not have favourites in a gang, but Ndede, chief paddler of the freight canoe, was a gem. Cheerful and soaked to the skin he toiled mightily at launching, paddling and beaching to bring catches ashore. Officially on the books as 'office orderly' he fitted the description not at all. His grin and muscular body would appear around my office door now and then – leaving a puddle – to report on fish boxes landed. A crowd, mostly women, competed to carry the fish to be weighed, and it was hard to know who were genuine *apaafo* (people paid in fish to do this job) or who were merely scroungers.

Another gem was young Gabriel. The variety of fish trawled up from rocky places was astonishing, and for the first time I became interested in fish, the science of ichthyology. Gabriel had been one of my 'recorders' on the Volta. He had a good eye for sorting fish and his bright intelligence noticed details. He went through the catches and pulled out any species strange to us. In no time, he was counting scale ratios, gill rakers, fin rays and spines, and identifying species from taxonomic descriptions. This was not exactly relevant to the job in hand, but out of interest we made a respectable list.

The people of Axim with nothing to do, apparently the majority of the population, gathered outside my office in the afternoon. A few 'important persons' hung around looking for a 'dash' of fish as reward for services rendered, or that might be rendered. There were relatives of crewmen, beggars and many children. At the fringes, petty traders sold food to the crews because there were no shops in Miemia. The densest scrimmage was around the landings, where traders raised their voices in bargaining, crewmen kept an eye on their own catch, buyers took fish away in basins on their heads, and others amused themselves shouting and shoving.

By custom, canoe fishermen got their living by dividing a catch into individual shares. Each man then made his own arrangements with his wife or sister, or some other woman, to take and sell his share for him – keeping a percentage for herself. She could process it by drying or smoking, and pay the fisherman maybe days later when the sale was completed. With our boats the procedure could vary, so that, for example, a bosun could sell his entire catch to one or more trader mammies, settling accounts with his men. Thus various sorts of understanding prevailed about sales among the MFVs, and it was hard for me to be sure what was going on. I had to put it together from crew records, the clerk's notes and, usually the most reliable, Ndede's fishbox counts.

Mannah reported the *Kanfla*'s catch, which was duly sold and paid to the office account. He never quite understood, or pretended not to, why the sales of his catch had to be paid back to the government. Government of course paid us wages regardless of the catch. In vain I repeated it was to help prove whether MFV trawlers were economical businesses, and we needed to be sure of that in terms of earnings. His invariable reply was 'plenty money there for government' (i.e., why worry, the government has stacks of money). I thought this was probably part of his wheedling game to get more of the catch for his crew than they normally kept for themselves. Only later did I understand the significance of his attitude – the notion, held widely by thousands of canoe fishermen along the coast, that government loans need not be regarded as real money to be repaid. Government could afford to lose (unlike you and me) and so was fair game. As it turned out, defaulting on repayments for boats and outboard motors was one of the main reasons why, in succeeding years, it became impractical to extend reasonable terms of credit to fishermen. The growth of the industry suffered accordingly.

As a first year went by it was clear the technical side of training crews and proving catches were not major issues in switching from canoes to MFVs. The men quickly got the hang of working from a diesel-powered boat and were certainly able to do the job. They could repair the net and keep the engine running – as long as nothing much went wrong. A more important problem was keeping them up to scratch, working regularly enough to make a profit. The so-called businessmen representing the boat companies knew little about fishing and could not motivate the crews – another fundamental problem in future development. But I could not find fault with the fish mammies. They were invariably first on the beach to inspect catches, their sharp eyes missed nothing and they bought, processed and sold through family links. Handling the commercial side seemed naturally the women's affair, following tradition. They not only knew about money but also observed the catching efficiency of each boat. It seemed the obvious way for a small-boat business to develop would be through a partnership between a fish mammy and the boat bosun, with the former responsible for financial matters and enforcing regular work.

The major question was whether Fante society would adopt these powered trawlers, and the loan system, as steps to building a commercial fishery? I say society because the roles of women and relatives were important; fishing was an affair of the whole family and kinship usually determined who was employed. But was routine commercial work acceptable to them? As I found for myself, it was a pretty monotonous life to sit beside a thumping engine through the long hot day, breaking off only to bring up the net. There is nothing like the regular drone of an engine to push one over the rim of sleep. The dull regularity of daily routine as a wage earner, contrasted with traditional fishing for food and the excitement of chasing schools of fish, sailing or paddling, depending on sea and weather, each man seeing himself a shareholder in the catch. Traditional fishing was also seasonal and desultory, with plenty of time off for personal activities.

From a social viewpoint, the traditional canoe man was part of a village community. If he owned the net and canoe, or represented the owner, his relationships with others in his crew derived from a web of obligations, family connections, rituals and rights. Could this arrangement and sense of status be duplicated with a commercial boat? Who would manage it, a seagoing skipper or an onshore investor? Could ingrained tradition based on catch sharing and the well-being of the community be incorporated into business? To what extent could the state manage the fish resource through laws and subsidies? Or would it turn out a free-for-all, with the market and private business running things? In a nutshell, would fishing carry on as a livelihood based on traditional village organisation, or would it become a complex of businesses dealing with a commodity and paying wages?

These sorts of questions churned in my mind. I was starting to understand a basic truth – that introducing technical improvements to a traditional society is only the beginning of a long journey. Questioning my crew about village life and fishing did not get me far. Our usually cheerful relationships relied more on smiles and gestures than on the exchange of ideas and confidences. They were probably constrained by working in an environment unusual to them. It may not have been easy rationally to compare life in canoes using *adii* nets with what we were doing now. At any rate, they seemed unprepared to analyse the difference, or to see matters otherwise than in terms of the prevailing assumption that mechanised methods must be better.

I found it revealing to attend occasional meetings with Gordon, at the house of the chief fisherman of Sekondi near Takoradi. The head fish mammy, and other advisors of that substantial fishing community were present. There was clearly a complex social structure with established procedures. The chief fisherman himself had considerable status and authority, while we from the department were evidently regarded just as advisers and innovators and possible sources of funds. The Fante to me seemed excellent fishermen with independent traditions. They were well able to adopt new fishing methods. With a large inland market served by improving roads their future looked promising.

Party members and politicians from the new government were busy at these meetings promoting their connections with the fisherfolk. One could only hope their promises about future development would work out well. Change was certainly in the air, together with expectation of financial largesse. It seemed our MFV project depended more on social than technical factors, namely the assimilation of commercial business into the traditional scene. It also depended on the policies of the new national government.

Fante fishing: Traditional to modern

The social evolution of the Fante fishing people in the past century has been volatile, as they attempted to incorporate technology with tradition. Interestingly, certain traditions have long persisted; in particular the practice of 'sharing' catches from the sea, the importance of kinship, and the dominant role of women in business.[3,4,5,6,7,8]

From earliest recorded times the Fante were established as traders and fishers for some distance inland to the forest belt. An account in the early eighteenth century speaks of thousands of fishermen who traded by sea along the coast from Accra to Axim (see Figure 2). In the long period before harbours existed, Fante men crewed for lighterage companies, plying to and from foreign ships anchored offshore. As late as the 1950s this centuries-old method could be seen at Accra, where dozens of surf boats were paddled, each by about 12 men, to and from cargo ships. Outboard motors had not yet come; nor had the port of Tema near Accra been constructed. These broad, planked craft were manned by strong fellows, who manually filled and discharged their boats with bulky sacks of cocoa beans and other primary products. The boat skipper operated a steering sweep, and thrusts of the characteristic three-pronged paddles carried them through steep waves and surf.

Cargo being taken by canoe to ship off Accra

Until the late nineteenth century the Fante fished with only simple methods – cast nets to catch schooling fish at the surface, simple gill nets set along the bottom (tenga nets), and hook-and-line – all worked near shore in less than 30 m depth. The cast net was thrown by an individual from the bow of a canoe. For the gill nets, usually a group of fishermen each owning one or more nets would cooperate for efficiency, setting a string of tenga nets from the same canoe. Each man kept the catch of his own net, and on landing gave it to his wife (or sister or other woman relative). She processed the fish by smoking, salting or drying, and traded them, settling accounts with her fisherman later. The early tenga fishery was one of subsistence and petty-commodity trading, changing little over time. In an explicitly Marxist description,[5] the traditional society has been disparaged as 'stagnant' 'and pre-capitalist'; in fact it was vigorous and complex in organisation.

Sexual division of labour and kinship linkages underlay all fishing activity. In a sense, husband and wife were an economic unit. Adding complication, each had a separate set of family obligations to their 'own side' of the family (his direct relatives and hers, respectively). Married couples generally lived apart, each in their own or in matrilineal relative's homes, children being brought up with the wife. Wife and husband kept separate purses, but each contributed in various ways to the upkeep of their children. The special form of distribution of work and responsibilities in Fante society (resulting in relative independence of a woman's economic activities) is thus closely linked to their kinship system. Exchange relationships between husband and wife contributed to general welfare, in helping to maximise earnings from fishing and spread earnings between households.

Disputes or matters of negotiation between fishermen were taken to the chief fisherman (*apofohene*) of the community, a hereditary position. Similarly, a woman of status (*konkohene*) regulated women's affairs. There was also a system of elders and advisors, as well as a third element termed '*asafo*' companies (formerly military divisions, but persisting as important community organisations and 'brotherhoods'). Thus power blocks and pressure groups existed in a community through which disputes and negotiations operated. It is interesting to note that the fishing segment of Fante towns and villages has always tended to be conservative and tradition-orientated; old social structures have influenced Fante fishing society up to modern times.

A significant change in technology came in the late nineteenth century with the introduction of twine to make nets, and lead weights and corks. Around 1890, the herring drift net appeared and was gradually adopted along the coast (the *adii* net). Of a kind known in Europe for centuries, it was a much bigger fishing instrument than any in West Africa. Two hundred or more metres long and ten metres deep, it was set at the surface and formed a wall into which schools of sardinella swam and were gilled. It increased catches greatly during the sardinella season, but because of its size could be afforded only by the relatively rich.

Adii nets required larger operations and bigger canoes; seasonal commerce increased. Bumper sardinella landings were made from August to October. In fact, the season could be extended to April by canoes moving to different parts of the coast. To distribute the benefit of good catches over time, the need for preservation grew (many more smoke ovens), along with more extensive marketing in which independent fish traders emerged. The roles of women in the latter activities increased.

For a man, *adii* fishing meant to some extent losing his individuality as the owner of a small net, and adapting to the role of a crew member operating a big net. However, his characteristic independence and notion of self-employment was carried over into a system of dividing catches into equal shares. The net owner, who was perhaps not a fisherman, generally got two shares, and the crew leader or *bosu* (bosun) got two. Outside the high season, the men individually fell back on small-scale tenga fishing. With time, *adii* nets grew longer and deeper, requiring much bigger canoes, and correspondingly the share system altered so that owners or investors received many more shares than a crew member. Even though productivity increased, the balance of advantage tilted in favour of those with financial capital.

Since the *adii* accumulated wealth, it brought forth categories of owners and workers. With bigger operations, labour started to become dissociated from the means of production (nets and canoes). However, transformation to a fully capitalist/labour division was incomplete because the system of shares paid in kind, reinforced by the trading role of family-related women, allowed crew members to retain their feeling of independence. But the *adii* stage is of importance because it marks the first step in a sequence of dissociation from independent subsistence to wage labour.

The implications of entrepreneurial advantage, and inequity through limited ownership of *adii* equipment, were not lost on the traditional leaders, many of whom opposed its use. They were supported by majorities who could not afford the big net. So began a famous internal controversy, lasting more than two decades before the 1920s.

Some chiefs issued by-laws banning the net, while those in favour of it took the matter to court. The case of the chiefs was probably not made convincingly because of the social complexity of their root objections. They expressed fear of destructive effects upon the fish stocks (which could not be proved); but in the main their complaint arose from 'unfairness' – some people catching much more than others, and consequent discontent. Very likely the new nets did promote internal conflict, and also involved a loss of authority for the chief fishermen.

The colonial authorities, on the other hand, had an official policy of 'no interference' in such matters. They probably knew they had not got to the bottom of the argument, but seem to have held the rather European point of view that, if new technology was more efficient, helped development, and in the end benefited everyone, there could not be much wrong with it. And so by a series of court judgements and steady unofficial persuasion, the contentious issue was put aside. From the early 1920s the *adii* became incorporated into usual practice.

This controversy would be an insignificant piece of history except that more and more innovations in the direction of entrepreneurial commercialism have, in hindsight, shown the chiefs' anxieties to be justified. They were concerned basically about disruption of tradition and their own authority, and feared for the integrity and welfare of their communities. The affair marks a turning point in Fante traditional life, and led to a more frankly capitalist market economy. Tradition nevertheless remained rooted.

The post-independence period 1958 to 1962 was pivotal. New technology flourished and political change came apace. Many significant things happened as culminations of trends or brand new developments.[9,10,11,12,13,14,15] Sardinella drift nets got even bigger, and in addition purse-seines evolved. It had become common to set the drift net around fish schools seen at the surface. Men would then jump into the water and drive the fish into the encircling net. Perhaps from this practice, or as a new introduction, purse-seines came into use. It is essentially a circularly set net with rings along the bottom, through which a line is pulled to 'purse' the net. Nylon webbing with small meshes was introduced, so the purse-seines trapped all the fish they encircled.

Greater mobility with outboard engines enabled fishermen to extend the sardinella season by 'following' fish schools. Outboard engines facilitated the Fante tradition of migrating from home villages during the sardinella season. It also made longer-term migrations to neighbouring West African countries more feasible. Migration can be seen as 'a strategy whereby the fisher people ... make the most out of the biological, social and economic resources that are within their reach'.[4] Close study of a Fante town revealed the primary goal of migration was to make money for investment at home, enhancing the well-being of their *ebusua* (matrilineage) and personal status. While abroad, the migrants live in communities following their own customary Fante institutions. Ability to migrate within a network of such places made the canoe fishery more resilient.

Outboard motors are said to have doubled catches. But they were just part of the increase in size of operations. Canoes grew bigger (to 15 m or more), nets larger and heavier to handle, and crews increased to 12–14, even 18 men per canoe. Of course, costs per unit grew many times. Indeed the entire pattern of financing and marketing took on new forms; a result being that market women became powerful as creditors and central in the fisheries economy. In many communities they owned the means of production (canoe, motor and gear). In the course of the 1960s, paddles and sails largely gave way to mechanisation.

Around the same time the small MFVs (such as I worked on at Axim) came into their own. Their numbers shot up to a remarkable 200 in the early 1960s, as Gordon's boat-building school expanded. However, 10-metre boats were found too small for going regularly to the edge of the shelf (50 km offshore), so larger boats up to 30 metres long were built as well. These trawled more deeply; consequently the 'alternative' fishing method I had been seeking at Axim turned out not to be shark catching with hook-and-line, but deeper trawling. The charter-party scheme, giving loans for vessels on favourable terms, expanded and numbers of boats climbed to 300 in 1965 and averaged 400 in 1970–74. The 1960s to mid-1970s were years of explosion in fishery development. It seemed to prove we had been on the right lines with the small boat scheme, based on step-by-step improvements on traditional life within a parsimonious budget.

However, this expansion was only partly due to profitability. Nkrumah and his party fervently wanted to industrialise quickly ('the big push' mentioned in Chapter 7). Colonial gradualism was rejected in favour of a drive inspired by Marxist ideology and the notion of modernising. The historic example of Russia was invoked, and Soviet financial support given. Indeed, international aid from many sources augmented abundant finance released from the government's inherited credit budget. In effect, the state gave out assets on easy repayment terms, along with subsidies and grants (e.g., subsidised fuel oil). In these boom years (so-called 'Klondyke period') there was no shortage of investors. Unfortunately many were not genuine entrepreneurs

Ghana, by independence in 1958, was relatively well off. It was the world's leading producer of cocoa, and traded in minerals, especially gold and timber, and had substantial currency reserves. Its road network, education system and general standard of living were comparatively high for the West Africa region. Parliamentary traditions of government had been introduced, and its civil service was acknowledged as one of the best among colonial administrations. The future looked promising.

Then power was centralised, as socialist theory required, and the instruments used to mobilise funds and administer loans were state corporations (along the lines of the old Cocoa Marketing Board inherited from colonial times; in fisheries it was the State Fisheries Corporation, SFC). Such corporations involved the state in almost every aspect of investment and commerce.

Eventually, limits to growth in the fishery were imposed by poor management and lack of skilled manpower at lower levels such as trained crew and especially mechanics. It was one thing to take delivery of a new boat on mortgage and another to operate it profitably. Supply of spare parts became a bottleneck; costs of these rose drastically in the 1970s along with a declining general economy. Widespread defaults on loans for boats and motors turned into a financial disaster. The Fisheries Corporation was incompetent and corrupt. In these circumstances, the development drive was bound to collapse, and a fall in catches in 1973 triggered it off.

The late 1970s were a time of general depression in Ghana. Dictator-style governments came and went (there were six governments after Nkrumah was deposed in 1966; the military heads of two of them were executed). The early 1980s brought more stability, and the World Bank assisted economic reform. This meant a long-term course of financial stringency, but large loans continued to be pumped in (foreign debt exceeded 4 billion US$ by 1990). Nevertheless, for the poorer members of society, there was hardship, unemployment, lower living standards and higher prices.

The nature of the rise and collapse of the small boat enterprise in Ghana led to undesirable repercussions. MFVs sharply changed the ethos of traditional fishing, with the pursuit of capital and use of quasi-wage labour. Concern over debt repayment and the accumulation of money to stay in business began to dominate over older concepts of participation, where shareholders were usually close family members. Community institutions were placed under stress. The challenge of continually having to increase catches and profits to match costs and running expenses shifted priorities to pecuniary ones. Defaults in repayments made credit harder to get, and the rates of money lenders were extortionate. In consequence, debt burdens came to override crew welfare. The old 'sharing' system became distorted as investors and boat owners cornered larger numbers of shares to cover costs. It became harder for crew members to retain the illusion of sharing in an enterprise though, strangely, some ambivalence and sense of personal independence still seemed to survive.

So in the end the plans of functionaries like me to progressively replace canoes with mechanised vessels did not succeed. Catch per boat fell steadily with diminishing fish stocks. MFV numbers fell drastically, and those still working now do so in constrained circumstances of low productivity and indebtedness. This once promising sector now catches less than 2% of the country's marine production.

In contrast, the fishery of outboard-driven canoes rose to over 8,000; manned by some 100,000 fishermen. Less financially encumbered, the artisanal canoe fishery proved to be resilient, persisting through many ups and downs despite much less government support than that given to mechanised boats. Catches grew until lately (62% to 76% of total marine landings over the last two decades), and they diversified to include large quantities of species other than sardinella – such as anchovy. However, this sector too is in danger. Profitability fell through multiple rises in costs of imported gear, spares and fuel through currency devaluation and the removal of subsidies. As fishing rates intensified – partly, unfortunately, by use of destructive methods such as smaller-mesh nets, beach seines and explosives – fish abundance fell and prices for the ordinary consumer steeply increased because this sector supplies the domestic market.[16]

In recent times, industrial trawlers and tuna vessels have increased in numbers and efficiency, contributing 36% of the marine catch, mostly exported overseas. In addition, distant-water foreign fishing vessels from the EU and other countries are present off Ghana. Officially they should remain outside the 200-mile exclusion zone, but it seems some intrude because law enforcement is weak. Thus it has turned out that a modern, capital-intensive sector, operating mainly in deep water, has been given priority by government.

To summarise, the Ghana fisheries steadily intensified but of late total catches have not risen. For canoes and MFVs, catches per vessel and per man are in decline. The resource is overfished and cannot absorb further intensification.

Discussion

'In the drive to modernise the economy of a developing country through technology transfer, how can we ensure that the new technology can be effectively integrated [without] becoming an instrument for perpetrating social disorganisation, exploitation and a new form of poverty?'[10]

This question was asked in an analysis of events at Mumford, a small fishing village west of Accra. Mumford passed through the kind of transformation described above, from a canoe fishery with *adii* nets, through use of outboard motors to small diesel-powered fishing vessels. Life changed from a stable traditional model to one with acute social problems. At individual level, the story can be summarised in parable form:

> A certain man was head of an extended family and fished with his kinsmen for a living, using a canoe and nets. At the end of each fishing season the family met together and the fishwives rendered account of their trading, dividing profits among the fishermen, who received equal shares, and repaying all debts. One year, they took advantage of a government loan for an outboard motor. This made their heavy labour with paddles and sail much easier, and they caught more fish. So they bought a bigger canoe and recruited more kinsmen to work a bigger net. And they prospered. In a few years the chance came to buy a fishing vessel with a diesel engine, getting loans from a bank and a moneylender. In taking this step, the man mortgaged his house, put his son in charge of the vessel and saw to his business onshore, making sure his income covered the interest payments to his creditors.
>
> Then he was beset by many troubles. The diesel engine often failed to work. They did what they could but to little avail – it needed a

mechanic, and anyway spare parts were difficult to get and costly. When not fishing, the crew still turned to him for food, so he fired his kinsmen and took on wage labourers as needed from nearby villages. With rising running costs it became harder to make a profit. Loan repayment was short-term, and the moneylender required 100% interest. So the man borrowed more from his relatives, and in exchange gave both them and the moneylender shares of the catch. But the remaining shares for the crew were too small, and they were discontented. Then came lean years when fish were no longer abundant in the sea. In the past, the man's cares had been for his family, but now the family were dispersed and his worries centred on money. His house also was threatened by debt.

Obviously there is more involved here than just 'transfer of technology'. The crucial question is the *integration* of the technology into the traditional local scene. The context is not just Mumford village, but overall the people of the Ghana coast have lived through a succession of outside influences and ideas, sweeping over them like tides ('isms' like nationalism, socialism, capitalism, as well as modernisation and market economics). Slowly evolving tradition had merged with colonial gradualism. Then came nationalism and the boom of Nkrumah times followed by a bust of depression, re-adjustment of government structure and slow economic recovery. To the villager it was a bewildering succession of new hopes while local circumstances failed to improve. Poverty still characterises the coastal fishing villages, and there are now more mouths to feed – Ghana's population has trebled in 50 years.

To a general observer outside the industry, the original idea was to assist coastal people to build up their fishery and supply fish for the domestic market. Development accelerated at independence then collapsed. With 'structural adjustment' in the 1980s, market orientation crucially shifted from the home market towards exporting fish. Related to this, development priorities switched from the inshore fishery to a growing, heavily capitalised industrial offshore fishery of big boats, with storage and processing facilities concentrated at ports. That way, the government earned foreign exchange. For the past two decades the industrial fleet has prospered, mostly in joint ventures with foreign companies.[17] Monitoring and surveillance of their activities is not good (unknown amounts are transhipped at sea and landed in other countries). In contrast, in the lower socio-economic artisanal sector, standards of living are falling, alternative livelihoods are scarce and unemployment is a serious problem.

Along the way, interesting paradoxes have cropped up. The socialist drive to industrialise and raise standards of living ended, ironically, by encouraging petty capitalism (and permitting large-scale corruption). The fishing boat project, which was to offer the canoe fisherman an opportunity to get modern, turning him into a small businessman, failed. And here the paradox is that while boat and methods were efficient, and theoretically within the reach of a competent fisherman to acquire ('appropriate technology'), the scheme did not work out because commercial and financial exigencies did not match traditional attitudes and practices.

A more general paradox is presented by the current artisanal fishery, which employs as many as 120,000 fishermen. It represents an important livelihood for the Fante people, and supplies the country with most of its fish. Nevertheless it remains poor though it has expanded and intensified. Outboard motors and nylon nets were imported and fuel subsidised, but the continuous improvements in method and technique were innovations by the fishermen themselves.

The most fundamental question lies in the mismatch between traditional and modern paradigms.[14] As described above, traditional Fante institutions acknowledge lineage and kinship, have their own ways of resolving conflict by negotiation, have particular concepts of gender duality, and are based primarily upon the notion of the welfare of local communities. Their integrated way of life works through a complex system of alliances, tributes and reciprocity. On the other hand, 'modern' systems emphasise technology, the manipulation of capital, the discipline of work, and individualism – where the more efficient individuals become the principal beneficiaries of the resource.

If the experience of 50 years is anything to go by, money and technology from abroad are not by themselves solutions leading to a better life for the fisherfolk. After national independence too much money was thrown into the industry, which was not well administered. More lately, resources have been (mis)directed to encouraging big industry, largely foreign-owned, while neglecting the local fishery which employs and supplies a large number of people. The question posed in the above parable about integrating new technology into an old social environment takes in the dilemma of the gulf between traditional and modern attitudes. Perhaps the question is, how can traditionally based artisanal systems flourish in an equitable relationship with industrial systems, or are they by nature incompatible?

I have overrun my tale and must return to 1958. My vagueness about the large political affairs going on about me now seems curiously unthinking. I should have comprehended the significance of the times, because Ghana was then the forerunner of nationalist movements in Africa. These few years of the late 1950s – early 1960s covered, as I've indicated, a historic watershed, a time of sea change. Britain was evidently pulling out, for good or ill, and it was said the French were considering leaving West Africa too. Except for India in 1947 nothing like it had happened before (Indian independence was attended by terrible violence). Ghana was the big experiment in African decolonisation; the first splitting off of nation states – which of course had never previously existed as nations.

Furthermore, by 1958 it had emerged that Nkrumah's vision was not limited to Ghana. He talked about African unity as a goal, and African socialism, whatever that meant, as a method. A cloud of political theory had descended upon Ghana, which was hard to interpret in terms of concrete plans. Nkrumah's statue erected in Accra (pulled down within a decade) had inscribed on it the parody 'Seek ye first the political kingdom'. No details, just doctrine.

The idea of accelerated change and expenditure to match came only a few years before independence. Whether the old scenario of gradual progress under tutelage would have continued to work, we shall never know. But the pressure for change was not a general revolution. It came from radicals rather than the body of the population. Indeed, I think now the underlying cause of change was a weakening in Britain's desire to rule; acceptance that the time of Empire was drawing to a close. The heart for it had gone, and the home establishment realised that dependent colonies were simply not affordable.

As far as the new Ghana was concerned, I undoubtedly belonged to the years before and around national independence – the end of the colonial era. My contract was up and time had run out. I'd been deeply interested and would gladly have carried on, but expatriates in government departments had no future. As a relative newcomer, I could accept events and see the political steamroller with detachment. I left Axim in an optimistic mood knowing the work would go on under a capable colleague.

Obviously, all did not view cataclysmic change in the same way. A few long conversations with FRJ near the end, remarkable because of his normal taciturnity, indicated the frustration, even bitterness of old-timers. His feelings were more intense than mine. As head of a department he was in the thick of change in Accra. He knew where the country had come from, but couldn't see where it was going and was anxious. Especially, he feared the likelihood of extravagance and corruption. After decades of service, the Gold Coast had become his life. Periodic leaves in England served only to confirm an increasing distance from home and greater affinity with Africa.

But the new regime was distinctly different from the step-by-step mode of indirect rule the old-timers knew, with its limited finance and largely rural view. They could only climb the great mountain of development at a moderate pace.

Notes and references

1. See Matthew Arnold's poem 'The Future':
   And the width of the waters, the hush
   Of the grey expanse where he floats,
   Freshening its current and spotted with foam
   As it draws to the Ocean, may strike
   Peace to the soul of the man on its breast:
   As the pale waste widens around him –
   As the banks fade dimmer away –
   As the stars come out, and the night wind
   Brings up the stream
   Murmers and scents of the infinite sea.'
2. Conrad, J. (1900). *Lord Jim.* Blackwood. 451pp.
3. Christensen, J.B. (1977). Motor power and woman power: Technological and economic change among the Fanti fishermen of Ghana. pp.71–95 In: *Those Who Live From the Sea* (Ed. Estell Smith), Monograph 62, The American Ethnological Society. West Publ. Co.
4. Overa, R. (2001). *Institutions, mobility and resilience in the Fante migratory fisheries of West Africa.* Chr. Michelsen Institute, WP 2001:2, Bergen, Norway.
5. Vercruijsse, E. (1984). *The Penetration of Capitalism: A West African case study.* Zed Books, London. 180pp.
6. US Country Studies – Ghana US Country Studies – Ghana. www.mongabay.com/reference/countrystudies/ghana/all.html
7. Walker, B.L. (2002). *Colonial history of marine fishing and property rights in Ghana.* Conference on Marine & Environmental Politics in 21st Century; Institute of International Studies, UC Berkeley, USA.
8. Walker, B.L. (2001). Sisterhood and seine-nets: Engendering development and conservation in Ghana's marine fishery. *Professional Geographer, 53*(2): 160–177.
9. Koranteng, K.A. (1992). *The marine artisanal fishery in Ghana: Recent developments and implications for resource evaluation. Proceedings of World Fisheries Congress (Athens 1992).* In: Meyer, R., Zhang, C., Windsor, M., McCay, B., Husack, L. & Muth, R. (Eds.), Science Publishers, Lebanon, USA.
10. Ninsin, K.A. (1991). Economic modernisation and social change: Evidence from Mumford, a Ghanaian fishing village. *Africa, 61*(1): 99–116.
11. Hernaes, P. (1991). *Modernizing Ghanaian Fisheries: The need for social carriers of technology.* Chapter 2. Tapir.
12. Hernaes, (1991) p.115
13. Christensen (1977), p.90; quotations:

'While no structured sample was taken regarding marriage and divorce, data available indicates that divorce is common, even to the extent of being the norm rather than the exception. One contributing factor is the economic independence of women. With the practice of each canoe selling fish to one particular female, the fisherman and his wife or wives no longer constitute an economic unit to the former extent. If the wife of a non-owner fisherman wishes to deal in fish she is likely to have to buy from some other woman. If the woman has the capital to obtain two or more pans (or basins, generally carried on the head), and can realise the minimal 25 percent profit (and most make at least that gain) she will make more from selling fish than her husband will from catching them.'

'This picture of economic and organizational misery which the history of the SFC represents, appears to have been all too common among Ghanaian State Enterprises. The major problem was that many of them were set up primarily as a result of political ambitions; they were not based on thorough economic planning or analysis or the feasibility of the projects. Never forced to function on strict commercial principles, they were kept going for political reasons and allowed to drain state coffers – decade after decade. In reality they became public utility services whose main practical purpose was to serve as a source of employment.'

14. Bennett, E. (2001). *The challenges of managing small scale fisheries in West Africa.* CEMARE Final Technical Report, Fisheries Management & Science Programme, MRAG Ltd., Queen Street, London.
15. Bennett, E. & Bannerman, P. (2001). *Country Report (Ghana). CEMARE Report on The Management of Conflict in Tropical Fisheries, Fisheries Management & Science Programme.* MRAG Ltd., Queen Street, London, p.64: 'These were the well-known "structural adjustment" policies associated with the International Monetary Fund and the World Bank, and applied in other collapsed economies of developing countries to get them out of the red. In Ghana's case, the resulting Economic Recovery Programme involved, as well as fiscal stringency, dismantling the system of State Corporations, devaluing the currency, focussing on exports and slimming down internal spending on imports, government departments, subsidies etc. It has been claimed that Ghana is a model case of structural adjustment, and while the economy as a whole became more efficient the equity issue (poverty) has not been addressed.'
16. Atta-Mills, J., Alder, J. & Sumaila, U.R. (2004). The decline of a regional fishing nation: The case of Ghana and West Africa. *Natural Resources Forum, 28*: 13–21.

    Interesting statistics from Atta-Mills et al (2004) are that the fishery sector in Ghana supports 1.5 million people, of which 27% are directly employed. Annual total landings are about 360,000 tonnes, most from a continental shelf of 23,700 km^2. Annual demand approximates 600,000 t. Ghana imports about 170,000 t. of low value frozen fish, and exports about 54,000 t. of high value fish. Ghana is a net importer of fish.

    Industrial fishery: Total landings have decreased since the mid-1980s, but fishing effort increased over the same period; e.g., trawler effort increased from 500 days in 1974 to 5,500 days in 1990.

    Artisanal fishery: Catches increased up to 1992 and then generally declined (the catch is prone to natural fluctuations). Numbers of fishermen increased from 97,000 in the 1980s to 123,000 in year 2000. In the same period, canoe numbers rose from about 8,700 to 10,000 (and larger canoes came into use requiring more crew). Catches fell from 35 t. per canoe in 1992 to 23 t. in 2001.

17. Seini, A., Nyanteng, V. & Ahene, A. (2004). *Policy dynamics, trends in domestic fish production and implications for food security in Ghana.* ISSER Univ. Ghana – Cornell Univ. Conference, July 2004, University of Ghana, Accra.

3

Apprenticeship

This chapter is a rather personal account of journeys from Cape Town, South Africa, to Northern Rhodesia (now Zambia), and then to the Zambezi River, the Bangweulu Swamps and Lake Tanganyika – I was to work at one of these places. The period covered some 15 months in 1959–60, and for me was a time of adjustment to Central Africa and to research – hence an 'apprenticeship'. I participated in a project to study the Bangweulu Swamps, and here include an account of the fishery of the Unga people of the Swamps.

Choices

'Where are you going with that, eh?' said the man who hoisted my car from ship to wharf at Cape Town.

'Lake Bangweulu,' I said.

'Where's that?'

'Oh, Central Africa,' I replied. We gazed at my little car, ridiculously top-heavy with oversize roof rack tapering down to tiny wheels. Its faded wishy-washy pink colour in the bright morning sun ('arundel-lilac') gave it a down-at-heel, second-hand appearance. He grinned in a friendly way, 'Sooner you than me,' adding a note of uncertainty and spice to the prospect.

The vehicle had been bought duty free from the factory in England in a flurry of arrangements, the smallest cheapest Ford available. Driving it to Liverpool for the same ship as us it had broken down in the Mersey Tunnel. Vital wires of the dashboard had apparently disconnected themselves. We were rescued from among whizzing traffic by the Automobile Association. The roof rack was my masterpiece of planning to carry bulky essentials, for there was little baggage room in the miniscule boot, and Dianne (not yet two) needed the entire rear seat to live and play in. Other worldly goods were dispatched in a crate labelled 'Samfya, Lake Bangweulu, Northern Rhodesia', where months later it turned up.

Figure 3. Sub-Saharan Africa

The morning in Cape Town was stunning. It must be one of the nicest places on earth to approach by ship. The spectacular mountain background draped in white cloud, crystal light, warmth, and gracious buildings, give the city a buoyant welcoming air. The 'Cape of Good Hope' indeed. Founded in 1652, it felt startlingly like Europe. I bought a map, and it showed the drive to Northern Rhodesia would take a week or two. At that time, new cars had to be 'run-in', which meant travelling under 80 km/hr for the first 1500 km. However, my new organisation had said simply 'make your own way up from Cape Town'. I was to find that trust in personal initiative was typical of the system we were joining. The prospect of finding our own way was in any case exciting.

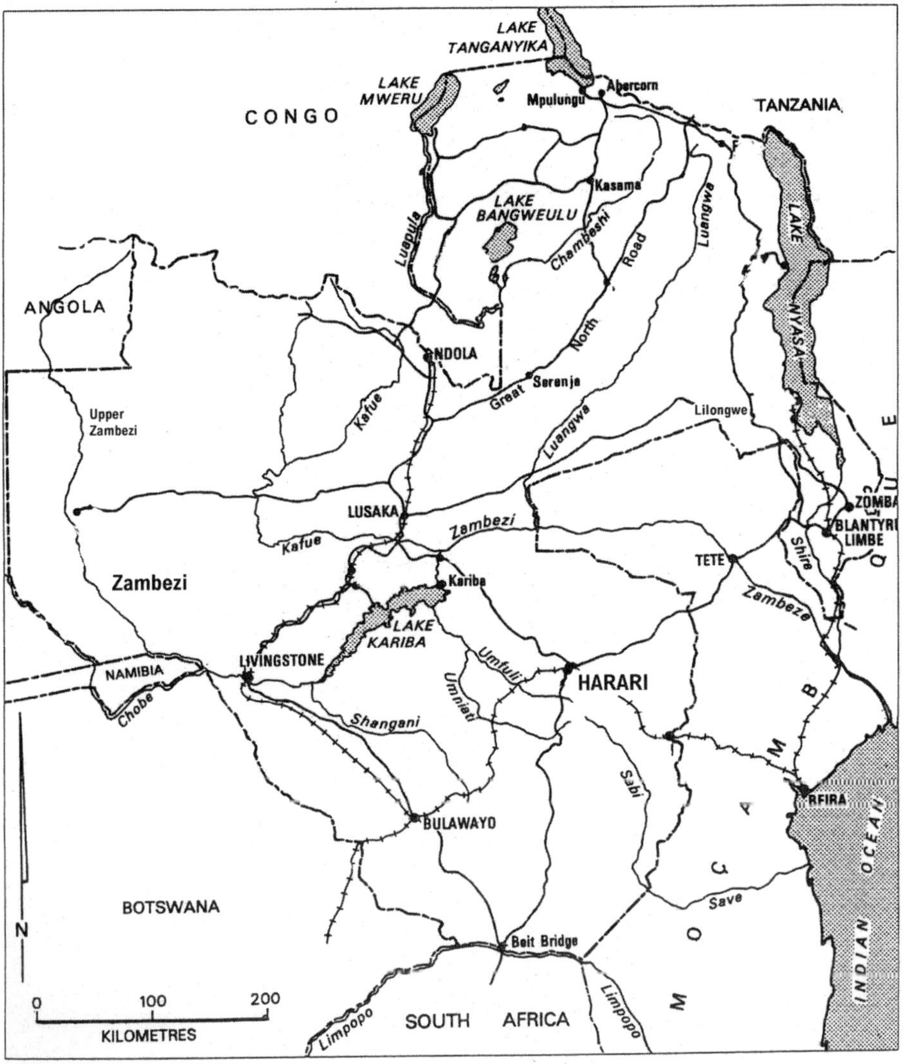

Figure 4. Territory of the former Federation of Northern and Southern Rhodesia and Nyasaland (1953-63), which became Zambia, Zimbabwe and Malawi, respectively. The work of the Joint Fisheries Research Organisation (JFRO) extended from Lake Tanganyika to Lake Kariba, and from Lake Nyasa/Malawi to the upper Zambezi River. From Jackson (2000).[1]
(Country border ---------- railway ++++)

Remembering the Mersey Tunnel breakdown we took it easy, venturing little off the main road. This enchanting hinterland of vineyards, with substantial farmhouses and old towns such as Stellenbosch, is of a piece historically with Cape Town. From there we crossed the mountains and plains of the Great Karoo, a place of marvellous spaces and far views. We'd decided to stay only in small towns or dorps, avoiding cities where possible. On our second night I went for a walk, and in a short distance left houses and lights behind. The silence was complete, no sight, or sound of man and, unlike West Africa, no night noises of insect, bird or frog. It had rained, and the stars were brilliant in clear chill air. This utter stillness and awareness of space was a new experience for me. Far away the hoot of a steam railway engine came faintly, followed briefly by a clatter of carriage wheels, then silence again – moments that crystallise in the memory.

The hotels and houses where we stayed contained something of this pervasive stillness. I remember cool rooms, high ceilings, old furniture of stinkwood and wax-polished floors. The hotel bar in the evening would be occupied by a few men, heavy-looking farmers who kept their hats on. Some played chess. No music, no women, only desultory exchanges in Afrikaans. They were formally polite, without going beyond simple greetings. I contrasted it with the chat and bustle of English pubs.

After Bloemfontein we circled Johannesburg and dawdled through the broad streets of Pretoria, not a busy place then, and on to the high veldt. Our daily routine was an early start with a long break at noon in a road lay-by. These are considerately designed in South Africa to be well off the road with ample shade for picnicking. Dianne could run around and play. Where the road branches east to the Kruger Park we had an incident in a rather rough lay-by with long grass and shrubs and a stone wall. After lunch, spread on a cloth on the ground, we sat back sleepily – in Margaret's case she leaned against the wall. In a while, feeling movement between herself and the wall, she became uncomfortable. I think the same thought struck both of us at once, and leaping up we beheld our first puff adder. It is a thick, patterned snake, poisonous but slow moving – except when it strikes. The creature had evidently been snoozing at the base of the warm wall and was beginning to wake up, or snuggle up

We had to cross the Limpopo, Zambesi and Luapula Rivers (see Figures 3 & 4). The Limpopo at Beit Bridge is not impressive but a historic boundary. Entering Southern Rhodesia (now Zimbabwe), we headed northwest to Bulawayo on an excellent sealed highway with little traffic. My photographs show roads deteriorating thereafter. Confidence in our little car had grown on good roads, but after Bulawayo the sealed surface shrank to two narrow

Roads of varying quality

A highway in South Africa.

Zimbabwe.

Zambia.

Burundi.

strips on which the wheels had to be carefully aligned. When another car approached on the same strips, one simply moved over, keeping two wheels on a strip. In Wankie Game Reserve the first buck I saw was a sable. Strangely, only twice in future years was I to see that splendid antelope again. No elephant were visible, just their significant deposits on the road. The Zambezi at Victoria Falls was in tremendous flood, its spray limiting the view. The photographs show aspects during the dry season.

A dramatic iron bridge spanning the Zambezi gorge below the Falls took

An unusual view of Victoria Falls, flying along the lip of the gorge in the dry season

Victoria Falls from the Zambia side (the rainbow can occur indefinitely)

us into Northern Rhodesia (Zambia) at Livingstone (see Figure 3). Hippo were grazing at the river bank. I suppose Margaret and I chatted about these while Dianne, in the back seat, looked and listened. Later that night as we passed the Kafue, one of the Zambezi's tributaries, a hippopotamus could be seen in bright moonlight standing near the road, its black bulk clear against a lighter background of river and grass. Dianne had an unexpected reaction. Perhaps some horror had grown from our conversations about hippos at the Zambezi, and now here was one up close in a ghostly light. She screamed inconsolably.

The Zambia 'Copperbelt' was a cluster of mining towns, a growth phenomenon mainly of the fifties. They looked what they were, raw boom towns, monotonously single-storey with corrugated iron roofs. Streets were crowded with blacks and whites. Other ethnicities were rare, but in reality of course we were looking at a society where both blacks and whites were diverse among themselves. Many tribes from Central Africa were attracted by employment at the mines, and most Europeans (many recent immigrants) were copper mine personnel too.

The only obvious racial rudeness encountered on our journey was in the Copperbelt. I had seen the labels 'blankies' and 'nie-blankies' at park seats and public toilets in Cape Town, but I must confess that to us at the time it seemed only some sort of legalism or by-law rather than offensive discrimination. Racial mixing in the city had a relaxed air. Strange as it may seem now, one tended as a first-time visitor simply to accept things in South Africa as the way they were. Of course, as residents we might have seen it differently. In Ghana I was used to different races co-existing. I don't think I had prejudice as such (was not a 'racist' in modern terminology), but tended rather to accept and adapt to what was manifest. The notion of legal separation of races (apartheid) was unfamiliar, but the subject had not then become a contentious theme. People in all their fascinating diversity were more interesting to us than politics. I realise this may sound disingenuous. Years of emotional anti-apartheid campaigns in Western countries have fundamentally changed our perceptions, so it is almost impossible now to disassociate matters of race and culture from politics and 'human rights'. We lived in simpler times.

Leaving Ndola (see Figure 4) the route north went through the strange geopolitical Congo 'pedicle' – an unlikely protrusion of land jutting from the Congo into present-day Zambia (Figure 3). No doubt its raison d'être was originally connected with possession of copper deposits. Cutting across it meant two inconvenient sets of customs and immigration posts. At the first I was summarily arrested by an agitated Congolese border guard, on charges of driving on the wrong side of the road and threatening to assault a policeman. We were detained in a hot room pending the return from his lunch of a Belgian official. I admitted guilt as to the wrong side of the road – it was so bad as to make no difference where one was on it – but had only tried to explain myself to his hysterical guard. The official grumpily let us go. I determined to avoid the pedicle in future.

On to a minor administrative station with a few stores (Fort Rosebery, now Mansa), where we turned down a bush track for another 80 km to reach Samfya at Lake Bangweulu (see Figure 5). The track, it seemed, could hardly have been narrower and still allow vehicles to pass, but according to our map it must lead to Lake Bangweulu. Eventually, the trees opened up to a large sand hill on which a dozen or so bungalows were perched, facing north over the lake. It had taken two weeks to reach this insignificant destination.

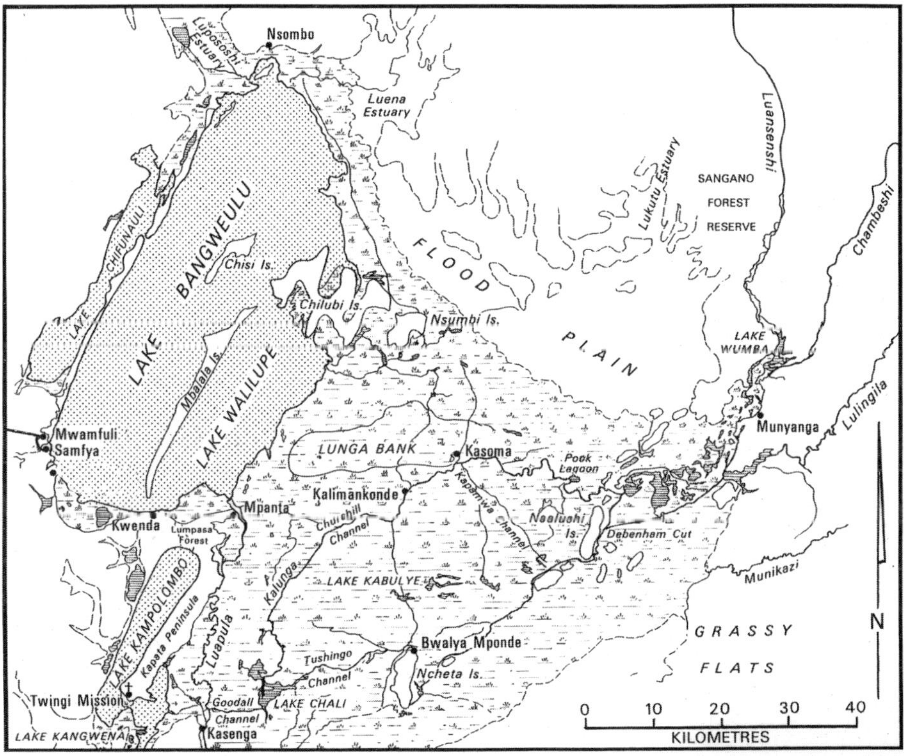

Figure 5. Lake Bangweulu and the Bangweulu Swamps, showing main villages, lakes and swamp channels. From Debenham (1952).
JFRO was based at Samfya at the southwest corner of Lake Bangweulu. Sampling circuits passed through various swamp channels between Mpanta on the Luapula River and Munyanga at the eastern side of the swamp.

Half a century later the diversity of this journey through southern Africa remains clearly in mind: the tranquil Cape with its centuries-old vineyards and steep hinterlands, merging into the rolling plains and rocky kopjies of the austere Karoo. Beyond that, flat maize farms of the Orange Free State then the rolling high veldt of the Transvaal – vivid in colour and clarity. Southern Rhodesia (Zimbabwe), with great fertile farms of maize and tobacco, had towns obviously newer than South Africa connected by splendid roads. North of the Zambezi, forests dominated and European influence diminished. There were more villages and people beside the road. The remote corner where we finally fetched up was a tiny enclave of whites in a land of blacks, distant from shops, without telephones, connected only to the main road by a track that looked as if it might disappear in the rains. In compensation, the view over the lake was splendid. To the east, lay the great Bangweulu Swamps, one of the largest permanent wetlands of the world (see Figure 5).

At the first bungalow was a car with two legs in shorts and white stockings sticking out from beneath. A middle-aged man with round face, moustache and a twinkle struggled out. 'Hello,' he said. 'We've ... er ... been rather expecting you. My name's Tim and I'm the DC [District Commissioner]. Just been fixing the car,' he continued, in what I would later know as his vague way. 'Anyway, here's Betty my wife. Come in and have tea.'

We did not talk much about our trip; it would have been familiar ground to them. And our dusty appearance needed no explanation. We had a laugh about the previous occupants of the house in which we were assigned to live. They had been an odd couple. The man, who had a large beard and bald head, apparently slept naked at night. Waking up one night he heard his chickens squawking and, thinking it was a raiding leopard, went out with his rifle. Whereupon his wife panicked, cut the lights and locked the doors. Fortunately, the leopard made off.

Samfya, we found, was only these few houses, plus the DC's office, the JFRO research offices, a mechanical workshop and a forestry nursery. The village of Mwamfuli was near, and beside it a Plymouth Brethren mission and further a Catholic mission. At any one time, about half the government officers would be travelling in the District, leaving the social life of Samfya in the hands of their wives – five ladies of whom Margaret was the youngest. They would pop in to see one another for coffee, and in the afternoons gather at the beach with half a dozen children. A woman's life on such stations tended to be dull since it was rarely possible for a wife to take up work of her own. The husbands were much more in everyday contact with African people by the nature of their occupations.

H.M. Colonial Research Service theoretically meant switching from dealing directly with people, as I had done in Ghana, to biological research. But in fact no clear-cut difference was possible. My job would be to initiate a research programme, recruit and train helpers and see to their welfare, carry out field work and finally write up the data. From day to day this meant almost anything; for example, building some kind of laboratory, staff matters, ordering equipment, knowing enough about engines to keep them running, all at the same time as sampling and studying fish stocks. Life in the field involved being self-sufficient to a degree inconceivable in a research institute. Distraction was the common complaint of my colleagues in fisheries research.

In its wisdom the Colonial Office appreciated the great importance of the lakes and rivers of Central Africa in providing a food resource; but before investment in fishery development, research was needed. So a Joint Fisheries Research Organisation (JFRO) for Northern Rhodesia and Nyasaland was set up (Southern Rhodesia had no major fisheries at the time).[1] Figure 4 shows JFRO's extended parish. Its head office at Lake Bangweulu was a compromise; distant sub-stations were at the south of Lake Nyasa/Malawi (960 km), Lake Tanganyika (640 km), Lake Mweru (320 km), the Lower Kafue River (630 km) and beyond that the Zambezi. This small, far-flung organisation proposed to have at least one project and one scientist at each place.

The tale of JFRO's accomplishments between 1950 and its end in 1962 has been entertainingly told by Peter Jackson, the officer-in-charge.[1] Arriving in May 1959, I was fortunate to be given the choices of working either on the Zambezi River and new Kariba Dam, or Lake Tanganyika or to stay at Samfya and the Bangweulu Swamps. Clearly I had to get to these places immediately to see where my unproved talents might be useful. I shall always be grateful to Peter J. for leaving the options open, and I never regretted my choice.

Land Rover travel on unsurfaced roads, by the ubiquitous short-wheelbase version, was as comfortable as riding a camel, and directly to blame for the painful condition known as 'landrover spine'. Long distances required night stops in government rest-houses, small whitewashed brick cottages near a boma. Bed, bath and cook were provided. One was often the only guest in these oases of comfort and quietness. Different conditions prevailed in the dry and rainy seasons. Laterite roads in the dry were corrugated in ripples over which a Land Rover passed smoothly enough at 80 km/hr, but at speeds under that the impacts of corrugations were transferred to the driver's spine. In the wet season, pot-holes existed containing water of

Rough country in Middle Zambesi valley, before the Kariba Dam

Unselective fish sampling in a rock pool in the dry Zambezi bed

Elephants in dry-season bush, Middle Zambezi

Operation Noah: activity in an animal corral – from a safe distance

unknown depth: hazards not to be taken head on. The good old PWD (Public Works Department) kept vehicles operational, and no doubt did their best about the roads.

Kariba Dam was then under construction. The part of the Zambezi to be flooded was the 290 km stretch between Victoria Falls and Kariba gorge. Though mighty in the wet season, the Zambezi was reduced in the dry to a small flow winding its way through rocky pools at the bottom of a steep, forested valley. From impoundment in December 1958, it took four years for the lake with its extensive side branches to fill. This so-called 'Middle Zambezi' region was remote, and tribal people there had lived practically undisturbed by traders or missionaries. Vehicle tracks were few, and larger wildlife such as elephant, rhino and buffalo fairly abundant. Our job in JFRO was to study the original fauna of the river, and eventually estimate the fisheries potential of Kariba Dam. A few fish-collecting surveys had already been made when river flow was low. These studies indicated fish predator–prey relations were important, and especially the ecological impacts of the 'tiger fish' *Hydrocynus*. The chief problem overall was whether any of the river fish species would flourish in the open waters of the new Lake Kariba and form a productive fishery. Or would it need to be stocked with species from elsewhere?

An interesting current activity was the rescue of wild animals from islands as the dam waters rose (the so-called 'Operation Noah'). Antelopes were entangled by nets, and bigger game anaesthetised by rifle-propelled dart. It was pioneering stuff, as very little was known then about the dosages of anaesthetics. Corrals had to be built and ways of transporting the immobilised beasts across water worked out – complications much greater than merely shooting them. It was slow and dangerous work. Results, however, were equivocal since the groggy animals fell easy prey to local hunters.

More difficult problems would beset the new lake which were not then foreseen; notably, floating masses of water weed (*Salvinia, Eichornia*) which blocked great areas of lake. On the human side, controversial re-settlement plans were in train to move people displaced by the dam. They had, of course, no choice but to go. Resettlement approaches were different between the south shore (S. Rhodesia) and north shore (N. Rhodesia), which increased complications and strife. Unhappy parallels with resettlement at the Volta Dam in Ghana came to mind. Frankly, I did not care for the Middle Zambezi Valley, at most times furnace hot and in parts resembling the surface of the moon. At Kariba itself where the dam wall was being built, a construction-camp atmosphere prevailed.

So I went north to Lake Tanganyika and promptly fell under its spell –

which has lasted the rest of my life. One cannot describe Tanganyika except in superlatives, such as the oldest and deepest lake in Africa with the greatest water volume, containing by far the most diverse array of aquatic species, many of which evolved there. Moreover it is beautiful. One arrives at a breathtaking view of wide blue water and distant mountains, just as Burton and Speke, the first European visitors, described on arriving in 1858 (see Chapter 8). The great chasm of the basin stretches northward for 640 km, and the Zambian bit at the south is 80 km wide.

Three government rest-houses stood on a promontory overlooking the lake shore. Thatched and attractively built of stone they were cool inside. One was to be my home for two weeks a month for the next year. The Tanzania coast stretched away on the northeast, and on the distant western side high mountains of the Congo formed the skyline. Niamkolo village was nearby. Its ruined church with an incongruous square Norman tower was built by the London Missionary Society in 1895. It would have seemed at home in England, but here was merely a desolate presence,[2] standing as a memorial to the tragically curtailed efforts of the first missionaries. The church would have had little future in any case, for in 1908 all the lakeshore population was evacuated ten miles inland because of the prevalence of sleeping sickness. One of the first things one notices is that the trees round this part of the lakeshore are cleared for 10 metres above the waterline to eliminate habitat of tsetse fly, the carrier of sleeping sickness. A few missions have survived from early times elsewhere on the lakeshore, such as at Karema on the Tanzanian coast.

My brief for research was broad. According to Peter Jackson, I was to 'do something useful; study the biological basis of the fishery and make practical suggestions for management and development'. An almost limitless programme, which of course had to be tailored to a small budget and my own energies. It was limited too by our ignorance of the immense ecosystem.

Nearshore the transparent water contained numerous coloured fish, members of the marvellous Cichlidae family, many of them located on mounds of sand and gravel which they constructed as nests and breeding territory. Around rocks swarmed myriad fish as on a coral reef, brilliantly coloured and patterned with conspicuous spots and bars. The real fishery, however, was out in deep water. It consisted of sardine (clupeids of the herring family) and four Nile perch species which prey on them. From my rest-house at night the lake was dotted with bobbing fishing lamps borne on canoes. Occasional distant rattling sounds came across the water as fishermen thumped their canoe sides with paddles, making sardine shoals rise to the surface. A traditional dip net (the lusenga – see this book's cover) was

The ruin of LMS Church near Mpulungu beside Lake Tanganyika; this is possibly the oldest church in Zambia

Bush clearance for 10 metres above the lake, a measure to reduce tsetse-fly habitat

The old Catholic mission at Karema has maintained its work at the lakeshore in Tanzania since the 1890s

Purse-seiner returning to land early in the morning, laden with crew and catch

used to scoop out the fish. In previous eras light was provided by bundles of burning sticks on the canoe bow.

As well, a commercial 'industrial' fishery was starting, funded by a grant from the copper industry. It employed a purse-seiner vessel, freezing installations on shore and refrigerated trucks to connect with the distant Copperbelt. A South African manager, Harry, and Scots fisherman, Tom, were the only resident Europeans. Tom slept during the day in a neighbouring rest-house and fished at night. Sometimes I went with him and his crew of thirty. Their fishing outfit had been purchased from Greeks operating in Burundi waters at the north of the lake where these vessels, seiner and lamp boats, were constructed. Crudely welded and functional they in no way catered for comfort. Such a large crew were needed for hand-hauling the big seine.[3] At about 10 km out, Tom would drop off the lamp boats, one by one. That done, he brewed tea, put in a spoonful of whisky, and curled up for a few hours sleep while fish gathered under the lamps. The crew slept too, aware of work ahead. As for me, I lay gazing at the stars as I would on many future nights.

Dense schools of sardine had accumulated around the lamp boats and we circled each in turn casting the deep purse-seine. Each haul took an hour. Tom was normally a quiet man, I think, but from the moment he woke to start fishing his voice was raised continually – orders, oaths and encouragement, he never stopped. By daylight we had a couple of tons of fish, at least half being good-sized Nile perch (some around 100 cm long). I was fascinated by the swirling masses of sardines under the fishing lamps. Small jellyfish medusae pulsated like gleaming coins. Occasionally fish-eating snakes – a tiny endemic one and a big cobra – wriggled across the lamp beam near the water surface.

I explored the coast with a borrowed launch. It was sparsely populated, the southwestern arm being a beautiful game reserve with animals visible on the shore. By day the transparent lake was apparently unproductive – little plankton to be seen – though in nearshore shallows a great variety of fish and invertebrates existed. But further out abundant evidence of life was given by gulls diving here and there. At these places the water boiled with fish, where pelagic Nile perch drove sardine schools up to the surface. All this – wave-crested water, fish schools and gulls – gave a strong impression of the sea, and it was obviously productive.

However, Tom and his diesel-driven vessel, big net and marketing organisation, would no doubt be followed by larger commercial enterprises. Only for the present might this ancient, diverse ecosystem be seen in its virgin state. I thought of it as the aquatic equivalent of the great mammalian fauna of Africa that existed before the gun.

Of course I hastened back to Samfya, euphoric with plans for the future; the only worry now that some obstacle might crop up to prevent assignment to Tanganyika. I could not bear to think of another posting. The little town of Abercorn on the escarpment above the lake seemed ideal. The district boma was there, and a small expatriate community, some farmers, shops, church, hospital, etc, even a golf course. Just outside the town lay a delightful little lake, Chila, surrounded by forest. At the far side were a few houses. Blessed are those, I thought, lucky enough to live there.

And so it turned out. Fortune smiled, and funds were available for a research vessel and a house beside Lake Chila, though the dream-come-true would take a while, as both boat and house had to be built. Meanwhile, I would commute by road from Samfya. It took about a year, until May 1960, but the delay was providential, giving time to learn the elements of tropical limnology and to recruit a team of assistants.

Attracting recruits was easy, selection was not. I was besieged by dozens of unemployed young men. Nearly all began with 'I have got a Standard Six certificate'. It was the same story as in West Africa. Missions and government elementary schools had for years turned out great numbers of youths who could read, write and count in English. But there was no work for them. Education made them disinclined to follow their fathers' life of farming and fishing. Naturally, discontent festered. Some went for spells in the mines to make money. These youngsters were obvious fodder for social unrest, and indeed by then were receiving attention from agitators. The political example of Ghana had quickly spread, and names of intending political leaders in Central Africa (such as Hastings Banda and Kenneth Kaunda) soon became familiar. A feeling of change was in the air (Harold McMillan's famous 'winds of change').

I simply wanted practical fishermen and would train two as lab assistants. Within a week the Police Special Branch told me one of those I'd engaged was a prime agitator they had an eye on, but he could of course continue to work with me. In no time this man was reeling off Latin names of fishes, crabs and molluscs, and keeping good records. He continued exemplary, and after some months the police said he had simply dropped out of their sight. Evidently, when kept busy, he stopped making trouble.

My little rest-house at Mpulungu might be dangerous, said the police, as government buildings were becoming targets for agitators.[4] It was easy to apply a match to a thatched roof at night. Sleep suffered, but in fact there was no need to worry. My presence represented employment, and so I was welcome.

Published work on Tanganyika at the time consisted largely of the results of British and Belgian expeditions to the lake. In the nineteenth century the unusual character of faunal collections gave rise to a theory that Tanganyika fauna had marine affinities and were relics of a Jurassic sea.[5] Further collections in 1904–08 rejected the marine theory.[6] A leap forward in knowledge was made by the Belgian administration of the Congo in 1946–47, which converted a lake passenger vessel for research and staffed it with scientists for a year. Numerous splendid tomes of this Exploration Hydrobiologique du lac Tanganika were published by the Royal Belgian

Museum of Natural History, Brussels. These became my field manuals and bible.

The Bangweulu Swamps and the Ungu people

The Swamps

While waiting to move permanently to Tanganyika I made two trips to the Bangweulu Swamps as part of a JFRO project. The fishes of Bangweulu had been pretty thoroughly collected and scientifically classified, and we were getting an understanding of swamp ecology and fish biology – including such things as breeding and feeding habits, age and growth. A comprehensive study of the 80-odd fish species in Bangweulu would have kept an entire institute of scientists busy, so we focussed on the primary ecological characteristics of just a few major species. Very important also was the fishery of the Unga people of the Swamps. Unfortunately they were shy, which is perhaps their character, but I thought also suspicious lest we were associated with fisheries laws.

JFRO used a special boat to get around in the Swamps, with shallow draught and propellers protected to avoid snagging in weed. It carried two scientists and a crew of three. We used gill nets for fishing, and measured oxygen concentrations since de-oxygenation under floating weed can crucially control fish habitats.[7] Our two week tour of pretty continuous work touched the main Unga fishing grounds. Nets could not be set at night because of crocodiles, and travelling by night through channels in the vegetation was slow. Crocs prefer to bask in the sun by day and enter water at night. They make a mess of gill nets, so we set nets close by and kept watch.

Probably few people outside Zambia know much about the Bangweulu Swamps, except for its great bird life and perhaps its association with the famous nineteenth-century explorer/missionary David Livingstone who died in dire conditions there.[8,9] The lake, swamp and its floodplains to east and south, can be pictured as a single aquatic system set in a vast, practically flat catchment saucer of about 15,000 square kilometres. It is fed by the Chambesi River which exits as the Luapula River (see Figure 5), which eventually flows into the Lualaba and mighty Congo River. The perennial Bangweulu Swamp of 4,000 to 5,000 square kilometres doubles in area during the rainy season, although the annual rise and fall of the water is only about 1.2 metres. In other words, it is a seasonally variable system in which quite small changes in water level have big effects on swamp area. This seasonality strongly influences the lives of the people there.

Most of the Swamp is an endless vista of low vegetation of reeds and sedges, interspersed with lagoons covered by water-lily. Channels and smaller passages, cut here and there for canoes and boats, tend to be fringed with papyrus and raffia palm.[10,11] Sandy islands are more pronounced in the dry season. This is not like the Nile Sudd, where channels are enclosed by walls of emergent vegetation. The swamp weed in Bangweulu is generally low and open to the horizon like a seascape. Beyond are vast peripheral floodplain flats of grass with an occasional projecting anthill. Even at the driest time of year the flats do not dry out but are covered with a mat of grass through which one can sink ankle-deep into mud. The flats are the special habitat of great herds of black lechwe antelope,[12] while the swamp itself contains marvellously diverse and abundant birds.

The majority of the population in the Bangweulu region live on the mainland around the lake or on islands. There are three principal tribes: the Kabende to the south and near the Luapula River, the Ngumbo on the west and large islands of the east side, and 10,000 WaBisa on Chilubi Island (Figure 5). Actual swamp dwellers are relatively small in number, possibly only 15,000. They are the Ba-Unga, about whose special way of life I am here concerned.

As a challenging place to live, a truly terrible environment, the Bangweulu Swamps can have few equals, especially in the wet season. The Unga people mostly live on sandy islands in huts packed tightly together. Land is sparse and rarely more than a metre above water; so living space is very limited. Near the middle of the Swamp is a large bank of alluvium and sand, the populous Lunga Bank. People also camp on floating aquatic vegetation in the main fishing season. The earliest, aboriginal people of the swamp were Batwa, of whom only few are left. Unga came there as part of a larger Bemba immigration from Angola in the eighteenth century, displacing and intermarrying with the Batwa.[13]

Curiously, the First World War had a major impact and lasting effects on this remote place.[14] In 1915 the possibility was recognised of using the Luapula and Chambesi Rivers, connecting through the Swamps, to transport war supplies to troops fighting in the then German East Africa (Tanzania). With a minor amount of channel cutting, a route was opened up for canoes. Stores coming from South Africa to the railhead at Ndola were carried overland to the Luapula River, then freighted by canoe upriver and through the Swamps to a point on the main road near Kasama (see Figures 4 and 5). The round trip for each canoe was about 1,300 km of paddling. Some idea of the scale of operations is given by one statistic: during a twelve-month period in 1916–17, 1,540 tons of goods were shifted by 1,885 canoes. Men with canoes were employed from all around Bangweulu.

From this wartime operation grew the realisation that future development of the region depended on a network of channels being cut in the peat of the perennial swamp, and being kept open. It became the main development objective of the next two or three decades, and by 1945 such a network had been created, at great cost for those days. It gave employment, since all was done by manual labour. Of course, the channels had continually to be kept clear or they would be blocked by drifting sudd and grow over. (The main wartime route became blocked a few years after.) Routine clearing was later done mechanically from special barges and the channels became an economic lifeline for the Swamp people, enabling them not only to export catches but also to import food, because they have insufficient land to grow enough for themselves. More recently, the problem of blocked channels has become crucial.[15]

Draining the Swamps for large-scale farming was one of the big development ideas that swirled around shortly after World War II. A 4-km channel was indeed cut to lower water levels around the important Lunga bank and allow more cultivation there.[16] However, a hydrobiological study by Cambridge University in the early 1950s[17] concluded against using the Swamps for a monster agricultural scheme

Mosquitoes in the Bangweulu Swamps are known for their extraordinary abundance and insatiable appetite for blood ('the quantity and viciousness of the mosquitoes are beyond description').[18] My colleague, Derek Harding, had a yarn about someone who, while working with fish in twilight, had the veins of his hands marked out by lines of mosquitoes. Rub-on chemical deterrents helped, but it was best to avoid night exposure and work only between dawn and dusk. How the Unga manage to co-exist with the mosquitoes I know not – perhaps smoke from fires in their huts gives protection.

Derek, a cheerfully pugnacious Welshman, was good company, and the crew were Nyasa men. Accustomed to that big open lake, they somehow managed to adapt to swamp conditions. Their English was good, and my involuntary habit at that time of falling into West Coast pidgin English caused much laughter. In contrast to the forceful Fante fishermen of Ghana and their big sea canoes, the Unga seemed gentle and distant. They would often appear out of narrow passages in the weed, silently paddling or poling their tiny dug-outs on errands mysterious.

By lucky chance my two trips in the Swamps were at different times of

Bangweulu Swamps. Fishing camp on floating weed mat (after Bertram and Trant, 1972)

A weir across narrow passage in swamp

year, each close to annual extremes in weather and water levels. On the first, peak level had been a month before and we were into the dry season. During high water, channels are deep with strong currents, and the water is crystal clear to the bottom. Occasional trading canoes passed full of goods and bags of meal, coming from the agricultural west side of Lake Bangweulu. At the same time canoes were returning stacked with baskets of dried fish. As the water fell, women were beginning to hoe meagre plantation grounds at the edges of islands and mudflats. Their technique was to build high mounds of peat, dug laboriously from the swamp, in which they planted cassava and beans. Planting had to be done early for crops to grow before the water rose up the mounds.

Emptying a basket trap

Men were making fishing camps here and there, erecting light grass huts upon compacted weed clumps. Stepping on one of these, the water immediately rose to my ankles. Such camps are only a temporary arrangement for shelter during the dry season when it is windy and sometimes chilly. They seemed most uncomfortable, but the Unga are truly amphibious. Bows of their canoes are often pulled right into the entrances of the shelters. Fish-drying racks stand outside. Conditions on such small weed clumps get very smelly and dirty as the fishing months go by.

On high flood, fish move out over the floodplains for spawning and their young grow rapidly. A few months later as the water drains back off the floodplains, the fish are trapped behind earth weirs. The only possible escape for them is through gaps in the weirs where basket traps are placed. During a month or so, huge catches can be made. This is the most productive fishing of the year. Livingstone described these weirs in April 1873, two weeks before he died.[19] The same method has recently been the subject of a thesis by a former fisherman.[20]

In the Swamp proper another kind of fish weir is used across narrow passages wherever a perceptible current exists. These are blockages made of dense walls of cut reeds reinforced by poles driven into the bottom. Cunningly placed baskets in the walls catch migrating fish.

A favourite fishing method using nets is called *kusakila* (*kutumpula* elsewhere in Zambia). Although it was illegal, we were able to watch it being done. A length of net, about 500 metres (made up of pieces belonging to individual fishermen), was set along the edge of a lagoon, reaching from surface to bottom. Men in six or more canoes spread out from the opposite side and advanced towards the net, splashing all the time with paddles and poles. They effectively drove fish before them into the net, which was then quickly raised. They made another setting soon after. A medium-sized species predominated in their catch, which, significantly, was not common in our own set nets – indicating the two methods had different selectivity characteristics. Each man took only the fish caught by his own bit of the net. Such cooperative drives are not troubled by crocodiles.

The energetic planting and fishing we saw all round us looked, to our northern eyes, strangely like spring activities. Yet in fact it was the start of the cooler season. Air and water temperatures were usually above 16 C, but at night it seemed chilly and wintery.

My second trip five months later corresponded with low water, just before the main rains caused levels to rise again. In fact, heavy sporadic rain storms were already starting. Thunder clouds loomed and dramatic lightening connected clouds and swamp. It was an uncomfortable thought that a metal boat, standing higher than anything else in the terrain, might attract one of these powerful bolts. Between storms the air was hot and oppressive. At this time, travel by canoe is problematic because of shallow water, except along channels and known passages. Travellers often have to get out and push their canoes over scarcely covered weedy bottom or mud. Few crops were visible. Fishing camps, so busy during high water, were deserted. Not only would the flimsy shelters have been even more uncomfortable, but good weather for sun drying catches was also over. The Unga catch fish for subsistence at this time near their home villages. Then it is most often the women who fish for the family. Working in groups they stand in shallow water simply scooping conical baskets over the bottom.

Derek and I helped set and haul the nets, but his expertise was essential when catches came in. Fish were separated into piles according to species, then individual lengths measured and stomach contents and breeding condition noted. Memorising the scientific names of the numerous species was a brainstorming exercise. Most were small and looked rather alike. At the same time, my memory was also exercised in identifying the myriads of birds in the Swamp. For the main groups it was not difficult – any ignoramus can tell a pelican from a heron, and spot flamingos, storks, cranes, spoonbills, geese, ducks and ibis – but, like the fish, there were a fantastic number of species (over 400 species are now recorded for Bangweulu). It is one of the hot-spots of bird diversity in Africa. Today, a valedictory feeling accompanies such rare sights as prolific nature shrinks before encroaching human activities.

With care, our nets escaped the attentions of crocodiles. At night a torch beam usually picked up several pairs of eyes glowing like cinders. The croc population was decimated in the 1940s and 50s by hunters. At first hunting was encouraged by paid bounties. But soon it became profitable to hunt for croc skins to make handbags, shoes, etc; but it was not easy money. Small and medium-sized crocs, more desirable for pliable leather, had been shot out in the Swamps. Those we saw were mostly big, perhaps their skins were too knobbly to be useful or they were just survivors. It is not easy to be certain of a croc's size in the water; one sees only two or three humps, the tips of head and back.

A surprise close-up came when we were coasting down the side of an island with the current, making very little noise. The top of the bank was at eye level, and we passed two very large crocs profiled along the bank edge. By the time we had reversed and got the rifle ready, one had disappeared and the other was launching itself down a muddy chute in the bank. Its whole body was steeply angled, tip of tail at the top of the bank and head in the water. It may have been 16 feet, the supposed maximum length, but chiefly impressive was its bulk. It was probably old and, like most animals, rate of growth in length decreases with age while bulk and girth continue to increase. Too late for the head, my bullet bounced off its armoured back. It dived under the boat and soon surfaced a distance off, regarding us malevolently. Several days before at a swamp village we had been shown the front and back ends of a small dug-out canoe found with no trace of its owner. Hippo, we thought. But hippo were rare in the Swamps. The croc we saw coming down the bank had a gape probably wide enough to bisect a small canoe.

The Swamps display contrasting moods. Though a wilderness of similar features, a mosaic of vegetation and lagoons lacking landmarks, certain snapshots remain in mind. The quality of light, the weather and the presence of life, determine a scene in which circumstances create a mood. Some days can be beautiful and joyful and others dismally bleak. I remember two such extremes.

A gusty southeast wind was blowing. We had been working since dawn, and now set off along a broad channel into the wind. Wavelets extending across the channel slapped the metal bows. The sky was cloudless, the air cool. Wind bent the tops of tall reeds and papyrus standing in dense walls either side of the channel. We turned into a side lagoon to rest and were immediately in shelter, the lagoon a tranquil mirror reflecting the blue sky. Tea was brewed and Derek got absorbed in paperwork spread over the engine hatch.

I observed our men in the stern. Putting another pot on the primus stove they continued the never-ending job of net mending, rather like knitting. Catfish are a curse in gill nets. Their needle-sharp spines snag and cut the net, and they usually live long enough to create tangled havoc. Fishermen break off the spines before disentangling the fish's body with great care because a punctured finger tends to suppurate. Spines are chucked overboard immediately. Mending holes in the net is a routine of cutting out loose ends and constructing new meshes. In our case the repairs had to reproduce original mesh sizes, to maintain the same catch selectivity. Derek cast occasional glances to see this was being done.

The routine movement of hands became hypnotic, so I sat on deck where my attention was at once held by the birds all around. Pelicans were fussing at the surface twenty or thirty metres off. Beyond them, numerous ducks and coots swam and dived, oblivious to the strange boat. These birds were not gun-shy as the Unga people probably saved their shot for lechwe antelope. At the end of the small lagoon a goliath heron stood facing us, still as a sentinel, his extraordinary height elongated further by the water's reflection. His head and beak tilted as his eyes searched the water at his feet. Malachite and coloured kingfishers flashed swiftly along the lagoon, diving to the surface occasionally for small fish. Above them rose a flock of flamingos, pink undersides outlined against the sky and long graceful wings beating to gain height. Far above again white ibises wheeled in wide circles. Then the scene was rudely interrupted by a formation of energetic ducks.

Some of the pelicans were drawn nearer by a light current, and they paddled to keep their distance. Some thrust to get behind others, but the current brought them on. Keeping side profile, they bumped together in rising agitation until two winged heavily off, their legs trailing. Then the others followed, trundling like old Sunderland flying boats of 1930s vintage. Were they ungainly because they had just fed? All wild things have a sense of propinquity, and when close to strangers feel compelled to draw away. Nevertheless one bird, reluctant to move, stayed to eye me steadily from a lugubrious face.

In fringing vegetation I tried to find the frogs whose chorus was with us at night. The immense cacophony that starts at twilight becomes an enveloping

Pelican flock taking off

A pelican reluctant to leave

wall of sound. There is no way to shut it off, and one must try to sleep despite rasping, grunting, sawing voices, as millions compete to be heard. At first I'd tried to identify choir members, trebles, baritones and basses, but had to give up. The uproar was indivisible. By daylight I had no more success in sighting them. Perhaps they were resting from vocal strain.

Across the lagoon came the highly distinctive call of the fish eagle *Haliaetus vocifer.* A beautiful bird with distinguishing white head and neck contrasting with a chestnut underside. It quickly makes its presence known

Fish eagle

by a unique, far-carrying, haunting cry, like no other bird (thus Livingstone's description: 'the fish eagle lifts up his remarkable voice. It is pitched in a high falsetto key, very loud, and seems as if he were calling to some one in the other world. Once heard, his weird unearthly voice can never be forgotten – it sticks to one throughout life').[21] To take a fish at the surface the eagle stoops in a shallow dive, decelerates with talons thrust out ahead of the beak, white tail spread and almost touching the water and grips its prey. Then the legs swing back and, without looking down, the eagle puts its strength into rising, often going straight to a tree top. Here in the Swamps there were no trees, so it was a mystery where they perched.

It was a beautiful day. The steady murmur of net mending continued in the background, and I thought of our damnable European habit of perceiving time in terms of past and especially future, which prevents us from enjoying the moment. For example, we had divided our two-week journey through the Swamps into compartments of daily distance to be run and amount of work to be done. We were trapped in a programme 'time-frame', an abstract boundary encompassing our plans and ambitions, erected to ensure certain objectives were reached. Means and methods held our concentration, so that ends were lost in the fuss. Evidently we could not look at life in existential terms – 'consider the lilies how they grow . . .'. This moment of unwonted idleness was surely excusable given the exuberant life of the birds and the setting – the brilliant sky and lucid water and wind in the reeds.

I was reacting of course against our busyness, which gave little opportunity to enjoy the surroundings. As well, there may have been some apprehension in my mind as to the futility of our plans in the face of a huge ecosystem. This monotonous, interminable water and vegetation was obviously full of complex dynamic life. We had much to learn. Was it reasonable to think one could understand the Swamp well enough to predict the effects of thousands of people fishing? It was not hard to dream up a plan of research, but how big must it be or how long to become an effective operation?

Another example of mood, this time contrasting, was on an afternoon in the rainy season. The day had started fine, but later cumulus began building and towered up until the entire sky was heavily clouded and rain was imminent. We decided to pull in for the night, and went through the motions of stowing gear and starting to prepare food. But I wanted to watch awhile. There was very little sign of life, even the frogs seemed hesitant to begin their serenade – perhaps sudden darkening had taken them by surprise. Soon the first heavy drops turned into a chill deluge driven by fierce wind. One would have been soaked outside our boat roof, instantly. Soon the storm eased and moved on, but another was approaching. The Swamps took on a look of extreme desolation and menace. The reeds looked disordered and crushed by the downpour, while a few erect stands of papyrus were threshing in gusts of wind. Beyond, the unvarying landscape felt completely unsympathetic; one could not imagine walking, swimming or sailing across it, nor was there any sense of a direction to take. No village was in sight. The locals did not stir much at this time of year ('all the voyage of their life is bound in shallows and in miseries')[22] and were in permanent huts on patches of land with the food they had stored. Exposed out here we were at odds with custom.

It occurred to me David Livingstone had travelled by canoe through the Swamps at the end of the rainy season in 1873, when water level was at its highest and food very difficult to procure. It may have been on a similar stormy evening, perhaps not far from the very spot we were anchored, that he came upon a providential islet 10 yards across. As he and his men landed, 'a pitiless pelting rain came on. We turned up a canoe to get shelter.'[23] Having had their tent torn down by wind, they spent the night under the upturned canoe, lying on their soaked loads, bitterly cold and uncomfortable. These dispiriting circumstances would surely have disheartened any traveller. The baneful foreground of mud and whirling weed with no other prospect must have seemed appalling; and he was dying of dysentery. But in the morning his journal records a resolve to go on; written despite the slight chance his pencilled notes would ever come to light. I had never imagined a situation so demanding of courage and persistence, nor understood the strength an inspired human spirit is capable of. Closing the flap with a shiver, I went into the forecabin for a cup of tea.

The big news for us at Samfya was that Margaret was expecting our second child. Circumstances were better than the first time in Ghana for she was not alone; two other ladies at the station were in the same interesting condition and expecting about the same time. They went to Fort Rosebery together for check-ups, although it was a delicate business getting them there and back over the 80 km of bad road. On one occasion when none of the husbands was available to drive, a young bachelor (Derek) was pressed to take them. He gallantly did so, apprehensive of having to deliver three babies in the bush.

A disturbing incident happened in Samfya one morning. A great crowd of people from local villages, at least five hundred men, women and children, came and sat down outside the boma offices. It was unheard of; and even more remarkable they were completely silent. A few apparent leaders strolled among them to ensure not even a baby cried. Inside at their desks were Tim the DC, two District Officers and a Cadet, along with several local clerks and half a dozen uniformed District Messengers (DC's assistants in general duties and policing).[24] It was about 8 am. Tim, of course, saw what was going on through his open windows, the crowd being seated on the ground only yards away. He continued quietly at work. After an hour of growing tension, the Cadet (who told me the story) came to Tim's office and nervously asked what to do: should he, for example, unlock the magazine and issue rifles? Tim said firmly, 'Do nothing of the sort. Go back and get on with your work; no fuss.' After a further hour the strain was palpable. The sun had risen high and it was hot. Tim called out 'Messenger', and the senior messenger came from his accustomed perch on the verandah.

'What are the people doing out there?' he asked – his voice carrying clearly outside. 'They are waiting to see you, sir'.

'Well then, go and tell them I am busy now. They should come back and see me later in the week, in small numbers.'

The messenger, an unflappable, long-service man, told the crowd just that. Whereupon they arose and went away. An agitator's game had been to bully the docile people into this demonstration, in order to draw Tim or one of the other officers into a public harangue. Tempers could have flared, and the quiet crowd been transformed into a mob. There was no possibility of getting outside force. Everything depended on the calm assumption of authority.

To put this in the context of the moment: a short time before, a District Officer on routine duty at the east side of the lake had been speared. Disorder until then was virtually unknown; the only violent incident in the District record had been back in the 1920s. Of course, investigation ensued and police arrested the offender, but it showed that the UNIP political party might be prepared to be rough.[4] No doubt Tim had to ponder this on that morning.

All was ready for Margaret to go to hospital when the time came; however, almost simultaneously with the first birth signals, I fell ill with hepatitis and was banished to hospital in place of Margaret. Fortunately, a friend and neighbour was an experienced midwife and Margaret had the baby at home. In the hospital I shared a room with a Belgian Catholic 'White Father', who had the same illness. We had long conversations, and during visits from other fathers of the mission I got to know them too. Their conversation was almost entirely about practical things – Were crops in the villages growing well? Did so-and-so get his roof finished before the rains? Was a bridge over some stream holding up? Such seemed the substance of their lives. I'd heard that these men rarely went back home, if ever, and lived their lives virtually in the villages, saying Mass, baptising, and teaching as well as helping in material matters. I had visited their big church, Lubwe. In one conversation I was prompted to ask my friend a perhaps impertinent question. Could he, I said, looking out from the steps of his church, which had been standing over 50 years, see any obvious evidence of change?

'Not really,' he replied, 'people live in their traditional ways; of course the Sisters have helped with hygiene, and we also make some improvements. But you see,' he continued, 'we are not working entirely for this generation, or even the next.'

This gave me much to think about. Despite preoccupation with crops, corrugated iron and such, their real priorities were on distant spiritual goals. I wondered how many of my own activities, or those of others like me, would be tangible after a generation or two? One cannot help wanting to make a difference here and now.

The Unga people and their fishery

> [Traditional fishermen of African swamps] 'are better integrated into a natural ecosystem than most human beings at the present time' (Beadle, 1975: p.258).

The Unga are well integrated with the swamp ecosystem of Bangweulu. In the past, oral story indicates they were ruled by semi-independent chiefs, none of whom paid tribute to the other. Quarrels and wars took place between them; but more important they were raided from time to time by the much larger Bemba tribe of the adjoining northeast plateau. Raids often occurred in the dry season when invaders could pass on foot over the flood plains. As a defence, the Unga surrounded their villages with stockades of euphorbia hedges, a quick-growing plant (there being little timber nearby), but their particular refuge was the interior of the Swamps. After 1899 the Bemba came under administration and the raids stopped. Soon afterwards, the British South Africa Company pushed into the Swamps, and internal disputes were then settled without war. However, along with peace came taxes, first paid in otter skins in place of money. From 1902, administrative boma posts and missions were set up on the Swamp fringe. Their work was always fraught with difficulty because of the inaccessible terrain and the independent nature of the Swamp dwellers. The giving and taking of slaves in restitution of wrongs was still going on among the Unga as late as 1922, according to Magistrate's Case Records of that period.

Information about the Unga exists in professional journals or books now out of print. Brelsford's monograph[10] is the only comprehensive account. He was an administrator concerned with local government and development in the Swamps, and brought to his description a good deal of field experience and familiarity with the people. The following outline is taken from various accounts,[25] especially Brelsford's, supplemented by my own observations.

Early in the twentieth century Unga were mainly hunters of lechwe antelope on the floodplains, chasing them into staked-out nets in communal drives. But from the time labour began to concentrate on the Copperbelt in the 1920s–30s, a substantial market grew for fish. Thus fishing and trading became their chief livelihood. Through the twentieth century they kept their customs, but also built up a big trade in dried fish. The product is packed in standard home-made baskets of leaf and fibre, and brought out by canoe. Some even transported their fish baskets to the Copperbelt by bicycle. (Interestingly, each man traded his catch on his own account; there seemed little marketing cooperation.) Later, outlets were developed near Samfya,[26] but getting fish to market generally means a long paddle, 80 km or more. Traders now enter the Swamps, when seasonal high water permits access for big canoes, bringing goods to sell or barter for fish.

As interdependence grew between the mines and fish suppliers, the government encouraged fish production over all the country. And as the pace of change quickened with post-WWII enthusiasm for faster development, road communications got better and new fishing technologies (e.g., nylon nets, motors) were introduced. So it became important to safeguard the natural fisheries from over-exploitation. There was some evidence that fish in Bangweulu were getting smaller, a possible indication of overfishing[10], but little knowledge existed on which to base management laws. Various restrictive measures were introduced as a precaution in default of fishery data.

In 1960 the JFRO hosted C.F. Hickling, Fisheries Adviser to the Colonial Office, at Samfya. He was particularly interested in biological productivity in tropical waters, and had had opportunity to see personally many African and Asian freshwater fisheries. He described examples of very high yields in the tropics under fluctuating environmental conditions, i.e., high annual pulses of production of small fish, and suggested such conditions would require different approaches to management than used in the northern hemisphere.[27]

Some of the old ad hoc legal frameworks have been retained to the present day.[28] But there has always been an element of the ridiculous in trying to enforce these laws in remote places like the Bangweulu Swamps. Consequently, legislation has been largely ignored by the fishermen. Government has been an onlooker not a manager. Only now, half a century after JFRO began studies, are we reaching enough understanding to define what if any fishery restrictions are necessary.[29] Of course, no one anticipated today's huge demand for fish and exponential rise in human populations.

The following notes indicate a largely traditional scene in the 1950s (all quotations are from Brelsford). Things have not changed much.

Rises and falls of swamp level strongly influence Unga life. Water level, rather than seasonal temperature and rainfall, determine cropping and fishing. The rainy season (January–April), when levels are high and most biological productivity takes place on the flood plains, does not favour Unga methods of farming and fishing. When the floodplains start draining in May, fishing begins at the peripheral earth weirs and soon afterwards in the shallow water around the Swamp fringes. As levels continue to fall during the subsequent dry season up to September, fishing intensifies using nets and weirs in the Swamp itself. Fishing camps are built, sometimes considerable distances from home villages, and there is a good deal of coming and going between them as fish are transported in one direction and food for the camps in another. ('The Unga is a restless man in the dry season.')

Meanwhile, cultivation continues in the swamps by the 'mound' method, mentioned above, and in addition migrations take place to cultivate areas on the mainland. Frequently, whole villages are deserted as the men go fishing and the women leave in other directions for farming. Not only young and active men and women work – some kinds of fishing, like tending basket traps in weirs, can be done by older men, and children are employed in small tasks. So entire families, except the sick and infirm, are busy. Grain harvested on the mainland by non-Unga peoples in July–August, is brought into the Swamps to trade for fish. Dried or smoked fish are sold or bartered from villages or taken to trading depots outside the Swamps.

Apart from seasonal fluctuations, there is historical evidence of long-term cyclical fluctuations at intervals of about 35 years (on at least three occasions). Low levels when more cultivable land is available have corresponded to times of relative prosperity, but high levels mean relative hardship and hunger as villagers are driven away from their homes by flood water. Population of the Swamp must ultimately depend on land available in it for villages. The 'land hungry swamp people' are thus highly sensitive to level changes, which control life and livelihood far more obviously than rainfall affects people on the mainland.

Levels also influence ecological production and fish distribution. Fish are scattered over a great area in the flood period and more concentrated at low water. Biological productivity in the sense of general growth in biota is almost certainly highest during the rains,[30] when only little fishing occurs.

'The whole life of the Unga centres around fish.' This has undoubtedly been so since the start of a commercial market in the 1920s. Nets were made from natural fibres before nylon came in the 1960s. Earth weirs have certainly long existed; Livingstone observed them in 1873.[19] But neither the weirs nor other methods – gill nets, basket traps, hand-baskets, long-lines, spears (17 methods have been noted) – appear unique. On the other hand, adaptation to Swamp conditions and fishing strategies do show specialisations. The outcome is that, 'their own [Unga] fishing methods have proved to be very efficient within their own terrain'; and 'the common methods of netting and weir-making give such good results from the family and commercial standpoint that the effort necessary to evolve other methods ... would not be worthwhile ...' Plant-cropping strategies, as on peat mounds, also show specialisation.

Rules of tenure and priestly ritual surround fishing practices. While netting grounds are traditionally open to all, the Unga like other tribes of the region, by custom gave a tribute of 'first fruits' to the chief. The tribute system broke down when fishing licences were introduced in the Bangweulu region in 1943. Fishers claimed that payment of tax absolved them from tribute, so the custom became courtesy not obligation.

Definite rules of ownership exist for weirs. Only Unga may build a weir in the tribal area. There is only one owner of a weir, a descendent of the original builder. The owner may invite whom he likes to repair and fish the weir with him (largest weirs take as many as 20 men). Each man comes with his own basket/s, sets them in place in the weir, and keeps his own catch. In explaining the tenure difference between netting and weirs, the people hold that 'weir fishing success does not depend upon the efforts or skill of the man. The fish either come to the weir or they do not, whereas in netting a man has to go out and hunt the fish.' Perhaps connected with this belief, there is also a strong spiritual association with the ownership of weirs and ancestors. Thus a priest is called to bless the weirs at the time water levels drop and weirs start functioning. A priest may be responsible for a number of weirs. He calls on the ancestors of each weir owner to give good catches to the living owner, and he performs set rituals.

Discussion

Unga fishing life is difficult to study. In routinely touring the Swamps we (JFRO) followed the usual pattern of officialdom, i.e., getting a picture at regular intervals. Weaknesses in this approach were that one saw only relatively small parts of the vast swamp region, in fact only areas adjacent to channels, and little of the activities in the rest. Thus the changeable swamp environment was probably not fully sampled. To give a wider view of human activities, an aerial census of canoes and fishing weirs was made in 1964, followed up by personal interviews in sample areas.[31] (Interestingly, this came 10 years after a pioneering aerial count of the black lechwe antelope on the Bangweulu floodplains – which seems to have been the first aerial census of wildlife in Africa).[12] In an overall sense, JFRO's work at Bangweulu was inconclusive because of the size of the task. Similarly, research monitoring in succeeding decades has yielded patchy results.[32]

A very useful micro survey was made by Ichikawa[25]; 'micro' because he lived with one group of fishermen in a fishing camp for three months, observing their daily strategies closely. In this group were 19 canoe units using different forms of *kusakila* (driving into set nets), gill netting and seining. He found there was no significant difference in efficiency between the units in terms of catch per day. This was the outcome of remarkably deliberate allocation of effort in a strategy, which took account of choice of fishing ground, water level, particular characteristics of each fishing method and the overall most effective distribution of fishing effort among the group. Cooperation for mutual benefit was evident. For example, the group acted to reduce any disturbance that might occur between various fishing operations going on at the same time. Ichikawa stressed the importance of kinship relationships in a fishing group.

More is therefore involved in the equation of output than ecological and fishing variables. There is a cooperative effort factor. Unga fishers in camps evidently have agreed strategies. In addition, Ichikawa suggested that social aspects not directly relevant to the optimisation of fishing efficiency needed to be taken into account.

Lately, modern stock assessment methods have been employed.[29] Using data going back to the 1960s, an in-depth analysis provided surprising conclusions. In Bangweulu fish catches seem to have remained stable for the past 50 years (around 1,100 tonnes per annum) and numbers of fishermen have remained around 5,000. Also, it seems that fishing intensity is very close to the biological optimum. These results pose interesting questions.

How do the Unga people live in a seemingly well-balanced relationship with their resource? Is it by deliberate self-management? ('The local fishermen ... know what they are doing.'[29]) Or does it reflect a degree of adaptability in which optimum effort is deployed within some overall bounding constraints, which are part of the nature of the environment and the fishing methods? Why has Bangweulu not followed the pattern of increasing fishing effort and instability of stocks seen in almost all African fisheries? Why have mounting fishing pressure exerted by foreigners around the Swamps, and strong market demand not been reflected in overfishing?

The resource is not 'managed' by authority in any effective sense. There certainly have been no capital investments for development (if the expense of making channels long ago is ignored). Biological overfishing appears not to have happened to the majority of species comprising the bulk of the stocks. The fishery has mostly been shaped by the efforts of resident fishers and the opportunities open to them. Routines and methods reflect a steady subsistence life among the Swamp community. But there is no conservation ethic at work, rather – as Gordon[33] put it for the neighbouring Lake Mweru – 'traps and nets were to catch everything they came across, like a hen that pecks at every last scrap, as indicated by [a locally] popular fishing song'.

Findings of different researchers have in the main been consistent: Brelsford thought that output depended on fishing grounds – some areas being better than others. Skill and technique didn't vary much, and the catches of individual men in the same areas were surprisingly similar over time. Ichikawa found a close relationship between individual catches and fishing days, so that catch and effort were strongly correlated in the long run. However, he thought also that deliberate strategies were adopted in group fishing, combining various methods. Finally, Kolding et al.[29] suggested fishing patterns have evolved over time from trial and error. Increased effort would not raise catches much because natural mortality rates are high in most of the fish species. More effort would simply result in diminishing returns. In short, the existing fishing yield balance is the result of a finely tuned exploitation regime giving close to maximal yields.

Weir basket fishing is a different case. It relies, as the Unga tradition has it, on 'fish coming to the basket traps'. The catch of the peripheral earth weirs must depend on biological productivity in the flooded area cut off by them. On the other hand, catches in the weirs of reeds set in swamp channels depends on the migration of fish along the channels. If floods do not vary much from year to year, then given the fixed nature of weirs and the fact that weirs account for the majority of the total catch, these factors should help explain the constant nature of annual catch from the Bangweulu Swamps.

Lastly, I return to factors determining human population numbers: The difficult terrain of the Swamps and limited amount of land on which to build, effectively excludes outsiders except in certain months. Pressure from the surrounding mainland to exploit the Swamps has probably increased two- to three-fold in 50 years (assuming similar rates of increase as in the rest of Zambia). The population of the Samfya District now stands about 200,000. Migrations by outsiders into the Swamps for fishing and trading occur mainly from April (after the mainland agricultural season) to November, i.e., during the dry season. These migrations seem to be largely into the western side of the Swamps, nearest the densest mainland population. Numbers actually living in the Swamps have changed little. Hereditary tenure of earth weirs and also of reed weirs within the Swamps, should both act to exclude outsiders and stabilise output.

That accessibility is a key factor, is indicated by comparison with Lake Mweru further downstream on the Luapula River (see Figure 4). It is of similar aerial size to the perennial Bangweulu Swamps and subject to the same annual flood pulse, but it is an open lake permanently accessible in every part to canoes and served by roads along the lakeshore. Fishing activities there have grown enormously in the past 50 years in response to market demand from the Copperbelt and Katanga (Congo). Mweru now produces several times the fish catch of Bangweulu. A recent publication describes the situation with its title: 'Mweru-Luapula is an open exit fishery where a highly dynamic population of fishermen makes use of a resilient resource base'.[34] Bangweulu might have attracted similarly intensive exploitation but for its physical character, poor communications, and the local conditions of tenure.

We may only guess the perspective of the Unga themselves; in particular, how residents see the balance between their secure livelihood and cultural integrity against the difficult and unhealthy[35] living conditions of the Swamps. Development and transition to modernity are constrained by these conditions.

Notes and references

1. Jackson, P.B. (2001). Freshwater fisheries research organisations in central and eastern Africa: A personal recollection. *Transactions of the Royal Society of South Africa, 55*(1) Special Issue, Cape Town.
2. Brelsford, W.V., Phillipson, D.W. & Hickman, A.S. (1965). Niamkolo Church. *Northern Rhodesia Journal, 6*: 147-152.
3. For details of traditional fishing and purse-seining in L. Tanganyika, see Coulter, G.W. 1991. [Ed.] *Lake Tanganyika and its Life.* Oxford University Press. 353pp.

4. Later events in the 1960s confirmed the readiness of intending politicians to use violence; e.g., their suppression with many casualties of the splinter movement of 'Alice Lenshina'.
5. Moore, J.E. (1903). *The Tanganyika Problem.* Hurst & Blackett, London.
6. Cunnington, W.A. (1920). The fauna of the African lakes. A study in comparative limnology with special reference to Lake Tanganyika. *Proceedings of the Zoological Society of London, 3*: 545-622.
7. Beadle, L.C. (1974). *The Inland Waters of Tropical Africa.* Longmans.
8. Jeal, T. (1973). *Livingstone.* Putnam, New York
9. It is hard now to realise how popular a hero Livingstone was in late-Victorian times. After his death in 1873 he came to be elevated almost to sainthood. This was partly because he personified the national ideal of a moral mission to carry the gospel, plus trade and Empire, to backward parts of the earth. Personal note: Livingstone was one of my father's heroes and Bangweulu was therefore a familiar word from childhood conjuring stories and mental pictures of the swampland. Family history relates that before marriage my father's mother, Elizabeth Hill, desiring to be a missionary, had stayed with Livingstone's daughter, Agnes. After his death she was a magnet for such missionary-minded volunteers.
10. Brelsford, W.V. (1946). *Fishermen of the Bangweulu Swamps.* Rhodes-Livingstone Papers, 12, Rhodes-Livingstone Institute, Livingstone, Zambia.
11. Burgis, M.J. & Symoens, J-J. (Eds) (1987). *African Wetlands & Shallow Water Bodies. Section 7.1 Lac Bangweolo.* pp.404-411. Editions de l'ORSTOM. Institut Francais de Recherche Scientifique. Col. 211, Paris. (NB. This publication lists some of the great variety of vegetation types in the Bangweulu Swamps.)
12. Vesey-Fitzgerald, L.D. (1955). The Black Lechwe and modern methods of wildlife conservation in Africa. *Northern Rhodesia Journal, 6*(2): 25–32.
13. There were remnant settlements of Batwa in the Swamps at the time of Brelsford (1946). He stated the Batwa 'did not cultivate at all, but fed on fish, lechwe meat, and on the roots of water lily (masanga) and on roots of papyrus (luko). They were expert at diving for these roots which, when split and dried, were pounded into a flour. In times of famine the BaUnga too go back to these roots which may be used as a sweet-tasting relish.'
14. Marshall, H.C. & Lobb, G. (1957). Water transport in the Bangweulu Swamps. *Northern Rhodesia Journal, 3*(3): 189–199.
15. Anon. (2004). *Civil Society for Poverty Reduction (CSPR) in Zambia: District Report for Samfya.* [http://www.cspr.org.zm/about.htm]
16. Pook, J. (1953). Making the Debenham Cut. *Northern Rhodesia Journal, 2*(2): 56–64.
17. Debenham, F. (1955). *The Way to Ilala; David Livingstone's pilgrimage.* London.
18. Brelsford (1946), p.30.
19. Waller, H. (Ed) (1874). *The Last Journals of David Livingstone in Central Africa, 2 vols.* Livingstone's notes on the Swamp fisheries read, 'The number of fish caught by weirs, baskets and nets now, as the waters decline, is prodigious. The fish feel their element becoming insufficient for comfort, and retire from one bouga [flooded plain] to another towards the Lake; the narrower parts are duly prepared by weirs to take advantage of their necessities; the sun heat seems to oppress them and force them to flee.'

20. Chanda, B. (1998). *Effects of weir fishing on commercial fish stocks of the Bangweulu Swamp fisheries.* MPhil thesis. Dept. Fisheries and Marine Biology, University of Bergen.
21. Waller, H. (1874) XI, p.296.
22. W. Shakespeare, *Julius Caesar*, Act V, Scene III.
23. Raids by tribes outside the Swamps had taken the food stocks of the Unga, and Livingstone found it hard to get supplies. Waller (Ed). (1874), XI, p.288–9.
24. Brelsford, W.V. (1954). The Boma Messenger. *Northern Rhodesia Journal, 2*(3): 34–42.
25. In addition to Brelsford's (1946) monograph, information on the Bangweulu Ungu and Swamp may be found in the following:
Debenham, F. (1952). *Study of an African swamp.* London, H.M. Stationary Office. 88pp.
Bertram, C.K. & Trant, J. (1972). *Letters from the Swamps 1936–37.*
Dr C.K. Bertram, Ricardo's, Graftham, Petworth, Sussex. 127pp.
Hill, H.C. (1962). Bangweulu and the surrounding mainland. *Northern Rhodesia Journal, 1*(5): 44–49.
Macrae, F.B. & Paine, N.D. (1952). Lake Bangweulu: Its fish and its fishing. *Northern Rhodesia Journal, 6*: 3–19.
Ichikawa, M. (1985). A comparison of fishing strategies in the Bangweulu Swamps. *African Study Monographs, Universities of Zambia and Kyoto, Suppl. Issue 4*: 25–48.
Jackson, P.B. (2001), see Note 1 above.
26. Fryer, G. (1957). Mwamfuli's village: new fulcrum of the Bangweulu fish trade. *Northern Rhodesia Journal, 3*: 483–488.
27. Hickling, C.F. (1961). *Tropical Inland Fisheries.* Longmans, Green & Co. Ltd., London.
28. Malasha, I. (2003). Colonial and post-Colonial fisheries regulations: the cases of Zambia and Zimbabwe. In: Jul-Larsen et al. (Eds.) *Management, Co-Management or no Management?* FAO Fisheries Technical Paper 421/1. FAO, Rome.
29. Kolding, J., H. Ticheler & Chanda, B. (2003). The Bangweulu Swamps – A balanced small-scale multi-species fishery. In: Jul-Larsen et al. (Eds.) *Management, Co-Management or no Management?* FAO Fisheries Technical Paper 421/2. FAO, Rome
30. For fishing in the shallow margins of the Swamps, see Ichikawa, M. (1985) (Note 25). More generally, see also:
Tourcara, S.B. & Quensiere, J. (1996). *Floodplain systoms.* ACP-EU Fisheries Research Report No.2 (Dakar-Senegal), Brussels.
Welcomme, R.L. (1979). *Fisheries ecology of floodplain rivers.* Longman, London.
31. Carey, T.G. (1965). Survey of the Bangweulu fishery. *Fisheries Research Bulletin, 3*, Government Printer, Lusaka, Zambia.
32. Ticheler, H.J., Kolding, J. & Chanda, B. (1998). Participation of local fishermen in scientific fisheries data collection. *Fisheries Management and Ecology, 5*: 81–92.
33. Gordon, D. (2003). *Technological change and economies of scale in the history of Mweru-Luapula's fishery. Management, Co-management or no Management?* FAO Fisheries Technical Paper, 426/2. FAO, Rome.
34. Van Zwieten, P.A., Goudeswaard, P.C. & Kapasa, C.K. (2003). *Mweru-Luapula is an open-exit fishery where a highly dynamic population of fishermen makes use of a resilient resource base. Management, Co-Management or no Management?* FAO Fisheries Technical Paper 426/2. FAO, Rome.

35. Brelsford (1946) devoted his Appendix 2 (entitled 'Ill-health: the penalty of swamp life') to summarising the results of various medical surveys in the Bangweulu Swamps in the 1940s. Malaria, jiggers, tuberculosis, worms and under-nutrition of children were the dominant sicknesses noted. Some 60 years previously the lake population had been almost wiped out by a smallpox epidemic. On the positive side was noted the absence of human bilharzia. Recent reports by the Civil Society for Poverty Reduction in Zambia (e.g., see http:/www.cspr.org.zm/about.htm) indicate that the above medical problems still exist – and in addition there is HIV/AIDS.

4

Lake Tanganyika – Zambia

'If truth were always what it seemed, how impoverished would be the imagination of man.'

Lawrence Durrell, *Balthazar*

Liemba – The Great Lake

One cannot describe Tanganyika without repeating superlatives. In our hyper-technical age we like to express the essence of things in numbers and statistics. But though data may quicken the blood of scientists, they may not completely express reality. The setting has to be experienced aesthetically; Tanganyika is particular in sense of place, beauty and atmosphere. History has left an echo. There is also the personal element, the perspective determined by one's interests, circumstances and experiences. Whatever the reasons, there began for me a close association with Lake Tanganyika in 1959, which has remained a lasting theme in my life.

It is perhaps to the Victorians we must turn for imaginative impressions of Tanganyika. Today's visitors and foreign workers are usually driven by programmes tied to deadlines, whereas the first visitors often spent years at the shore, travelling by foot or by canoes and small boats while slowly establishing themselves in missions and government outposts. Explorers had long waits for change of weather or the arrival of supplies, and early writers had more time to stand and stare and let their imaginations run loose in prose. The new and mysterious loomed large for them. Of course they were also occupied with practical expedients for survival, and lived uncomfortable, unpredictable lives burdened by frequent illness. But the scene on the lake has not changed much, though it is important to remember they saw it with different eyes. Burton[1] was closest to a poet. He was also a thorough and original ethnographer, though personal dislikes distorted his views. Livingstone, too, was an acute observer of detail.[2] He was a curious mixture of devotion to humanity and Christian mission on one hand, and on the

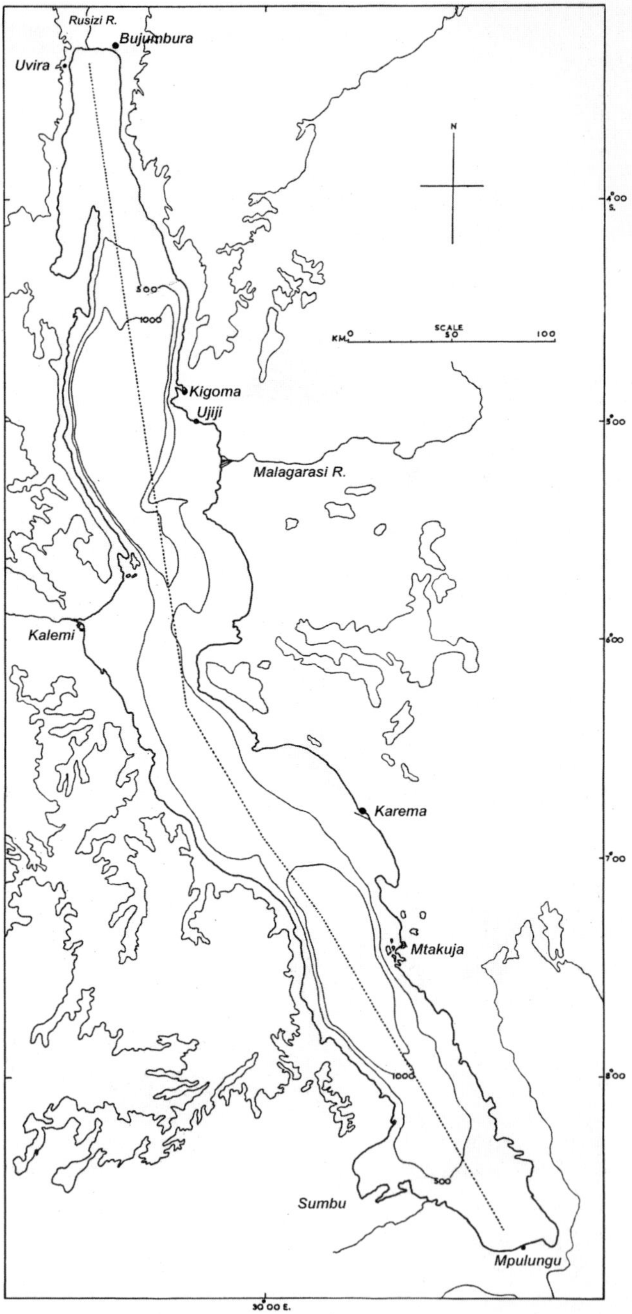

Figure 6. Lake Tanganyika. Isobaths at 500m and 1000m depth, and land contours at 1500m altitude are marked. The mid-lake course taken to study 'the Big Wave' is indicated by the dotted line.

Research vessels

Limnothrissa

Dame-des-Iles

Lady Alice

other to geographical problems and fantasies concerning the origins of the Nile and Congo Rivers. Stanley,[3] a tough professional explorer, Cameron,[4] a naval commander cum explorer, Hore,[5] a master mariner and missionary – these and others gave personal glimpses of Lake Tanganyika in flights of the imagination.[6] In my own time, I have seen hard-nosed, budget-conscious scientists react to it with awe.

The first of English writers to describe it, Sir Richard Burton, compared the lake with the Mediterranean. For his readers in the 1860s that would have been the epitome of natural beauty in a sunny clime. Tanganyika was then utterly remote and inaccessible, and Burton had the difficult task of conveying an understandable picture. He spoke with insight about a vast sheet of deep water contained in a dominating mountain background ('whilst continuous parallels of lofty hills, like the sides of a huge trough, close the prospect and suggest the idea of confinement'). Tanganyika is indeed quite different from a watery expanse in a flat setting. The scene has three major components: the lake, the surrounding steep mountains rising range upon range to high horizons, and the cloudscape above. Towering cloud masses move over the mountaintops, or join across the chasm of the basin reflecting light downward. Coleridge's words are fitting: 'Clouds which image in their bulk the mountains and the lake beneath.'

Changing cloud colours and reflected light create moods; pale cool dawns, sultry afternoons in the rainy season when massing legions of cumuli burst in furious storms along the sides of escarpments down to the beach; and, at the end of the day, glorious sunsets intensified in colour by reflection from coloured strata in the mountains. For instance, high layers of red rock along the south coast glow richly through evening mists. On the lake one passes rocky promontories or sandy beaches, interrupted here and there by stony outcrops or massive semi-submerged boulders bearing tidemarks of previous lake levels. The densely forested slopes stretch up in a monotonous green belt. There are few islands and these are generally near-shore and rocky without much vegetation. Clusters of thatched villages are tucked into folds of land beside beaches.

Lubugwe anchorage

The walls of the rift are everywhere fairly close, especially at the Mahali Mountains halfway along the east shore, which is cleft by deep ravines through which waterfalls plunge in the rains. Anchorages are sometimes hard to find because the bottom is steep. In one favourite anchorage where the Lubugwe stream enters, chimpanzees perch in tree branches stretching out to the lakeside. It seems they feel the little bit of intervening water between the boat and them keeps them safe, and we gaze in mutual curiosity at each other. There is a coastal park reserve just north of Kigoma (see Figure 6) made famous by Jane Goodall's studies on

'Help me down'

chimpanzees. More distant vistas open up on plains or hills in parts of the shoreline.

Some villages have a distinctly East African Coast atmosphere – Swahili culture evident in the square tidy houses, the minute Islamic mosque and abundant palm and fruit trees. Such is Mtakuja, Tanzania, where fish-traders with lighter skin, and in skullcap, smock and sandals, could have been Omani Arabs. Such villages were doubtless lake depots of the slave trade where Arabs settled and intermarried. Using skills from the East African coastline, planked boats are made (pit-sawn planks are shaped by adze, and ribs formed from natural bends of tree branches). These boats are common as 'water-taxis', carrying about 20 passengers or sacks of dried fish. Driven by outboard engine, they play an important part in local transport and trading since land communications are poor. Lake steamers for public transport and freight have existed since the 1920s. (The first steam-driven vessel was the mission boat *Good News*, which was launched in 1885. The first passenger and cargo vessel was built in Germany, brought in pieces to the lake and launched in 1913; see Chapters 9 & 12.) Isolated missions on the lake shore depend on its regular appearance. Some of these Catholic missions have seen several lifetimes of missionaries. The first, at Karema, was established in 1885, and with a few others have quietly persisted through slaving times and colonial and national eras. Encountering some of these mission buildings comes as a surprise. Karema's architecture would look at home beside one of the Italian lakes. On calling, one is made welcome (the Sisters have rather more comfortable living rooms than the Fathers), and given glimpses of settled lives in remote environments. Their story from early times, no doubt in Vatican archives in Rome, would make interesting reading about the long cultural interaction with local people.[6]

A mosaic of tribes have traditional locations around the lake. According to Burton, from Arab sources, 16 tribal districts were represented in 1858. The missionary Samuel Hore, who sailed frequently around the lake in the steam vessel *Good News* in the late 1880s and knew the settlement pattern well, reckoned there were a dozen tribes. The lake would have constituted a barrier to migrating peoples in the past, who may have tended to settle beside it. Indeed they probably struggled to claim part of the shore, for access to water and fish. With the lake's long periphery (c.1,820 km), it is not surprising so many tribes are represented.

Effects of political change on the lakeshore people have been complex over the past century. Colonial powers divided the lake into three administrations (German, Belgian and British). After the First World War, German possessions were divided between Belgium and Britain so there were, and still are, four national sectors, two anglophone and two francophone (see Chapter 11). Intercourse between these has tended to be influenced by official language; for example, lake steamer traffic is largely between Zambia and Tanzania on one hand, and French-speaking Congo and Burundi on the other. In post-independence times the former two have been relatively peaceful, but the latter two have endured successive waves of violence.

In the Congo strife and disorder commenced at independence. In 1960 European refugees were a common sight passing through Zambia in trucks towards South Africa. A United Nations peace-keeping force failed spectacularly to be of help, and the disorder spread. Eventually a military junta led by Mobutu Sese-seko took over government and managed to stay in power (with the help of foreign cold-war allies) over four decades. Mobutu's government looted the country and allowed civil infrastructure to decompose. Central government in Kinshasa had only nominal control at Lake Tanganyika. In 1964–65 came the so-called 'simba' or 'mulelist' rebellion, which was driven back into the eastern provinces of Congo by the army, generating large bodies of refugees of which many fled across the lake to Tanzania and Burundi. In the official story these 'mulelists' were notorious for frightful slaughter and atrocities. The situation has hardly improved. Outward fragmentations of populations from the Congo, and from Burundi and Rwanda into the Congo, have destabilised the lake region for half a century (see Chapter 6), limiting the possibility of international aid and development projects in the Congo sector.

Making enquiries

To return to the Zambian fisheries research project at the south of the lake begun in 1960, the essence of my terms of reference was to 'work on things of practical importance'. We had only vague ideas of the extent of fish resources. Numerous species of fish and invertebrates had been identified by British and Belgian scientists, but not much was known about their biology.[7] No continuous research had ever been based in the south lake. Compiling a feasible work project was difficult faced with the extraordinary diversity of this ecosystem. So we started with the general questions: Do distinct stocks of fish exist? Do they fluctuate, and are they sizable enough to support a bigger fishery? Do seasonal productivity cycles occur in this lake; if so what drives them?[7]

Answering these questions led to a five-year study of fish distribution, migrations, seasonal fluctuations and the impacts of growing commercial fishing. One fish community was in pelagic offshore waters, and another highly diverse one lived in shallows nearshore but seemed too sparse to support a fishery.

Lake Tanganyika has extensive southeast and southwest arms, where the bottom shelves gently. Beyond these shelf areas, it is precipitous. A survey showed a rich fish complex living on the bottom down to the limit of dissolved oxygen (about 200 m). Thus we set strings of nets along spaced bottom contours, sometimes 10 km from shore. Catches were examined in a grass shelter on shore or on the boat. My crew were divided into the strong, the fishing team, and the brainy ones who helped examine the catch. Fish were abundant and the crew well motivated because they kept what we caught.

And so lots of offshore sampling and laborious fishing on the deep shelves ensued. Data piled up too from the pelagic commercial fishery, and cried out for analysis. Also several lake-length journeys were made to study seasonal changes that fundamentally underlie the lake's productivity. Interesting topics often arose which had to be set aside – one never had enough time. But a story about fish communities and fishery possibilities emerged, which in 1964–65 were written up as a thesis[8] and later contributed to a book.[9]

Without delving into detail here, I will briefly describe work on the lake with a local team. Most of my own recollections are against a background of working with nets and water sampling equipment, and between-times bowling along in a boat. In the early days we had a 10-metre wooden boat (*Limnothrissa*). A canopy over the working space did not entirely protect one from the sun, which also reflected cruelly from the water surface. Sun and its reflection enclose one in a furnace of radiation. The shirt sticks to the back, and any exposed skin burns. I often envied the apparent tolerance to radiation of my black helpers. Now and then we would roll into the water (27°C) to cool off. Gill nets were set in the evening; an easy job as the piled nets slid out smoothly from behind the boat. But hand-hauling the nets from depths to 200 m was heavier toil. Waves helped if not too steep; we just let the boat's buoyancy bring up the net a bit then hauled in quickly while descending into a trough. During the day, nets were repaired and stacked ready for the evening setting.

Nights on the lake deserve mention, for then most sardine fishing took place. Except during spells of bad weather, the lake is usually still in the early evening. Later light thermal breezes blow from shore. Cries and conversations between fishing canoes tell how the night's fishing is going. As the stars pale, the lamps go out one by one as canoes are paddled home to the women waiting to spread the catch on the beach at sun-up. The smell of drying sardine was pervasive at the beach, but out on the lake at night offshore winds brought fragrant whiffs of flower scent from the land, which I guessed was produced by the native nindi (a plant from which an essential oil for perfumes is made).

My echo-sounder was designed to pick up schools of fish, but registered disappointingly little. Yet catches showed fish were abundant. However, the sounder showed big comet-shaped schools over short time spans, exactly at dusk and again at dawn. The sardines lay dispersed at depth by day, came together in tight schools and ascended to the surface during twilight and then dispersed. Similarly at dawn, schools formed, descended and disappeared. By day, the fish apparently spread out near the bottom or in deep water and so didn't register. Daily migrations appeared a response to predation by the Nile perch – simply, the sardine had to keep in dim light for protection and move only at dusk and dawn in schools.

Traditional and religious practices seemed not to interfere with fishing, but local people were reluctant to venture far into the lake in dug-out canoes and so could not exploit the main stocks offshore. Using a stone anchor fishermen customarily remained within a kilometre of shore. They obdurately refused to accompany our boat further. My first windy season showed

The mountain Kapembwa at the south end of Lake Tanganyika

why. From May to late August, strong southerly winds blow as part of the monsoon system. They are channelled up the great canyon of the basin in an unimpeded fetch of over 600 km (see Figure 6). These winds come characteristically in bursts lasting two or three days, raising steep seas and tempest conditions. Small dug-outs must of course be paddled to shore quickly or they would get blown far up the lake into foreign territory and an uncertain fate. They had reason to be careful.

I came to associate strong pulses of south wind (so-called *kapatas*) with the high escarpment between the southern arms, and on the lake used to look apprehensively towards it for first signs of a gale. The scarp is most impressive, high cliffs rising successively back from the lake. The most striking cliff at the south, called Kapembwa, is locally revered for the power of the associated god over the lake. The crew's attitude indicated respect and humility were due. Bad luck could befall; thus no talking, or waving of arms or taking photos. A former boat employer, I was told, habitually put a five-pound note on the waters for good luck every time he passed that way. The mountain was a baneful presence even at night, and in the rainy season when rainstorms gathered round, it seemed the particular source of thunder which rolled in great echoes, while the mountain faces were lit up by lightning flashes. For the sake of morale if nothing else, we kept well away.[10]

It is a curious fact that though the crew chatted a great deal as we measured fish, looked at stomach contents and so on, few enquired why we

Winching up sampling instruments

were doing these things. More obviously, we were demonstrating that if you had a boat to go offshore, with an engine and set of nets, you could make a good living from fishing. But no entrepreneurs were around either to catch or buy on a commercial scale. The villagers had no cash. We also spent a lot of time winching thermometers and water sampling bottles up and down, which was harder to explain. I did not know myself what the data might show.

Evenings after work was the time to fish with rod and line, trolling a lure just above the rocky bottom nearshore where lurked the main inshore fish predator *Boulengerochromis*. Spitted and smoked above a slow wood fire on the beach overnight, they were delicious eaten cold next day. The crew slept ashore, but I generally stayed aboard in one of the quiet bays celebrating the going down of the sun in the usual way. With sunset an offshore breeze started hesitantly then freshened, infinitely soothing after the heat and glare of the day. Wavelets lapped the bow, and the anchor chain clattered as the boat dragged it over the bottom (curiously amplified in the boat). From shore came bursts of human chatter, a hippo snorted, and the frog and insect choir sang their incessant song. In anchorages remote from settlement, wildlife could be seen close up. They came to drink at the lake edge in the evening or early morning. The boat did not alarm them provided the wind was offshore, perhaps because it was white and merged into the gleam of the lake. The behaviour of species differed: antelope would appear suddenly, take a quick drink, look around, then reassured go on drinking slowly. Elephant and buffalo in herds approached deliberately. Lion came unhurried. I was enchanted at being taken for granted.

With dawn came the crew, a few with hangovers. The senior man, Hindson, focusing attention on the job to be done, sorted out malingerers. Those complaining of 'coughing and sicking' might require aspirin or castor oil. Over the years a candid relationship developed between us. I planned the programme, Hindson pointed out any snags or excessive demands, we compromised and he got on with it.

One fisherman, Shadrack, I came to know well. He did some carpentry and asked to be paid as a carpenter. I told him government only gave me enough to pay him fisherman rates, and he replied irreverently, 'Well, maybe its time we got a new government.' I got him a pay increment, and thereafter he worked well, simply requiring recognition of his skill. Another man, Sam, was elderly and arthritic. He could have been a night watchman, but he wanted to keep up with the others. Always in attendance, never late, he did his best. Unfortunately he tended to catch the blame when anything went wrong; but he had a most disarming smile. It is strange how a nice smile sticks in the mind. One day he disappeared off to prison for three months for not paying his tax. To keep him on the payroll, head office was informed Sam was serving the Queen in another capacity.

I was lucky in day-to-day relationships with a group of fifteen or twenty locally recruited men. Africans are very perceptive in social matters, such as customary procedure or seniority, and the Lungu tribe are much given to elaborate politeness, with ritual hand-clapping and bowing. Some of my crew were Malawians or came from non-local tribes, and so habitually kept a low profile. Morale depended on having a core of good exemplars. Some I had to part with, mutually or otherwise, but most stayed amicably for years. This is the more surprising considering they were under much social pressure in those days of political change, which at times threatened to amount to rebellion. They were subject to noisy agitators in the villages and propaganda on the radio. For months in 1960–61, uproar could be heard and seen on parts of the shore – bonfires, drumming and shouting. But our work was not interrupted. Administration and police officers had hectic moments; though it should be said they enjoyed loyalty and support from their own staff and district councils. In my own heart I felt, 'Oh dear, here we go again, just like Ghana,' but in fact there was still about a decade to go before expatriates such as me began to leave.

In the run up to independence in 1964 agitators used any weapon, including racial incitement. It had been peaceful for so long. Sixty years of quiet times separated the young from knowledge of tribal fighting, stockaded villages and slaving raids. Only the elders remembered. Would-be politicians focused on young jobless men, aiming at disaffecting them from the status quo. One evening on the way home I stopped at a political meeting addressed by Simon Kapwepwe, later to become the country's vice-president. He was impressive. Years later, when I was elevated to membership of the National Council for Scientific Research, he was its chairman, a job he handled well. Not long after, he died in jail – perhaps his ability was perceived as a threat by some. At the roadside that evening I came to appreciate the emotional stress ordinary people might be under. Nevertheless we continued to work detached from potential revolution as though it were all brewing somewhere else. Doubtless they would vote for independence when the time came, though some may have realised nothing much would change.

Investigating the Big Wave: A sub-project

Despite 'endless summer', distinct seasons of wind and rainfall occurred in Tanganyika, as well as cycles of fish and plankton. In certain months the lake grew green with plankton. Swarms of little sardines appeared nearshore at times, and catches of bigger sardine offshore had an annual peak. Were such cycles brought about by fertilising nutrients washed in during the rainy season (November-April)? Or did the lake get stirred and nutrients circulated, possibly by the strong monsoon winds of May-September?

Belgian research had shown the lake was permanently stratified in three layers. Imagine Tanganyika as a sandwich, long and narrow like a bread baguette, with layers of different thicknesses. A top layer about 50 metres thick is exposed to sun warming and wind mixing; a lower, cooler and very deep one mixes very slowly and temperatures remain virtually unchanged. Between them is a layer where there is a temperature step. These are really density layers, sitting one on the other, because in Tanganyika temperature chiefly determines water density.

Plants and animals in the sunlit layer eventually sink and decompose, so the deep bottom layer has become chemically enriched but is without oxygen. It constitutes a great reservoir of nutrients that, if leaked upwards, would fertilise the sunlit layer.

I began once a week to record temperature and oxygen profiles. The top layer cooled in the dry windy season, and it seemed that deep water upwelled. For the rest of the year, the middle layer rose and fell in huge 'internal waves' of 50-metre amplitude, cycling every 25-30 days.[11] In nearby Lake Malawi/Nyasa (see Figure 4) a colleague, David Eccles, was getting a similar picture. Like me, he was at the south end of a long narrow lake, where it seemed upwelling occurred during the south winds, and for the rest of the year these great internal wave pulses were prominent.[12] The fanciful analogy occurred to us that we were each located at the big toe of a recumbent giant measuring its heartbeats.

Papers by Beauchamp,[13] who visited the lakes before World War II, gave inspired glimpses of what we were dealing with. He was thinking about our two vast tropical lakes in terms of what happens in small temperate lakes, which also stratify in summer into three density layers. When such lakes are long and narrow, like the UK's Windermere or Loch Ness, the upper two layers get tilted by strong winds, while upwelling occurs at the windward end where the deepest layer may come to the surface. When the wind relaxes, the tilted upper layers then rock to and fro, generating 'internal waves' until interrupted by further wind forcing. However, we did not know if something similar could happen in Tanganyika and Malawi; no internal waves of the size and duration we were measuring occurred in any lakes in the world. But if some kind of analogue with temperate lakes existed, then a great deal of familiar physical theory might apply.

We decided to investigate the circulatory systems of the 'sleeping giants', by trying to get 'instantaneous' pictures of temperature in both lakes when tilting might occur, i.e., during the strong southerly winds. This meant going right up the middle of each lake, as near simultaneously as possible. David would cover the length of Lake Malawi first, and then hasten to me at Tanganyika and we would go north along it together. It was an ambitious plan, because each lake transect would take three or four days and nights of continuous work, stopping every 10 km for a temperature profile down to 150 m (see Figure 6). In the strong winds of May it would not be easy to halt and lower an instrument vertically.[14] In the event, David got about 250 km up Lake Malawi before rough weather forced him to stop. He arrived at Tanganyika and we set off, but after 15 hours one of our two engines broke down. The vessel could not manoeuvre with a single engine. We cut the instrument cable and lost our temperature probe.

At this point there was little to show for our labours. But we had an engineer along, George Hutting, loaned from the Public Works Department (PWD). He decided to return and take the failed engine to his distant Lusaka workshops. It seemed too great a job, given our crucial dependence on timing. We did not know George previously. He seemed a quite ordinary sort of man. Back at Mpulungu, he immediately set to work, hauled the heavy engine out with pulleys and manpower, and put it on a truck. He drove south all that day, worked on the engine all night, and drove back the next day, reinstalling the engine at dawn. By noon we were off again. The turn-around had taken only two days due to George's unbelievable effort, driving some 1,500 km mostly on bad roads. Such heroism does not usually find its way into reports, but we appreciated him.

Kinder weather enabled us to go on steadily for four days and nights, the full length of the lake. Bujumbura, in Burundi, lay peacefully before us and we felt elated. A quick scan of our temperature/depth data indicated an overall downward tilt of the middle layer to the north, and there had been signs of upwelling in the south. David's Malawi results gave a similar picture. Responses of this kind to wind had not been measured on such scale elsewhere, and it seemed to parallel the classic response of smallish temperate lakes. If so, both the upwelling and the internal wave should be associated with turbulent mixing between deeper layers and surface water, and this had important implications for biological production.[15] We made our happy way into Bujumbura port, tired and desiring only sleep. Alas, it was not to be.

Deserted wharfs, moored steamers and barges, idle cranes, closed warehouses – no one was in sight in the middle of the day. Not quite – a squad of soldiers marching up the quay. We stepped ashore to introduce ourselves. The NCO, a corporal, halted them smartly. They lined up and raised automatic weapons. Though dozy, we could see this was not a friendly reception. The corporal spoke Ki-rundi, French and a little Swahili. He demanded passports, and as he brusquely took them I asked what was wrong. We were made to understand that today was the celebration of Independence Day in Burundi. The significance sank in. International heads-of-state, foreign representatives, plus anyone who was anyone would be gathered, very likely in a stadium, for the celebrations. As far as the corporal was concerned, literally all the world was assembled for *les manifestations*, while he was stuck to guard the port. No wonder the city, large for East Africa, had seemed peaceful. What a day to choose to arrive! '*Exactement*,' agreed the corporal.

This no doubt explained their truculence. But there was something more; the NCO was looking wildly around for orders, evidently loath to receive us. As always, suspicion dawned. We must be 'mercenaries'. In the mid-sixties European soldiers of fortune/mercenaries were creating a violent rumpus in the Congo (its mountains visible from where we stood). It was headline news; everyone knew what they looked like. Shaggy and nondescript, we fitted the description. Our men were from strange tribes. Last, but not least, George's passport was recognised to be South African. It must be so. Panic . . .

The corporal dashed to and fro making phone calls, but no one was at work or at home. After a couple of hours, during which the armed guard had not relaxed, we three Europeans were put in a jeep with two of them, leaving our men on the wharf under guard. We drove through empty streets, from one deserted office to another, arriving finally at what looked and smelled like the jail. But the NCO in charge there would not take responsibility for us. So, back again to the port. By now our corporal was a dangerous man – bloodshot eyes and speechless. He gestured with his pistol at his watch and at the lake, giving just two minutes for us to make ourselves scarce. We made good use of them to put as much space as possible between ourselves and what Burton in 1858 had called 'that inhospitable land'.[16] After a while we stopped in mid-lake and slept. Later, one of our crew picked up a radio broadcast in Swahili from Bujumbura. It described how, during the Great Day, three dangerous South African spies had tried to infiltrate and been successfully cast out. The corporal must have found someone to report to.

Two more south–north voyages were made in subsequent years, but no more attempts to land. From the three trips and regular records at a station in the south, a pattern emerged consistent with the hydrodynamic model.[9] A fuller picture obtained by scientists in the 1990s confirmed our basic propositions. They also showed close connections between the internal wave and biological productivity. (In scientific terms they 'showed strong coupling between physical processes and nutrient dynamics in the pelagic waters'[15].) One might be excused for wondering what is the practical usefulness of studying the hydrodynamics of Lake Tanganyika? Well … hundreds of thousands of people in the region get their main animal protein food from the lake, and it is useful to understand the mechanisms underlying its productivity.

Notes and references

1. Burton, R.F. 1860. *The Lake Region of Central Africa.* 2 Vols. London, Longmans Green.
2. Waller, H. (Ed.).(1874). *The Last Journals of David Livingstone in Central Africa.* 2 Vols.
3. Stanley, H.M. (1878). *Through the Dark Continent.* Sampson Low, Marsten, Searle and Rivington. London.
4. Cameron, V.L, (1877). *Across Africa.* London.
5. Hore, E.C. (1892) *Tanganyika: Eleven years in Central Africa.* Stanford.
6. Abbe Lechaptois (1912). *Aux Rives du Tanganika.* Rome
7. The most comprehensive Belgian work on Tanganyika was their *Exploration Hydrobiologique* (1946–47), published by the Institut Royale des Sciences Naturelles de Belgique. The research topic in fashion early in my time was the interrelationships among fish species complexes. Classic studies had been done on the tilapia of Lake Malawi by R.H. Lowe, and by G. Fryer on feeding linkages between the numerous endemic cichlid fish. H. Greenwood was busy describing the famous species flock of haplochromine cichlids in Lake Victoria. I might have tried following in their footsteps, so to speak, with the very colourful inshore cichlids of

Tanganyika, but unlike Malawi and Victoria, the Tanganyika cichlids are not of much exploitation value. Offshore sardine and Nile perch are the main targets. For a scientific bibliography on Lake Tanganyika, see Note 9; also *The State of Biodiversity in Lake Tanganyika: A Literature Review* (1998). Natural Resources Institute, London.

8. Coulter, G.W. (1966). *Hydrobiological processes and the deep-water fish community in Lake Tanganyika.* PhD Thesis, Queens University, Belfast.
9. Coulter, G.W. (1991). [Ed.] *Lake Tanganyika and its Life.* Oxford University Press, 353pp.
10. The only written description of Kapembwa I know of was published by a friend, John McCrae, in the *Northern Rhodesia Journal* (1963) *5*(3): 246–250. As he was born in the country, the son of a long-time official, he was well known to the local people. He was given permission to visit the place on the mountaintop where, in former times, sacrifices were made to the god. Macrae describes how in an annual ritual, when it was believed the spirit deity was temporarily absent out on the lake, a maiden selected for sacrifice was cast from the summit.
11. To be clear, the so-called waves were not surface waves, but internal 'wave-like' displacements (internal seiches) of the 'middle layer'; specifically, where the temperature boundary between it and the upper layer is sharpest (the thermocline).
12. Such internal seiches could not continue long in high latitudes because inertial force from the earth's rotation (Coriolis Force) diverts and dissipates the wave energy. We now have theory explaining why the giant internal waves set up by the south wind persist through the rest of the year in Lakes Tanganyika and Malawi. Essentially it is because inertial forces from the earth's rotation are small at these latitudes not far from the equator; and also because of the long narrow shape and great depth of their basins.
13. Beauchamp, R.S. (1939). Lake Tanganyika. *Int. Rev. ges. Hydrobiol. und Hydrograph, 39*(3–4): 316–353.
    Also: Beauchamp, R.S. (1940). Chemistry and Hydrography of Lakes Tanganyika and Nyasa. *Nature, London, 146*(3695): 253–256.
14. David's procedure for rough weather was to measure the angle of the cable, from which the true depth of the instrument could be calculated. Mine was to manoeuvre the boat to keep the cable vertical. We had trained hard at this in all weathers, especially at night. David had a trusty vessel and I borrowed a 15m yacht *Dame des Iles* from the district administration.
15. Langenburg, V.T., Sarvala, J. & Roijackers, R. (2004). Effect of wind- induced water movements on nutrients, chlorophyll-a and primary production in Lake Tanganyika. *Journal of Aquatic Ecosystem Health and Management, 6(*3): 279-288.
16. Burton, R.F. (1860), p.106.

5

Expats and Experts

Working in harness

In 1965 I found myself working with a new UN-FAO fisheries project to advise on Zambia's various fisheries. As co-manager, with responsibility also for departmental fisheries research, my two roles represented a fusion of old and new styles; the department continued to work from outstations whereas UN staff resided at a central institute in Chilanga, near the capital Lusaka. A new world of working with colleagues in an institute opened to me.[1]

The old system was inherited from colonial-type administration. Although it meant being out of touch with colleagues elsewhere, it also meant being in daily touch with the people of the country. However, political independence involved changing senior government personnel from whites to blacks. It could not be done at once because of the shortage of blacks with professional qualifications. International 'aid' was recruited to speed the pace of development and accelerate training of nationals. Whatever the intentions when this aid started, it has grown not diminished over the decades.

Colonial administrations in Africa in the first half of the twentieth century acquired departments staffed with professional officers, for example in agriculture, fisheries, medical, veterinary, etc. They were not subordinate to the District Administration, and had their own chief officers and directors. In the main they were graduates from British universities, had similar backgrounds, and were used to working in a chain of command (especially the ex-servicemen). The hierarchy, however, gave plenty of room for personal eccentricity. This was the colonial structure, and the Game and Fisheries department in Zambia was fairly typical.

Foreign aid arrived first in the form of individual consultants for specific jobs; and then the project formula became popular, each project being staffed with a team of 'experts' who stayed for the life of the project (several years). In country-to-country (bilateral) aid, the experts might have been all, say, Norwegian or German. On the other hand, a UN project usually employed different nationalities. A principle was to train a local 'counterpart' for each expert. The most promising trainees would often be sent to overseas universities – with the intention, not always fulfilled, that they would return.

At the beginning of the foreign aid era, colonial professional officers were often cast uneasily in the role of 'counterparts' of foreign 'experts'. This led to invidious situations in which the old expats were more competent than the new experts, and in addition knew the country. But in Zambia we rubbed along in harness with a fair amount of mutual benefit.

I must confess it took me some time to comprehend the purely information and advice nature of aid-funded projects. The work of the Zambia fisheries institute, from bacteriology to fish biology and commercial preservation techniques, was indeed useful. We in the service tried to ensure the work was all relevant – 'keeping feet on the ground'. The basic difference between us expats and the project experts was that we were members of a service with a long-term point of view, aware especially of the time it took to get new practices established. We worked with local people. While already on the way out, we still kept some 'permanent and pensionable' attitudes; which meant, among other things, that what you accomplished mattered. They on the other hand were there to do research and provide advice about methods, without direct responsibility for outcomes.

Later, on joining a UN agency myself as a project manager, I came to understand better. If stuck with a problem I went to the senior agency man in the country. In the particular case, I received counsel from a very experienced Belgian who had worked many years in Africa. He would listen to me carefully, occasionally interjecting '*D'accord*' or '*Voilà*', expressing agreement and understanding. When I'd finished, he would invariably reflect, shrug and say '*C'est comme ça*' (that's the way things are). This was not what I wanted. I was looking for specific advice, solutions. But in a while I understood he was implicitly saying, 'OK, these are indeed the circumstances, and you are more or less on the right track. Just keep on doing your best.' He knew very well my power to act was limited; there were no quick fixes I could carry out. He also knew that giving me more advice would not materially affect outcomes. So best just keep on working with the plan of operations agreed with the government.

Having this plan of operations, the international expert's job is then to work towards the plan's completion with government officers. Much depends on personalities and local policies but in the end it is their (the country's) project. The expert's advice might not be taken. Some political discontinuity might cause the ruin of what has been built up. But the expert must be prepared to come back to the ruin and keep on trying. He lives in the 'now', but paradoxically must be prepared to work in terms of 'the long haul'. He must care, but not get discouraged; he must be an active agent but accept that he is an indirect one. These are the practical realities of aid-funded projects in developing countries.

It often happens, and was the case in the Zambia FAO project, that experts personified their own national characteristics. Stereotypes can be funny. Those like me, ex-colonial British, probably appeared as stereotypes to them. As for us, we were suddenly surrounded by foreigners whose thinking and methods were strange. While it is dangerous to generalise, the following few examples indicate how different national attitudes of aid experts may mightily influence approaches taken on the ground.

One would often hear from North Americans: 'Technology, that's all they need, technology; just feed 'em that and they'll see the point and run with it.' Recommendations therefore went forth for complicated equipment without much regard to local preferences or maintenance capability. Similar attitudes prevailed in scientific methods; for example, I found myself with US biologists in a little boat on the Kafue floodplains. It was high flood and we were surrounded by dense emergent vegetation, which limited our movement. We stuffed an electronic bleeper into the stomach of a captured catfish, with difficulty. Theoretically its movements could then be traced around the vast stretches of flooded plain. The first bleeps came as we gazed into the control box, and then were heard no more; the fish had taken off through the weed where we could not follow. The next loaded fish went to ground right below the boat, so its bleeps meant nothing. But at least we had taken a modern technical approach and had two data points. A few more bleepers and we could build a statistical model.

On the other hand, Germans put stress on efficiency and will: 'Anything is possible if you work together with a will.' This was true enough if a task was tightly supervised, or a new method suited local environments. It is a sad story but I had a friend, Sturm, who was expert in planning and budget control of small businesses. After a while, he had a nervous breakdown from frustration over lack of progress. 'Take it easy for a while,' he was told, 'do something simple like working in the garden.' Sturm's wife being a friend of my wife, I was able to see him often during his convalescence. His garden quickly became a new project and progressed. Under his careful hand, level lawns were laid out, intersected with paths well trimmed along their edges and dividing at exact angles. Disciplined lines of little bushes sprouted that could be manicured. A miniature Versailles. Unfortunately, when the rainy season finished there came the long dry and unproductive period. The garden wilted. Sturm did not get better, and had to be sent home.

On the other hand, an English friend favoured persuasive discourse. He explained, 'You must talk and listen to the people, exchange views, arrange meetings, get consensus, all must participate; then at that point move the community forward in the way they want to go.' He was very busy and for a short time caused quite a stir. The trouble he found was that management by foreign social notions about community and organisation can clash with local custom and expediency, and it can get political – which is a minefield for foreign advisers. I believe he eventually wrote a book about it.

The Irish tended to see the funny side and could discover an absurdity in the dullest document. In contrast, Swedes and Russians took things very seriously; they would thoroughly evaluate and assess situations, then solemnly pronounce, '*Probleme*'! The Japanese found it difficult to communicate with anyone else.

I enjoyed working with Yuri, sincere and likable. We went to see the film of Pasternak's *Dr Zhivago*, and our personal friendship was good enough to discuss it from different sides – he didn't think it properly presented 'the spirit of the Soviet people'. We worked together on the adaptation of the Lake Malawi *chirimila* net to conditions in Tanganyika. I did the field trials, and Yuri the technical description.[2] Our 'international' effort was successful and the device proliferated, catching tons of Tanganyika sardines for years.

I said we rubbed along with mutual benefit. Let me describe an instance that indicates the context in Zambia. Often one had to make long road trips by Land Rover on unsurfaced roads. Rest stops were few because the country is mostly bush with only rare places to spend the night. In the dry season red laterite dust penetrates to the hair roots, encrusts eyelashes and fills the nose and throat. Open windows cause the body to dry out. Speed must be kept at 80 km/hr at least to 'smooth out' road corrugations. In the rainy season, craters and ruts full of water have to be skirted. In these conditions, one carried for sustenance just water, nuts and perhaps bread rolls.

I took Yuri for a first trip to Tanganyika, and since we were in a saloon car brought Margaret along and Yuri's wife Olga, who offered to bring a bite of lunch. At midday we stopped under a tree, laterited all over as usual, and took the customary comfort walk in the bush. Returning minutes later we found Olga and Yuri spreading a banquet on paper mats placed on the car – salami, sliced ham, caviar, smoked salmon, cheeses, pickles, biscuits, cakes and fruit, with white wine from a cooler box. They had concealed all this in their baggage. We did not want to appear surprised, or explain such procedure was unusual, in case they would be embarrassed. So we showed appreciation by making the feast disappear quickly, before it could be ruined by dust from passing vehicles. In due course they became experienced travellers and adopted travelling austerities. What remains in mind is the contrast in our ways, and the generous Russian impulse.

Another 'joint' exercise with the Institute was the transfer of Tanganyika sardine to Lake Kariba. This turned out to be a very significant operation, because the sardine (*Limnothrissa*) flourished and for decades has yielded catches from Kariba of the order of 30–40 thousand tons per year. From pre-Kariba Zambezi studies, my former JFRO boss Peter Jackson believed that the open-water niche in the new lake would not be filled by any of the river fishes. It was suggested one of the Tanganyika sardine species might fill the ecological gap. At Tanganyika I had noticed that at certain times of year tiny *Limnothrissa* fry appear inshore in great abundance. Trials to catch and hold them in aquaria showed they were very delicate, and had to be caught before their scales developed. We had a Belgian biologist study sardine spawning and handling, but in the end feasibility of stocking seemed a matter of trial and error. Prediction of the biological impacts of introducing the sardine into the Zambezi system (below Victoria Falls) was too great a task, so the questions were simply could we fly them to Kariba (1,000 km), and would they survive there? They did not survive in the first (1965) trials, but died on release due, we guessed, to shock from temperature difference.

We had another shot in 1968. Graham and Barry in the Department arranged dawn capture of thousands of tiny *Limnothrissa* in plastic containers. A former assistant in the department, Andrew, made 29 transport flights in a light plane. At Kariba a second crew kept the containers in the water until temperatures equalised before releasing the fish. They 'took', i.e., fed, bred and flourished, and gradually fishery yields became substantial.[3]

Did such *ad hoc* action prove that introductions can be undertaken without secure prediction of effects? I don't think so. We were just lucky that Kariba was a new lake with an empty ecological niche to fill, and that the sardine were able to adapt. Current opinion is that the effects of transfer of alien species can be catastrophic; great caution is necessary. Introducing Nile perch to Lake Victoria in the 1960s is an example. Controversy still continues as to whether the growth of that fishery (now the largest in Africa) outweighs the resultant extinction of hundreds of unique native species.

Through the FAO Institute we also had access to short-term consultants, a group of whom assisted in studies of the Kafue River floodplain; laying the foundations for managing this important fishery near the Zambia capital, Lusaka. The extensive Kafue flats or floodplains had long been used for cattle ranching. Great herds of red lechwe antelope there originally occurred in tens of thousands. Their semi-aquatic habitat provided a degree of

Captive lechwe antelope

protection from predators, but early ranchers had struggled against large numbers of lions. One ranch, Lochinvar, became a wildlife reserve that provided us with opportunities to study Kafue fish.

This great plain was vividly green when inundated by the flooding river. In contrast, in summer it was dry and brown. Enormous populations of big aquatic birds, such as pelicans, gathered in flooded shallows, and with the lechwe herds were important components of the ecosystem. Prodigious growth of young fish in the flood months makes the fishery a very rich one, and the activities of local fishermen intensify as flood waters recede from the plain and they take their annual fish crop with traditional nets and baskets. In this changeable environment our research had to be opportunistic, so short-term intensive studies were suitable.

Another short-term consultant studied the Upper Zambezi Barotze floodplain, working in harness with our departmental scientist concerned with the biology and distribution of the well-known tiger-fish *Hydrocynus* in the river. Tiger fish burgeoned too in Lake Kariba, feeding on the ex-Tanganyika sardine, and became an important sport fishery. In the Upper Zambezi, sandbanks emerge from the river at low water providing perfect conditions for catching tiger-fish by rod and line. At that time of year the *Hydrocynus* were in good condition, having fed on young-of-the-year prey fish

A tiger-fish; note the metal tag on its gill-cover

on the floodplains. The ecological impact of tiger-fish upon them was great. My colleague devised what seemed to me an idyllic work programme, catching and tagging tiger-fish by rod and line, so migration and growth could be traced.

Our visiting consultant on the Barotze floodplain had a passion for hunting. Around the Upper Zambezi that could only be done by the permission of the paramount chief of the Lozi people, a very powerful personage, whose word on the matter was strict. If he agreed, it was customary to return some meat to him. The consultant sought and got permission and I was invited too. We chose a spot where Zambia is bordered by wild parts of the Congo and Botswana (see Figure 4). Driving into sparse forest and open parkland we were faced with an astounding sight. A great range and number of animals, including some rarer species. Most remarkably, they seemed little afraid and did not immediately flee, though neither did they stand passively as do animals accustomed to harmless tourists taking pictures from minibuses. These were just not accustomed to encountering humans.

It was a rare privilege to witness a scene from Africa before powder and shot. This was how it had been for timeless ages, and it felt sacrilege to shoot. In the event, our consultant friend soon disposed of all the animals our helpers could cut up and carry away. In fading light he dropped a running pig from over 200 m: I had not seen telescopic sights used until then. But the abiding impression was the first 'moment of vision' when stepping into that wonderful place. It was an experience such as visual artists perhaps get when they see a composite image as a whole, the unity as well as the detail.[4] In our case, the individual animals were there as parts of an entire, ecologically integrated assembly of large wildlife.

I think of the period 1965–69 in Zambia as the last years of the old regime when professional posts were still staffed by colonial-service-type Europeans, who had been together for years, supplemented gradually by international then national personnel. I handed over to a Zambian colleague in 1969.

Lake Tanganyika provides an example of the subsequent institutional 'project approach' to giving aid. Since the 1980s three successful research projects have used teams from Finland (UN-FAO), Britain (UNDP) and Japan (University of Kyoto), respectively; making extended visits to the lake.[5] Another project on Tanganyika, run by the University of Arizona, USA, lasted ten years and was devoted to training in limnology. The result has been many scientific publications as well as training opportunities for young nationals.

Hail and farewell: Visiting academics

> The bird of time has but a little way
> To fly – and Lo! The bird is on the wing.
>
> Rubaiyat of Omar Khayyam

> 'I am just wasting my time,' a visiting scientist exploded, exasperated by delays. 'No, that is not the case,' retorted a local official. 'You are not here to serve your own purposes. You are here to help us.'
>
> (Overheard in one of the countries)

Foreign academics on brief sorties with their own specific goals are in a decidedly different category from experts working in a country-based project. There is indeed no shortage of scientists keen to come to Africa for research, but places to receive them with material back-up and local know-how are relatively few. I have taken part in short-term, hi-tech projects by providing the local back-up of a resident project and encouraging scientists

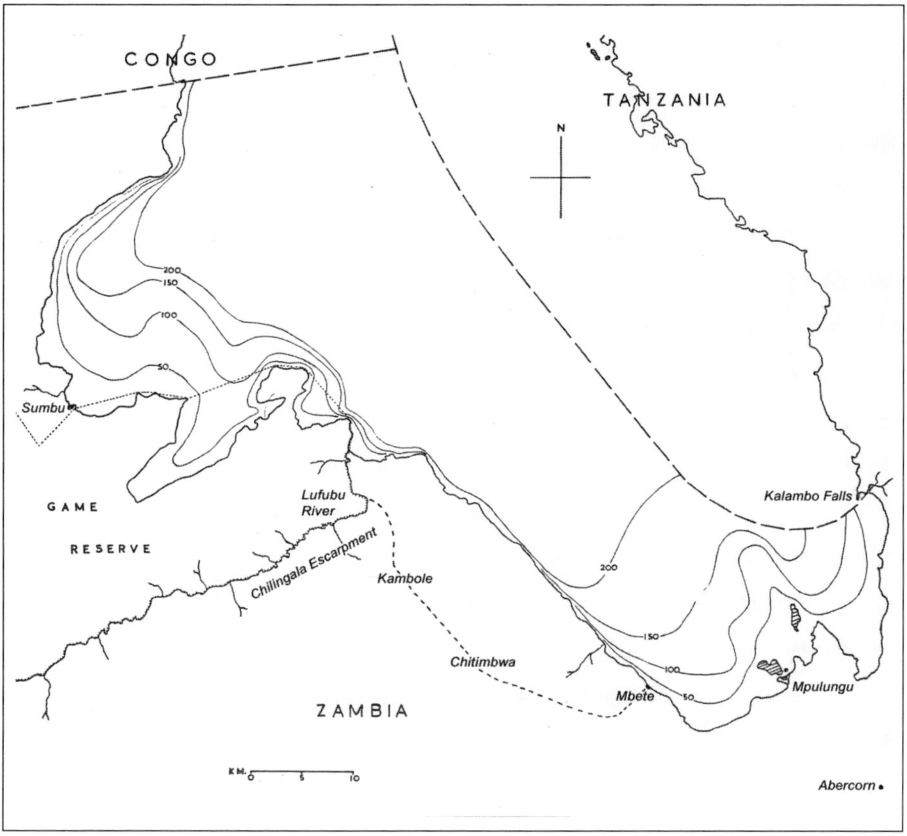

Figure 7. South end of Lake Tanganyika. Lake isobaths are at 50, 100, 150 and 200 metres depth. Dashed line indicates Livingstone's route between the Lufubu River and Mbete.

whose interests fitted within our general programme. They came on an expedition basis, mostly from North America.

My first encounter with American academics was in 1962. Daniel Livingstone and Jonathan Richardson, distinguished scientists, knocked on my door in Abercorn near the south of Lake Tanganyika, explaining they were on reconnaissance to get samples from the bottoms of African lakes. Lake sediments may contain the remains of aquatic plants and animals that have accumulated over time, and therefore comprise a record of past floras and faunas. Not only that but wind-blown particles such as pollen grains, persisting in sediments, can give strong indications of surrounding vegetation in the past (the study is called paleolimnology). My visitors went on to explain the most attractive target lakes are Tanganyika and Malawi. They are deep and ancient, the bottom is virtually undisturbed by wind and because it is deoxygenated no aquatic animals have disturbed the sediments. The steady accumulation of sediments over millions of years, possibly contain a long successional record of life in the lake and its surrounding land vegetation. (One interesting aspect is that these sediments might record the climatic history of mankind, since *homo sapiens* is believed to have evolved in tropical Africa.)

Cores would be shipped out for complex analysis overseas, but meanwhile Livingstone and Johnson were identifying feasible coring sites. Among other places they mentioned Lake Chisi in the Mweru-wa-ntipa area. I advised that Chisi could be risky in their rubber boat. My JFRO boss, Peter, had recently been chased there by aggressive crocodiles, and he was in a big canoe

So also it happened with them, in a very dramatic incident. Their rubber boat was attacked and punctured and they spent perilous hours in the water. It was not a trivial experience, and it gave rise to fascinating papers in learned journals about why crocodiles attack small boats.[6] On his next trip, Livingstone and another colleague came to get sediment cores from Tanganyika. They borrowed a steel catamaran, put a platform and coring rig on it, and disappeared out into the lake. When they did not reappear for days, I grew anxious and searched the southern coast by boat (as far as Sumbu). Finally, coming to the Kalambo river delta which in the east marks the boundary between Zambia and Tanzania (see Figure 7), I approached the shore intending to ask if anyone had seen the missing scientists. It was night and still, and a bright moon illuminated the deep canyon cleft by the Kalambo river. A light mist covered the flat lake. On the beach was a waiting party. It was a magical scene. Mentally I framed the question as I beached the boat – had they perhaps seen a Dr Livingstone around there? Then it struck me that David Livingstone had indeed passed Kalambo (on 11 November 1872).[7] I imagined the helpful reply: 'Yes, but it was some time ago.'

The catamaran turned up next day with a substantial core from a place where water depth was 500 metres. On examination the core proved a scientific triumph, leading to much further exploration. Also, it demonstrated the tenacity one came to associate with the best of such enquiring visitors.

It was with this memory I attended a meeting at the North American Great Lakes Centre, Milwaukee, Lake Michigan in 1968. C.H. Mortimer, director of that centre, kindly arranged a lecture tour in the USA and Canada to help pay my expenses. I gratefully accepted, innocent of the demanding system whereby visiting lecturers are whisked around a circuit of cooperating universities and institutes. To cut a hectic story short, I gave around twenty-five lectures in five weeks, and by my return to Zambia had made twenty-

Sumbu, southwest arm of Lake Tanganyika

Kalambo Falls, southeast arm; the second highest sheer falls in the world (233 metres)

seven flights. At about $100 plus short-hop travel for each talk, remuneration just covered costs, but I was dead on my feet.

At each stop one glimpsed a campus, usually of bewildering size, handed the lecture slides to a technician and, after a brief introduction, was suddenly face to face with a large audience of students and faculty members. One had to try to explain the African scene and lake science to people totally unfamiliar with it. The lecture was followed by questions, and sometimes discussion with a smaller group asking harder questions. Then to a hotel, more socialising, and next morning another flight. Towards the end I was living on adrenalin. On the New York–London leg of the return the plane flew a 'great circle' course, crossing Labrador and Greenland. Through a port I gazed at the big round moon, which apparently stayed still right where it was, during the whole night! In my exhausted state this phenomenon puzzled me.

American informality, I found, can be just that. One was on Christian-name terms surprisingly quickly, but it did not indicate intimacy or necessarily friendliness. It helped facilitate contact. Business is business and one was expected to give value. It was also expected that information should be supported in numerical, statistical, and if possible graphical forms. One journal editor told me he worked for a 'data-orientated constituency'. But they seemed to appreciate the beginning of my talk, with pictures of people and animals to set the scene, and perhaps that helped hold attention through the dry stuff that followed. Lack of knowledge about Africa was surprising, and there was even mild surprise that another set of Great Lakes might exist in the world. Most, however, had heard of the Nile, Congo and Zambezi Rivers. The basic frame of reference in all discussions was the North American lakes, and it seemed hard to get a different picture across – such as endless summer, year-round growth of organisms, permanent stratification in deep lakes. That fishing in African lakes was for food not sport was especially hard to communicate.

Few expressed an intention to visit Africa, and I sensed a reluctance to venture outside the frame of the familiar. My overall impression was of concentrations of scientific expertise – huge teaching faculties with flocks of post-graduates and astonishing scientific assets. Despite all this they were narrowly focused; and of course our situation in Africa was in utter contrast, with small numbers of scattered research personnel working in isolation. If only a tiny fraction of US or Canadian resources could be attracted to Africa, what a difference it might make, provided they were prepared to stay long enough (or come back often enough) to adapt to the different natural and cultural environments. I resolved not to let slip any future opportunity of capturing some of this expertise. Even small numbers, supported by academic grants, could boost African efforts tremendously. As it happened I did have opportunities later, and the outcomes were generally satisfactory. However, it was never easy to fit visiting scientists straight from home into the local scene.

As an example of such associations, a group came to Tanganyika from Scripps Institute of Oceanography and the Massachusetts Institute of Technology (MIT). They proposed to study the chemistry, including isotopes, of the deep water. It involved doing many analyses in the field, as well as air-freighting hundreds of water samples to the home labs. Sounds straightforward, but it entailed shifting a camp laboratory around distant points along the shoreline (tents, benches, generator, pumps, analytical equipment, food, sleeping and cooking arrangements). They made two expeditions, each of several weeks, a year apart. Naturally, it entailed improvisations and tribulations. The visitors were unused to what locally were regarded as trifles, like delays or the absence of conventional facilities. Snakes escaped from bunches of bananas, causing rapid exits overboard. Some visitors had neglected to take the necessary malarial prophylactics and paid the penalty. Incongruencies among personalities became prominent in the midday heat. Patience was taxed to the full and beyond. But remarkable work got done. There were only two unfortunate incidents with this lot.

One scientist and his wife parted company from the main body to go sampling out in mid-lake in a small launch. They were discovered at night by one of Mobutu's (Congo) gunboats. These hoodlums knew our main vessel, which flew the UN flag, but did not recognise the smaller one. They took it in tow to Kalemie (formerly Albertville) on the Congo coast. According to our crew an argument then took place on the gunboat about whether to shoot them (usual practice when canoes were accosted at night) or tow them in. A radio message to the capital, Kinshasa, eventually brought instructions to release the captives. After a day or two waiting in port they were towed back to the middle of the lake. There they could not restart the engine, and we found them looking harassed. Fortunately they had been unaware of the depth of their peril.

Finally, when leaving the airport with big wooden crates containing hundreds of invaluable water samples in tiny bottles, there was a bureaucratic hitch. Customs regulations required that each item exported must be declared on a separate form. In vain we pointed out it would take weeks to fill a form for each bottle. 'Why not,' suggested an official, 'just put all the little bottles into one big bottle, so you'd have to fill out only one form?' Considering this, our visitors searched for a deeper meaning, because he surely couldn't mean it? Then they blew their fuses. Unfortunately they mentioned the use of tritium isotopes in the water samples from the fall-out of atmospheric testing of nuclear weapons.[8] Official faces clouded with suspicion. The crates glowed with imagined radioactivity. Customs personnel went into a huddle, and presently I was beckoned over. They were desperate. A minor customs matter had suddenly taken on enormous significance. Nuclear weapons were being passed through their hands. The matter was elevated to a super-diplomatic issue. Big trouble for everybody! My heart sank; all that work for nothing. Our innocent efforts would certainly be misrepresented, and our distinguished visitors languish indefinitely in jail. Since all was lost, I suggested a quick illegal remedy. 'Get rid of these people and their baggage. Fill just one form and get them off. Then forget about the whole thing.' It worked, and to our relief the visitors were bundled off to Departures.

On our side valuable knowledge was gained about nutrient chemistry and mixing regimes in the deep water of the lake.[8] It could only have been achieved by analysis and interpretation far beyond our local capacities. It demonstrated the need for this kind of help to get breakthroughs. It also showed the necessity of a local organisation to receive foreigners and overcome logistic difficulties. Most science is done as joint effort. Ideas contributed in discussions with colleagues are vital. Lack of joint effort is especially acute in Africa where resident workers tend to get isolated. There are many little groups of graduates cut off in their countries from the mainstreams of their disciplines, underfunded and lacking injections of inspiration. They need contacts with researchers elsewhere. In aid projects, foreign scientists go on to resume their careers at home, leaving behind local co-workers without continuity in their relationships. Few expatriates can have worked in Africa without being struck by this dilemma.

A fundamental problem in getting short-term assistance from overseas is often the different viewpoints of the visitors and local officials (exemplified by the above case). In home countries, to raise grant money means that proposals must meet the criteria of their funding bodies, in competition of course with other applications. These criteria usually stress the value of the work to science, its place in that person's current line of research, advantages for the teaching of students, and so forth (motives distinct from giving aid to a foreign country). Success in meeting these goals affects careers and future prospects for further grants. The person is often in mid-career taking limited leave from a home university. So he/she is tightly time-restricted and narrowly focused in purpose. Circumstances determine that one is driven by personal motives far more than by idealism.

All this is pretty evident in the visitor's behaviour. To the local people he is a caricature – a phenomenon wearing a peaked hat, nervously stooping over apparatus or laptop, rising abruptly to look at his watch and stare expectantly to the horizon (for the people and supplies, which are late). Then he returns to his box for some minutes, only to jump up and stare into the distance again. He is a creature possessed and driven, troubled and irritable, in the frantic pursuit of data within his tight time schedule. In fairness it should be added that this is not always so. Repeated visits during projects of several years permit human contacts to be made, and give time for friendly appreciation to grow on both sides.

Strangely, the time–money problem was exemplified by one of the earliest visiting Europeans. H.M. Stanley was probably the most professionally successful of the explorer figures in Africa of the nineteenth century, but also the most controversial. To this day his methods are often mentioned with hostility, especially in Britain (where he was born and eventually returned after years in America). According to one biographer[9], Stanley's problems arose to a large extent from his substantial financial backing, which 'placed him under special obligation to his employers to complete his various missions with the utmost dispatch'. Hence the rude urgency of his conduct. He was out to get quick results. In effect, this led to his employing many personnel, requiring detailed organisation which he largely supervised himself, plus the best technology available. He was goal-orientated and always too much in a hurry. He was not inhumane, but 'time was against him; this was at the root of his frequent inability to foster friendly relations with the Africans'.

It is arguable whether the collection of data for science *per se* should have priority in present-day Africa. Connection to human welfare seems a vital condition. Yet how is science in a broader sense to be funded?

Notes and references

1. Anon. (1966). *Fisheries Research Bulletin, Vol.4.* Department of Game and Fisheries, Zambia, and UNDP/SF/FAO Central Fisheries Research Institute. Ministry of Natural Resources and Tourism, Zambia.
2. Coulter, G. & Y. Znamensky (1971). The chiromila net: A method for catching light-attracted fish on Lake Tanganyika. *Fisheries Research Bulletin of Zambia, 5*: 215–224.
3. Bell-cross, G. & Bell-Cross, B. (1971). Introduction of *Limnothrissa miodon* and *Limnocnida tanganicae* from Lake Tanganyika into Lake Kariba. *Fisheries Research Bulletin of Zambia, 5*: 207–214.
4. Clark, Sir Kenneth (1954). *Moments of Vision.* Clarendon Press, Oxford
5. (i) FAO/FINNIDA – *Research for the management of fisheries on lake Tanganyika.* GCP/RAF/271/FIN. FAO, Rome.
   (ii) UNDP/GEF Project – *Pollution control and other measures to protect biodiversity in Lake Tanganyika.* RAF/92/G32. UNDP, New York.
   (iii) *Multiple studies on inshore fishes of Lake Tanganyika (1985–2000).* Kawanabe, H., Department of Zoology, University of Kyoto.
6. Jackson, P.B.N. (2000). Freshwater fishery research organisations in central and eastern Africa. *Transactions of the Royal Society of South Africa, 55*(1) p.12.
7. *Last Journals of David Livingstone.* p.248 (Waller, Ed.).
8. Craig, H., Dixon, F., Craig, V., Edmonds, J. & Coulter, G. (1974). Lake Tanganyika geochemical and hydrographic study. *Scripps Institute of Oceanography, Series, 75–5*, pp.1–83.
9. Halladay, E. (1970). Henry Morton Stanley: The opening up of the Congo. pp.223–254 In: R.I. Rotberg (Ed.). *Africa and its Explorers.* Harvard University Press.

6

Lake Tanganyika – Burundi

The last of the projects I wish to outline was carried out by UNDP/FAO at the north end of Lake Tanganyika in Burundi (Figure 8). The fishery there is an important food source for this densely populated country, and the research and development project (*Projet Pêche*) was to devise a management plan and ways of producing nutritious and affordable fish products for the market.

The lakeshore people lived a self-sufficient subsistence life, growing their own food and supplementing it with fish. At night the men fished up to 3 km from shore in canoes and catamarans. Settlements tended to be in places where boats could be drawn up on beaches. Any catch in excess of family needs could be preserved by sun-drying on sandy beaches (the dried sardine called *kapenta*) and sold to familiar traders. This brought in a small amount of cash for items like tea and sugar, used clothing and kerosene.

On the other hand, a commercial, mechanised fishery, (so-called *pêche industrielle*), operated over the 2,000 square kilometres of Burundi territorial water. It was in the hands of resident Greeks who owned about 20 purse-seiners and trucked their catches daily from landing points on the coast to a central market in Bujumbura. The business was labour intensive (which was desirable), employing about thirty men per purse-seiner. It did not compete with the canoe/catamaran fishermen who lacked transport to get catches to market, although both sectors exploited more or less the same fish species.

The new project buildings went up in 1970, staff arrived, local relations were good and activities commenced as planned. Then the fishery was wiped out in 1972 by an invasion, civil war and genocide. After six months, project activities resumed but this time had in addition to help rebuild the artisanal fishery. So the project's story falls into three parts – initial activities, civil strife (*les événements*), and a recovery phase (which later went on to a remarkable expansion). This chapter covers only the first two; the recovery phase is dealt with as part of a discussion on development in Part III, in Chapter 13.

Since outbreaks of violence have checked development in many places in

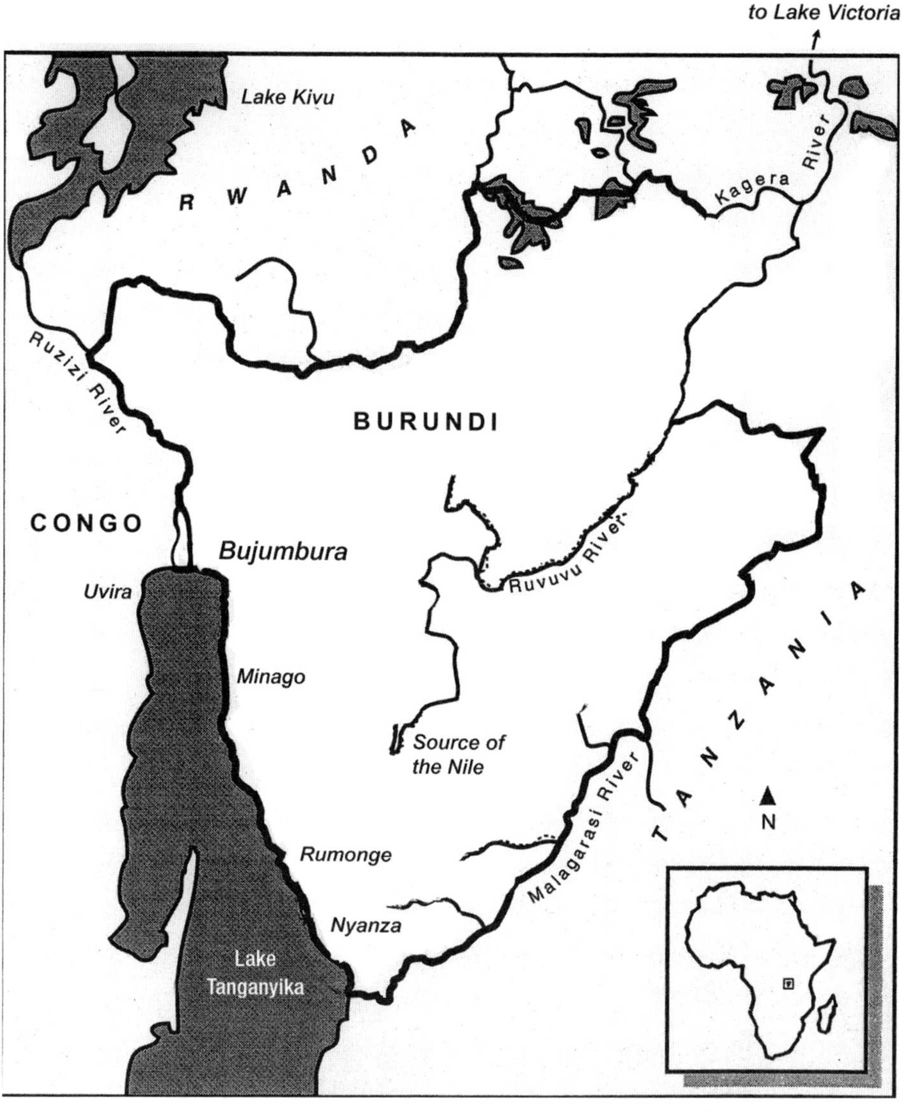

Figure 8. Burundi and north end of Lake Tanganyika. Note upper Kagera River system, putative source of the Nile.

Africa, I want to consider in some detail what the disruption entailed in this case. The Burundi genocide has not, as far as I know, been described by any outsider living through the events. What happened is significant also in a wider context.

Catamarans drawn up on a Burundi beach

Bujumbura fish market

Densely cultivated Burundi countryside

Twisted canoe in a small lake in Burundi interior

Project sub-station ('Chateau Akhenaten')

Kagera source of the Nile (from left: Guide, Keith Meecham, Eugene Balon and George Coulter)

A pleasant little country

Burundi is a small but intricate country, hilly with slopes intensely cultivated in terraces. The great majority of people depend on what they grow. Perhaps the best material legacies of German and Belgian colonial times were the countrywide development of hillside terracing to reduce land erosion, and the introduction of coffee as a cash crop for small farmers.[1] Coffee still provides the main income of the country. Population density is one of the highest in Africa, and the people among the very poorest. A newcomer is struck by the diffuse distribution of people over the land. Relatively few live in villages and more on tiny farm plots. People say they belong to a hill or a 'commune', rather than to a village or district. Although the landscape undulates steeply the scene varies little, because the various crops – beans, coffee, bananas, vegetables – vary little. Boundaries between plots are unclear to the casual eye; only the clustering of huts indicates ownership.

On the narrow unsurfaced roads snaking around and over the hills, one is constantly aware of human presence (voices), and a peculiar atmosphere of intimacy. Though not many people are to be seen at a time, they are there working among their crops, and communication is going on between them across a hillside or valley. One could imagine that rumour and mood might sweep quickly over this dispersed yet closely populated countryside. On Sundays especially, people are to be seen in groups on country roads on their way to church or to visit friends. Women carry baskets on their heads and dress in vividly coloured wrap-around clothes. The traditional baskets, globular and dark in colour, contain gifts for those to be visited. A little flag of banana leaf on the top of each basket is cut into a pattern denoting the status of the recipient.

There are several small lakes in the north of Burundi. Fishermen there have difficulty providing themselves with canoes because trees big and straight enough to make dug-outs have been cut down.

Bujumbura is the country's single city, with a cathedral, hotels, restaurants and many clubs. A pleasant enough place for the wealthy or visitors, but inequity is great in the population as in all African cities.

To a visitor then, in 1970, Burundi would have seemed a tranquil, closely-knit countryside. True it had a minority government (dominated by the Tutsi tribe who were only 15% of the population, the rest were Hutus), but superficially the appearance was of peace and stability. Poverty was evident in slums and townships around Bujumbura, but in the countryside was less obvious, the banana groves and crops giving an impression of self-sufficiency.

Since the Burundi fisherfolk were dispersed on the coastline with a few villages connected by a single rutted coastal road, the project needed a sub-station to work among them. Providentially, an empty villa stood on the coast near a village, Minago (see Figure 8). It was an extraordinary three-storey structure, topped by a turret, built by an eccentric businessman and philosopher, Albert Maus, for his retirement.[2] His naturalistic beliefs included sun-worship (thus a plaque of the ancient Egyptian pharaoh Akhenaten figured on the villa frontage).

It was the venue for a fisheries limnology conference in 1971 – a think-tank affair to which FAO invited some of the best brains in fisheries science from the USA and Canada. With splendid views over the lake to the cloud-banked heights of Ituri in the Congo, we pondered stimulating theory for several days, and its possible application to our project of Tanganyika. (We also took an excursion to the putative source of the Nile.) Perhaps our visitors benefited by seeing a situation widely different from their own. After all, the central problem to be faced was to find useful links between western culture and technology and existing circumstances at the lake; how to introduce modern methods to subsistence fishers.

Training nationals is a part, but by no means the entire, solution to becoming modern. At that time, we had only two Burundi (Tutsi) graduates in the project. They gave a good impression. Years at Belgian or French universities seemed to produce men of assurance and sophistication, with little trace of chip-on-shoulder attitudes. At that time also, tribal preference did not seem to matter – my co manager was a Hutu.

A project vessel was essential. The following details demonstrate the kind of logistics to be overcome by projects remote from the coast in Africa. The boat needed to be seaworthy, have working space for oceanographic equipment, a range of at least 640 km (length of the lake), reliable engines and living space for six. For political reasons such a vessel could not be brought up from South Africa; our other option was to import one from Europe and rail it across Tanzania from the East Coast – but that would seriously limit the boat size.

So a possible road route from the ports of Dar-es-Salaam or Mombasa had to be investigated. Quite big boats can be got across rough tracks, but a weak bridge, an extra-steep hill or some pot-holed stretch might cause disaster in a remote place. It took a month to check roads and trails through northern Tanzania and southern Kenya, variable terrain and at that time sparsely populated. Head office read my report with cautious interest but in the end settled for a smaller simpler boat to come by rail. Named *Lady Alice II* – in honour of the first craft brought overland to Lake Tanganyika for

Transporting a boat on an unsurfaced road – it can be done!

A bridge too weak for a heavy load

exploration long ago[3] – it gave years of multi-purpose service though never much comfort. There is a photo of the boat in Chapter 4.

Working on the lake had hazards other than physical ones; indeed most of it could be described as troubled waters. Clandestine movements of people across it have taken place for decades, especially in the northern half – migrating fishermen, refugees, dissidents, mercenary soldiers and revolutionaries (including even Che Guevara). Many migrants were destined eventually for camps run by the UN High Commission for Refugees (UNHCR) in northeastern Tanzania. Given the decades of turmoil in the Congo and scant administrative presence all around the shores, smugglers and raiders could escape to relative safety in another country. We commonly encountered water-taxis full of people out in the lake at night. Semi-permanent enclaves of Congo fishermen occur on the Tanzania shore. These and suspicious places known to our boat crew were avoided where possible.

In the early 1970s several gunboats were donated by US President Nixon to his client President Mobutu, with the object of patrolling the Congo sector of lake. No doubt it was welcome assistance and probably not a bad strategy, as long as no regard is taken of the grim fate of those intercepted. The gunboats roved at will in the other national waters, and we commonly encountered them in *Lady Alice*. Interceptions at night tended to be alarming. No words were exchanged, the gunboat merely inspecting us by searchlight. Soldiers stood on deck casually handling their weapons of mass destruction, and then moved away. At the US embassy in Bujumbura a naval captain explained to me the gunboats were US Coastguard ships, flown out in sections and assembled at the lakeshore. Continuous mechanical servicing was provided, and soldiers trained as the crews. The costs of this 'assistance' must have been large. Said the captain, 'Don't worry, I'll put up a photo of your boat in each gunboat, and tell them to leave you alone.'

During the 1972 *événements* in Burundi, *Lady Alice* was itself commandeered as a gunboat for several months by the government. Project crew were used to take Burundi soldiers on patrols with the object of preventing refugees fleeing across the lake and, especially, preventing insurgents crossing from the Congo. One often heard the familiar note of the *Alice*'s engine as it left Bujumbura at night. Its involvement in drastic activities was later disclosed by the crew; definitely not the sort of work we were there to do.

Genocide, 1972

The sight of soldiers being exercised was a normal part of the scene around Bujumbura. Platoons of tall young men under shouting NCOs panted and sang as they jogged along in full kit. Most wore parachute flashes on the shoulder. It was commonplace to see them dropping from the sky onto a plain near the city. Clearly Burundi had a competent and mobile little army – 'Dad's Army', we laughed as they played hide-and-seek in camouflage fatigues festooned with leaves.

The social and political contexts of the Burundi *événements* of 1972 *et seq.* have been examined by scholars,[4,5,6] whereas the viewpoints expressed here are those of an expatriate aid worker who witnessed without taking part, and was then closely involved in the recovery of one sector of the economy.

Two particular incidents of 29 April 1972 remain in mind. In the afternoon I had been at the chateau Akhenaten to see our project consultant, Jorge, who was living there for a few months. Jorge was born and raised in Angola where his family had lived for generations. His line was to teach improved techniques of smoking and brining fish, and his good humour and idiomatic English made him amusing company. Ethnically European, he was essentially African in background and quite at home living in the villages doing his job and happy to stay at chateau Akhenaten. On this particular day we had been stringing up a wire aerial so he could communicate by radio with the project offices in Bujumbura. Surprisingly, Jorge turned up later in the afternoon at my house heading for a hotel in town. I asked him why, but he just shrugged and said, 'Smells me something not good.'

My second memory was of returning that night with my family from the city. Alarming gunfire was going on and flares rising from the military barracks on a plain facing our house. Next morning, the radio announced martial law and dusk-to-dawn curfew. Troop movements and helicopter activity were intense. Apparently an insurrection against the government had taken place in the south of Burundi, with the assistance of refugees living over the border in Tanzania. This area near the border around Nyanza-lac (see Figure 8) was densely populated by Hutu fishermen whose catches we monitored. Many Congolese had settled in that area too, including, it was said, 'mulelist' rebels who had fled the Congo. It seems an anti-government, explicitly anti-Tutsi, insurrection had been whipped up, with vicious tactics employing drugs and 'magic' typical of the kind of deadly mischief that occurred in the Congo. About ten thousand Hutu and 'mulelists' were advancing up the coast towards Bujumbura, slaughtering all in their path.[5] Although knowing nothing of this, Jorge's instinct had made him move out just in time. His six trainees were killed at the sub-station that night.

Simultaneously, a separate party of rebels attacked the central radio station and military barracks in the city – the fireworks we had seen. These attempts failed, and in a vigorous counterattack the army put down the rebellion with indiscriminate slaughter. Thousands perished. Congolese troops suddenly appeared in Bujumbura, President Mobutu's willingness to lend them to Burundi being due to the presence of ex-Congo rebel elements in the insurrection. The Congo troops were to guard the airport (and no doubt the presidential clique) from potential internal threat, releasing the Burundi army for action against the enemy.

It was hard for us to comprehend the unexpected violence. Unbelief was followed by horror and then a protracted moral dilemma. One would have to understand the evolution over time of Tutsi–Hutu relationships (the history of conflict between the tribes differs in Burundi and Rwanda), but suffice to say these relationships are not simply tribal or ethnic, nor can they be explained entirely by social or economic stratification. They are deeply influenced by a history of atrocities, fear and failed hopes, which have produced ineradicable myths. Deep fear (*'grand peur'*), pervaded Burundi in 1972, and a smouldering after-shock has persisted for years, bubbling up in further episodes of violence.[6]

I'd been completely deceived by the 'placid' peasant people living apparently settled lives in the countryside! I was not alone in this. It has been said of Burundi that the game of politics often went unnoticed in the countryside, while at the same time ethnic polarisation could reach alarming proportions in urban areas. In fact, a situation had built up creating both the climate for massacre and the necessary instrument to carry it out. Indications of potential violence between Hutu and Tutsi were evident from the time of national independence (1962 for both Rwanda and Burundi). Tensions had exploded in the killing of many Tutsi in Rwanda in 1963–64. This created fear among Burundi Tutsi, which was heightened by an attempted Hutu coup in Burundi in 1965. Had that succeeded, a similar massacre of Tutsis would likely have happened. One of the military officers who put down the attempted coup, Michel Micombero, became president of the so-called First Republic of Burundi, in which a predominantly Tutsi elite held power.

Under Micombero, the army was gradually transformed from a mainly Hutu to a mainly Tutsi force. Recruitment procedures selected Tutsi, and Belgian military advisers (who might have resisted this) were dispensed with in 1967–68.[6] After another suspected Hutu coup was revealed in 1969, the rate of replacement of senior Hutu in political and military fields was accelerated (executions and disappearances). A power struggle took place even within the Tutsi elite itself in 1971, followed by a well-publicised political trial that effectively stepped up tension.

The government was able not only to quench the uprising quickly but also finally to purge Hutu within the army. With a reliable military instrument in hand, it was then only another step to secure the future by systematically eliminating all potential threat to Tutsi hegemony, i.e., killing all educated Hutu down to 12 years old. Seen in this light, what seemed completely indefensible genocide to us was in fact just the final step in an inexorable process of consolidating Tutsi power.

It was the first African genocide as such – if one may define the term as the deliberate execution of a selected sector of population on a national scale. Qualitatively resembling Hitler's or Stalin's exterminations, it was foreign in nature to the way disturbances or revolts occur in Africa where employment of violence is common enough. Well-organised rational killing on a scale designed to ensure continued domination by one tribe was a new thing. In hindsight one sees that the 1972 genocide in Burundi became a significant historic watershed in that country and in the region. Regarding Rwanda and Burundi together, nowhere else in post-independent Africa has so much violence killed so many people on so many occasions in so small a space of territory. Strangely enough the precursor, Burundi 1972, went practically unnoticed in the world, and its historical significance is still largely ignored.

As the actual insurrection subsided it seemed at first as if the violence was virtually over. Government statements spoke of a serious and well-coordinated attempted coup, involving plotters in high places including several Hutu government ministers, and said all subversive elements must be rooted out. Then it became evident no public political trials were planned, as in 1971. Instead, summary executions were to be carried out. While putting down the coup caused many deaths, this prolonged countrywide repression that followed was worse. For us it was hard to understand what was really going on. Most information came from government statements, and no independent observers had access to locations where executions were carried out.

I had occasionally played tennis with one government minister, now stated to have stored machetes at his house in preparation for an uprising. A mild man, he didn't seem the type. Discreet enquiries only led to a reply that he would not be seen again (*il n'en sortira plus*). Rumours circulated that hundreds of Hutu soldiers had been shot by their Tutsi officers around the time the army went into action. It began to appear that the 'rooting out' process was on a wide scale. Arrests were made openly in the street – I saw ordinary-looking young men grabbed by a party of soldiers and pushed into a jeep. In banks and commercial offices, like Sabena Airways where numerous clerks normally sat at the desks, seats were suddenly empty. Hutu doctors and nurses were taken at work in the hospitals. Employees started to go missing from our project. We feared particularly for the life of our project co-manager, a Hutu ex-politician and therefore an obvious target, and suggested to him ways he might escape. But he continued at work until one day an army jeep duly picked him up for execution. Almost as dreadful as the ruthless manner of arrests was the hapless acceptance by the victims of their fate. They seemed already to have accepted death.

Until that point the actions of government and army could be understood as maintenance of order and defence of the country against invasion. Foreigners in residence, like me, were thankful to have escaped violence. Several weeks passed before it was realised in embassies and foreign agencies that we were now into a quite different phase – nothing less than the extermination of all Hutu political threat in a foreseeable future. This meant the execution of all educated Hutu, right down to school children, throughout the country. It appears to have been a deliberate decision, taken in committee, then ruthlessly carried out. Trucks and Land Rovers were commandeered from aid-agencies to carry those arrested to places of execution. Bodies were moved during curfew after dark for mass burial outside the town. Our project vessel was taken to patrol the lake to see no one escaped that way. Naturally, many Hutu fled over the frontiers, to the Congo, Rwanda and Tanzania.

Much of the killing was done by '*Jeunesses*', a loosely organised pro-Tutsi semi-militia, who took a big part in the rounding up of Hutu in the countryside and villages. Trucks full of young *Jeunesses* passed my house daily on their way to gather up and bury the dead insurgents and victims. One could hear them singing in high spirits as the trucks returned, many still wearing the white rubber gloves issued for their grisly task. They were a nasty sight. Mayhem was created by them according to opportunity, by attacks on Hutu families and even villages with their machetes; and more purposefully by the army who went for targeted individuals in institutions like schools, businesses and churches. (The *Jeunesses* seem to have been a parallel of the *Interahamwe*, responsible for most killing in the 1994 Rwanda massacre.)

Late one afternoon at home, our house-help shouted '*Bagarre*' (disturbance), and a crowd were to be seen running desperately towards us across the plain between the military barracks and our road. I thought, of course, they were insurgents. The front-runners were close when, very suddenly, three helicopters appeared overhead and opened heavy fire. One after the other they moved up one side of the crowd, then down the other side. At once the mass of people was reduced to heaps on the ground. Another quick circuit, shooting continually, and the helicopters disappeared, leaving silence. Soldiers had done the shooting with machine guns through the open doors. The pilots were European.

It was a mass breakout of Hutu from the prison and a practised manoeuvre by the army. It helped to explain the recent rapid victory over mobs of insurgents coming up from the south, who, exposed on the coast road or bare hillsides to armed helicopters would have stood no chance. I waited about an hour and seeing no movement from the pathetic heaps went on to the road. A single army jeep stood there, and walking from it was an armed European officer, French I thought, along the grassy ditch at the roadside. We did not greet one another; he was intent on the ditch, obviously searching for any runners who might have made it that far. None had. In the morning the heaps were gone.

Our instructions from the local head of UNDP were to carry on as usual: 'Do not enter into discussion; just keep your hands at your sides.' Naturally I sought guidance from my head office in Rome, and received a reply by diplomatic pouch a couple of weeks later casually asking, 'What trouble?' Evidently we were expected to solve local problems. To a dismayed onlooker driving to work each day in an environment of fear, conscious of horrors but seeing little, life seemed unreal. We just got on with writing up the results of work so far, but these results appeared largely irrelevant, in that they concerned fisherfolk now killed or fled. So we held our breath. I drove to the project offices around the side of the city, past the *quartier asiatique* – whose inhabitants doubtless had their heads down hoping to stay clear of events – then out the other side towards the airport and Congo border. It was over six kilometres, and I often passed a small group of project labourers making the same journey to and from work barefoot. Sometimes I gave them a lift, but they were shy and reluctant, needing to stay inconspicuous. Their survival depended upon appearing too poor and unimportant to attract attention.

Colleagues in education projects spoke of mass arrests of students, at university, high school and even primary schools. From missionaries I heard heartbreaking stories of deaths of local pastors, deacons and teachers, representing the life's work and posterity of missions. Such Hutu were precisely the target of the army and *Jeunesses*. Tales circulated of the heroism of certain pastors in jail awaiting execution, comforting others with prayer and hymns.

It was probably inevitable that at some point things must come to a head for me, as for others seeking a personal position. Every Friday I had a routine meeting with my senior government contact, '*le directeur*'. He would drop in for a chat. We were on friendly terms; often drove in the same car to inspect progress, and had been together to a meeting in Europe. Our discussions were free, though it was our custom and perhaps character to remain semi-formal ('*Monsieur*'). He was imperious, sometimes haughty, overseas educated, sophisticated, suspicious but not lacking humour; a type among the ascendancy with the *je ne sais quoi* one came to recognise. In the middle of our bland discussion of work details, my anger and despair boiled over: the project was in ruins, staff murdered, vessel taken. Using his Christian name for the first time, I cried out, 'You people must stop this! It's wrong: it's impossible for you to go on.'

He rose at once, went to the window and said quietly, 'Monsieur, if the knife is at your throat, you do what you must.' I made no reply, aware I had broken instructions as well as transgressed our mutual protocol. He left and we never spoke of it again, though meeting weekly as usual. I am sure he understood my outburst was a personal *cri de coeur*. He understood too that I'd simply have to accept the way things were.

On reflection, I thought he was sincere in justifying the actions of government and army as simply self-defence – both the quashing of the invasion and the execution of potential Hutu dissidents. Had the boot been on the other foot, there would have been a general massacre of Tutsis. So for him it was a question of survival, whereas my family and I were under diplomatic protection and would eventually leave the country. More generally, I could hardly invoke 'civilised principles', remembering our own 1939–45 war which began with self-defence but ended with actions that might only be described as 'crushing the enemy' – such as saturation bombing of Germany late in the war, and atomic bombing of Japan after the course of the war had already been decided. Lastly, the organisation I worked for had not protested; rather it had fixed on a policy of non-interference and kept its people on station as onlookers. Other than personal conscience, I did not have a leg to stand on. The decision was whether to make my own protest by resigning, or stay on for the salvage operation as head office intended.

Conscience was continually aggravated by a sense of complicity. Is it possible to stand detached and objective in the middle of a massacre, at the same time reasonably assured of one's own safety; to view acute fear and suffering close up but do nothing, not even protest; to simply avert one's eyes? People in quiet countries remain detached from calamity happening elsewhere by thinking of it in the abstract. We do it almost every day as we register catastrophies on TV. At the time of writing, for example, the world is trying to avert its eyes from Darfur and the Congo. But if one is actually on the spot, it is necessary to disconnect somehow from manifest horror and outrage, or find some excuse that gives legitimacy to being there (our official position). The hapless onlooker inevitably becomes uneasy and begins to feel guilt. It is practically impossible to numb moral concern, ignore what is going on, and have everyday dealings with the killers.

There was plenty of opportunity to sound out the feelings of other expats. They talked of practically nothing else. But their views, varying between fatalism, unease and guilt, gave little comfort or direction. Official embassy attitudes seemed strangely unprincipled; their staff had to be guarded in informal conversation because of cold-war diplomatic positions. Burundi's main allies were Zaire and France; indeed the position of France was extremely ambiguous (as I'd observed in the helicopter murders). The American Embassy was well informed, as we know from embassy reports now published, but the US deliberately chose to avert its eyes.[7] Quite a few national interests were represented diplomatically in Bujumbura, including Russia, China, North Korea – the place was an important staging and listening post, adjacent to Congo and Tanzania. But evidently too little agreement existed between embassies about what could or should be done to bring convergence of opinion and a strong protest. Without concerted diplomatic effort to put pressure on the Burundi government, nothing indeed could be done. National interest overrode conscience, as usual.

Nor did any effective protest come from the Organisation of African Unity, which held a summit meeting in June and passed a special resolution on Burundi. Unspecific and meaningless, it might have been read as a message of support for Micombero.[6]

At the end of three months the curfew was lifted. The number of dead, by consensus between embassies, churches and aid-agencies, was estimated around 230,000. In addition, at least 150,000 people had fled over the borders. Other estimates, published later, vary between 100,000 and 200,000 dead. No one will ever know exactly. Nor can the broader social impacts be quantified – such as profound effects upon children and old people, or suffering within split and displaced families – which keep ethnic hatred alive. As to our project, the damage was considerable; the coast had been severely depopulated of fisherfolk and most canoes and catamarans had gone. On the other hand, our research vessel was returned undamaged. Overseas funds for general reconstruction in Burundi were boosted.

Personally I was due for leave, and left with my family by road as soon as the curfew was lifted. The Burundi countryside was weirdly still, an appalled silence over all. People walked in groups, not singly. It brought to mind, though I knew the comparison absurd, my feelings as a child in England in the very early part of World War II when waves of children, pregnant mothers and old people, about three million of them, were hurriedly sent out from the cities to escape anticipated German bombing. Here there seemed something of the same pervading fear of unseen threat, with disorientated adults and bewildered mobs of children. Over the border in Rwanda, where many Burundi refugees had gone, it felt similar.

In a day or two of driving the atmosphere eased, but little upsets still occurred of course. Stopping for petrol, I watched the pump attendant holding the gushing nozzle in one hand, while in the other he held a lighted cigarette – a reminder of the normal risks of life.

No account of the massacre in Burundi had appeared in the newspapers or on the radio abroad. Friends and family in Britain did not understand what we were talking about. It was perhaps naïve to think they were bound to know, and that in the world of the 1970s it would be impossible for any government to deliberately kill 200,000 of its citizens without some rumour or report coming out. Was it that Burundi was just too far away, too exotic, too small to elicit concern or compassion elsewhere?

These excuses cannot be the entire explanation. Even if a general averting of eyes took place, surely such a large atrocity should have triggered, say, an article by an investigative reporter somewhere? I remembered a significant remark by the old journalist, Malcolm Muggeridge, to the effect that there is no point in a reporter sending back articles from Africa that he knows his editor will not publish. The implication, that links between media and government policies can blanket reports of outrageous events, is a very unsettling thought. Yet I'd had the same thought during the Rhodesia crisis in the 1970s, handled by Harold Wilson's Labour government. It could not be doubted that the media were orchestrated at that time if one saw the events, as we did, from both ends. Still, the silence about Burundi in 1972 set a new record for inhumane disregard. My trust in the BBC collapsed.

One can get too close to intense experiences. Standing back gives perspective, although I cannot say it was so with me after returning from two months leave. But by then the time for protest resignations had gone. In any case, it would have made little difference if all aid-agency personnel had resigned. The government would not have been deterred from genocide by less than vigorous international protest and economic pressure. But was it right to keep us there and ride it out, so as to resume work immediately the emergency was over? The practical answer was, probably, yes. Projects in train are better able to continue, even though damaged, than if planning, recruitment, financing, etc. have all to be gone through again. Our project continued another two years, reaching most of its material goals.

Nevertheless, the genocide cast a lasting shadow. Morale within the expat community was slow to recover. More serious was the palpable feeling of hatred and fear abroad in the country, just under the surface, which would take ages to erase. The cheerful optimism of the project's first two years had gone. Foundations for a new start were poor, and ghosts hung around. These feelings were shared by most senior personnel in the UN office in Bujumbura at the ritual weekly meetings to keep up morale and unity. In fact, these '*réunions de coordination, cooperation et collaboration*' served only to highlight our futility.

There was an exercise of raising funds for orphaned children, so-called 'victims of the events'. Money was donated privately and from embassies, businesses and clubs, and raised by raffles, bring-and-buy sales and suchlike. A tidy sum was realised, which then, to the great disillusionment of the volunteer organisers, disappeared into the official distribution machine. It was said to have been used only for the Tutsi along Lake Tanganyika who suffered in the original Hutu attack.

Another interesting experience was a commemoration service, held in the cathedral in Bujumbura, for a person prominent in foreign aid and diplomatic circles who had died. The service was packed, and at the last moment government ministers filed in and solemnly took their seats at the front. I was especially interested in the bishop's homily, as it was probably the first public event he had addressed with members of government present since the official massacre. Perhaps my understanding was faulty for, despite careful listening, I heard no arrows of reproach aimed at those decision makers in the front rows. A marvellous opportunity missed, though I suppose the church wanted to stay on – like the rest of us.

To the question of whether expedience justified staying on, an answer becomes clearer in hindsight. The 1972 Burundi '*événements*' were deeply felt in other Central African countries. It was a key moment of history. If a real international protest, a stand upon principle, had been made promptly in 1972, the grievous turmoil and genocides of the following decades in Burundi and in at least two other neighbouring countries, Rwanda and Congo, would probably have been much less; might even have been avoided. To make this point, in the next section I take a quick look at the drastic sequences of recent history.

A painting by my daughter, Grace, aged 15, after the genocide. It is an attempt to convey the desolation and despair of that time.

Hindsight

> 'In the collective psyche of Hutu and Tutsi, two genocides compete for recognition and condemnation: the 1972 genocide of Hutu in Burundi, and the 1994 genocide of Tutsi in Rwanda. Far from cancelling each other, the result has been an unbridgeable moral distance between Hutu and Tutsi.'
>
> (LeMarchand, 1996, p.xii)

> 'Today as in the years that followed independence (1962), what happens in Burundi will be conditioned by what happens in Rwanda – and in Zaire [Congo].'
>
> (ibid. p.xxii)

For many years after 1972 the army held Burundi in a tight grip. Three military presidents succeeded one another – Micombero, 1965–76, Bagaza until 1987, Buyoya until 1993. In the Bagaza years ethnicity was 'de-emphasised', efforts were made to 'villagise' the dispersed rural population to improve access to government services and facilitate political control. The concept of a secular state was promoted and missionaries expelled. None of this was popular. In contrast, Buyoya's policies allowed more freedom of expression and normalised relations with the churches. Despite these more liberal trends, vicious disturbances erupted again. In 1988, burning with local injustices and memories of 1972, Hutus started to kill Tutsis in two provinces bordering Rwanda. The army responded, which in the context means indiscriminate slaughter (15,000 dead, 50,000 fled to Rwanda).

This time, however, there was strong foreign reaction; for example, a resolution was passed in the US House of Representatives that threatened severe costs for the Burundi government. Probably as a result, the army suppression did not spread nationwide. Also, concessions were made – Hutu representation in government was increased and a Hutu prime minister appointed.

But again, in 1991–93, insurrections broke out. They were located near Bujumbura in provinces which abutted on Rwanda. Many of the rebels were former Hutu refugees who had filtered back from Rwanda and Congo, and probably also from Tanzania. Tutsi civilians were killed in incidents, and stern reprisals by the army killed thousands of Hutu in an effort to 'cleanse' the suburbs of the capital.

Gradually, however, Burundi entered a power-sharing mode in 1993, influenced by a growing commitment of the intelligentsia, both Tutsi and Hutu, to the rule of law. A general election overwhelmingly voted in a Hutu president (Ndadaye), ending three decades of Tutsi hegemony. But within months Ndadaye was assassinated along with some senior members of his government in an army putsch. In immediate reaction Hutus rose up countrywide, and inevitably the army and *Jeunesses* responded. This time, 300,000 died and 1.2 million were internally displaced or made refugees.[8] There emerged in 1995 a 'thinly disguised military rule held together by networks of Tutsi politicians, youth gangs and armed militias'.[6]

Rwanda, on the other hand, had been ruled by the Hutu virtually since 1962. Inward flows of Hutu refugees from Burundi in 1972, 1988 and 1991–93, each time destabilised populations along the southern border. However, and very important, an army of the Rwandan Popular Front (RPF) made up of Tutsis who had fled to Uganda over the years, invaded from the north in November 1990. Seeking to strengthen itself against this external threat, the weak Rwandan government incited a general hatred of Tutsi, which eventually exploded in the 1994 genocide of 800,000 which reverberated round the world. The '*genocidaire*' Hutu, of course, vividly remembered that at least half a million Hutu had been killed in Burundi by Tutsi-led governments between 1972 and 1993.

Soon the Tutsi army under Paul Kagame broke through to the Rwanda capital, Kigali, and promptly assumed government, ending a Hutu regime of three decades. About two million Rwandan refugees precipitately fled to the Congo (most to Kivu province). Kagame had himself elected president in 2003.

These wretched sequences of Hutu–Tutsi conflict in two small neighbouring countries, resulting in colossal numbers of dead and displaced, show that genocides cannot quickly be forgotten. Such hatred and losses take generations to pass from memory. Ethnic, or more truly perhaps, group-stereotype hatreds seem to acquire, as time goes on, an internal logic and momentum that keeps them going. Poverty provides continual grounds for discontent. Tit-for-tat reactions explode into massacres, as in 1972 and 1993 of Burundi Hutu, and in 1994 of Rwandan Tutsi. There is no doubt that the latter and biggest holocaust was based to a large extent on the massacres of Hutu in Burundi between 1972 and 1993.

Refugee camps run by international aid bodies in neighbouring countries have become quasi-permanent settlements (as in northern Tanzania, for over 40 years). People in them have no future apart from return and resettlement, and the camps have served as centres from which continuous infiltrations or armed invasions are launched back into homelands. In densely populated Burundi and Rwanda where agricultural land is very scarce, the re-settlement of refugees in their places of origin can be very problematic. It is therefore remarkable that of the 431,000 Burundian refugees who have been living in Tanzanian camps, 271,000 managed to return between 2002 and 2005.[9]

The massive movements of almost three million displaced people triggered by the conflicts in Burundi and Rwanda in the early 1990s, still affect people living in camps in Tanzania, Burundi and Rwanda. Of course, these bare numbers are inadequate indicators of the effects. One has only to see the traumatised, malnourished and stunted people surviving on aid for years to realise that the timescale for them or their children to return to self-reliant community life will be very long.

Not all refugees enter camps. Spillovers of desperate people have destabilised the whole region. Seeking revenge on Hutu '*genocidaire*' refugees in the adjacent Congo in 1996, the Rwandan Tutsi army not only crossed the border but also pushed on to the distant Congo capital, Kinshasa, and installed a new president. Subsequently, war arose in the Congo, which brought in army contingents from Uganda, Angola, Zambia and Zimbabwe, leading to prolonged warfare and looting. Over 5 million people are said to have died from war-related causes in the Congo in the decade since 1998. UN 'peacekeepers' have been deployed, of course, but still no adequate government has emerged. There is an ever-present danger of further interventions from neighbouring countries, or even Tutsi–Hutu war within the Congo.

I went back to Burundi in the mid-1990s. Encountering friends from the 1970s was nostalgic, but it also made vivid their painful past. Still, I was struck by the busy intensity of life. After 20 years, both town and country seemed more crowded than ever. Certainly the coast of the lake was more densely populated and the fish resource more heavily exploited, probably overfished, as more people sought food. Subsistence fishermen had made a remarkable recovery – catamarans and canoes had, so to speak, out-competed the Greek purse-seine fishery, which became uneconomic and disappeared.[10] Overall one might say that more fish was being eaten, but the average fisherman was poorer and probably got less to eat. Despite losses from warfare and AIDS, the population had *doubled*; 70% were below the poverty line, and about the same proportion suffered malnutrition. Life expectancy was 43 years.

In the crowded city of Bujumbura I noticed tiny plots of beans growing on an unpaved sidewalk. Someone needed that space and food. The populations of Burundi and Rwanda (as well as the small country of Malawi in the lakes region) are the densest in Africa, and over 90% of the people live in rural circumstances. Cultivated family plots are very small, and there is little room to let land lie fallow between crops. Consequently the land becomes depleted of nutrients, and since the farmers cannot afford fertilisers their crops diminish. Intuitively one feels such overcrowded and overfarmed situations are not sustainable, and must give rise to social tensions. Pressure on land was probably one of the underlying causes of the waves of violence.

Regarding AIDS, two things in particular struck me. A large poster in Bujumbura had the slogan 'You don't need to die from AIDS', seeming to carry the inference that people were accepting the disease as part of normal existence. Second was the greatly enlarged cemetery, not far from where I used to live. Commenting on this to a fellow passenger in a mini-bus, he replied, 'People die easily nowadays,' and explained that AIDS weakened people so they died of common things like malaria or flu, which they otherwise would have survived.

Looking back over half a century one sees apparent links between events and wonders how it might have turned out otherwise. It is reasonable to believe that if an international spotlight had been put on genocide in Rwanda soon after independence or, particularly, the first deliberate government genocide in Burundi 1972, disastrous sequences of violence might have been avoided. In the case of Rwanda 1994, UN peacekeeping troops might have stopped that genocide at an early stage had they been given a firm mandate from head office to do so.[11] The perpetrators were doubtless counting upon another weak international response. In short, Burundi and Rwanda demonstrate the tragedy of just allowing events to take their course.

This chain of events has led to a large region north and west of Lake Tanganyika, especially northeast Congo, becoming one of those frightful basket cases in which international aid tries to assuage prolonged misery. WFP, FAO, UNHCR and other agencies have been looking after refugees in a long, costly humanitarian programme.[9] Recently the governments of Burundi and Rwanda have made progress towards national reconciliation and economic recovery. Tanzania has fortunately remained peaceful though poor.

Do nations have consciences? A suggested historic example

> 'I beg to explain to Lord Salisbury that here we contemplate no threat, but merely the principle that in foreign policy one is guided not by feelings, but by interest and reciprocity. Kindness without return only occurs in private life.'
>
> Chancellor Bismarck to Foreign Secretary Salisbury, 1887
> (Coupland, 1939, p.481.)[12]

> 'Insofar as it can be detected at all, what goes by the name of an international conscience is the expression of convergent national interests, not of a global commitment to moral values.'
>
> (Lemarchand, 1996, p.60)

> 'We have fallen back on the yardstick of national self-interest to measure which portions of the planet we will allow ourselves to be concerned about'.
>
> General Dallaire, force commander of UN Assistance Mission for Rwanda, 1993–94

There is little or no evidence of an international moral conscience. It is unlikely to come before the development of national ones. Do national consciences exist in issues that do not coincide with, or even go against national self-interest? Examples are probably rare. Had a powerful nation, say, one of the Security Council members, reacted strongly enough about Burundi in 1972, or 1988 or 1993, confident of moral support from their own population, it could have made all the difference.

The Commission for Africa in its 2005 Declaration hopefully makes the point that the world is now vastly different from what it was 20 years ago. Then it was, quote: 'locked into its Cold War political stasis, remained rigid in its competitive ideologies. The breaking of this deadlock, and the increase in global trade that followed, allied to new technologies and cultural shifts, have created a more fluid, less predictive yet more interdependent world.' Tony Blair[13] and the other members of the Commission evidently placed hope in the opportunities brought about by greater flux in the world. Consequently they hoped, in modern terms, for less self-interest and maybe an agreed bottom-line based on human rights ethics (if not moral conscience).

There is a relevant historic example where nations took a moral position contrary to commercial advantage. That was the suppression of the slave trade in the nineteenth century, in which several European nations took part. Is it valid to compare the slave trades with recent and current phenomena of social chaos and misery in Africa? The nineteenth-century humanitarian stand against slavery had to fight formidable financial vested interests in Europe and the Americas,[14] and it took a very long time to achieve its goal over the entire continent, most of a century. But it was a movement strong enough to keep up unrelenting diplomatic pressure, while at the same time forcing physical interventions (e.g., navy blockades on the Atlantic and Indian Ocean coasts.) Motives were not entirely idealistic, for it was clear by the 1870s that before commercial trade in Africa could proceed, the devastating slave trade had to be stopped.

In Britain the crusade against the West African trade had waned by mid-century, but was re-ignited for Central Africa largely by David Livingstone. His fiery speeches in the 1860s and his last letters stoked moral outrage to the point where popular feeling could not be ignored by the governments of the day. Was the drastic language used by Livingstone and many others about the slave trade very different from the language used now by the Declaration of the Commission for Africa? It starts with this statement[13]:

> The Commission ... finds the condition of the lives of the majority of Africans to be intolerable and an affront to the dignity of all mankind. We insist upon an alteration of these conditions through a change of policy in favour of the weak.

Looking at the atrocities of recent decades in the scale of millions of people – for example, the five million in the Congo since 1998, or at current news media figures for Darfur – 300,000 killed, four million refugees – are they not of comparable magnitude with the slave trade? If moral conscience was enough to quench slaving, could it not impel us today?

Difficulties particular to our day arise from the ways policy decisions are made and implemented by the United Nations Organisation. Consensual agreement is not reached quickly enough to prevent atrocity when it begins. The response must be more rapid because major genocide can take place in a few weeks, though admittedly it is not easy to get a clear picture at an early stage in densely populated places with poor communications. The international media have a responsibility to spotlight genocide quickly, so that events cannot be ignored or hidden as in Burundi in the 1970s, 80s and 90s. Attention was indeed called to Rwanda in 1994, but the full picture did not come out until much later.[11,15,16] Part of the problem, no doubt, is the reverence we give to the sovereign state concept, hence our tendency within the present international forum to accept as more or less 'normal', the maladministration and occasional genocides in failed states. There is a reluctance to intervene. But merely to send out UN 'peacekeepers' without a strong mandate to keep the peace is little more than a gesture.

Notes and references

1. Louis, Roger (1963). *Ruanda-Urundi, 1884–1919*. (Coffee was introduced during the time of German administration, p.174–175).
2. Maus had died by suicide 10 years before and was buried nearby. Apart from the removal of his books, pictures and furniture, the house had remarkably been left untouched. No one else lived there, and the local people avoided it. Another clue to his humanistic philosophy were words on the wall of the former library: '*Le fin de l'homme est d'être heureux sans nuire a autrui*' (The end of man is to be happy without hurt to others). We took the place with government permission, dubbing it 'Chateau Akhenaten'.
3. The explorer H.M. Stanley's boat *Lady Alice* was named after his fiancée, an American girl (who jilted him before he could return from his travels). Stanley designed and had the boat built in England. It was a long, narrow (40 ft × 6 ft) open boat, made of cedar, that could be dismantled into five portable sections. As it was not completed in time for his departure, it was sent after him to Zanzibar. There he found the sections much too large and heavy to be carried, so a carpenter and two of his expedition men, the brothers Pocock, cut the boat down to about half its original length and lightened the sections. It turned out very successfully. Stanley took it right around Lake Victoria and then Tanganyika, exiting by the Lukuga and then into the Lualaba and Congo Rivers (see Figure 11, Chapter 8). It had to be abandoned in the Congo. See also:
   Stanley, H.M. (1878). *Through the Dark Continent*. London & New York.
   Stanley, R. & Neame, A. (1961). *The Exploration Diaries of H.M. Stanley*. Kimber.
   Hall, R. (1974). *Stanley: An adventurer explored*. Collins, London.
4. Notably by Lemarchand: (1970). *Rwanda and Burundi*. Pall Mall Press.
5. (1975). Ethnic Genocide. *Society, Vol.12*, 50–60.
6. (1996). *Burundi: Ethnic Conflict and Genocide*. University of Cambridge Press (for 1972 *événements* pp.76–105).
7. Hoyt (1972), quoted in LeMarchand (1996).
8. Guest, R. (2004). *The Shackled Continent*. p.109. MacMillan.
9. World Food Program/FAO/UNHCR. *Joint Needs Assessment – PRRO Burundi, Rwanda and Tanzania,* 18 March–8 April 2008.
   See also:
   International Rescue Committee, IRC Special Report on Congo (2008). http.www,theirc.org
   Food & Agriculture Organisation of the United Nations, Operations & Rehabilitation Division (2007) www.fao.org/reliefoperations/burundi
10. Roest, F.C, (1992). The pelagic fish resources of Lake Tanganyika. *Mitt. int. Verein. theoret. angew. Limnol, 23*: 11–15.
11. Dallaire. R.A. (2004). *Shake Hands with the Devil: The failure of humanity in Rwanda*. p. 517. Arrow Books.
12. Coupland, R. (1939). *The Exploitation of East Africa*. p.481. Faber & Faber.
13. Commission for Africa. *Final Report (2005)*. (Introduced at the meeting of G8 Countries, Gleneagles, Scotland, 2004). http//.www.commissionforafrica.org
    Incidentally, one might note that in launching the Commission initiative on current African ills, Tony Blair followed a long line of British politicians, starting with Pitt

(the Younger) and Wilberforce in the 1780s. Distinguished later parliamentarians who were active to improve conditions in Africa included Palmerston, Russell, Derby, Gladstone, Clarendon and Granville.

14. Concerning the West African slave trade, there were large private European investments in West Indies sugar plantations. Slaves and ivory in East Africa were also very profitable. The two businesses were closely linked.
15. Rusesabagina, P. (2006). *An Ordinary Man.* Bloomsbury Publ. Co.
16. Wallis, A. (2006). *Silent Accomplice: The untold story of France's role in Rwandan genocide.* Tauris, New York.

PART II

Ancestral Voices: Times Past

7

Historic Paradigms

Part II provides a historic perspective by considering different epochs in the past and their dominant paradigms. The region considered is East and Central Africa, especially the area around Lake Tanganyika. The purpose is to link, in a general context, the development activities described in Part I and the ongoing transition to modern times addressed in Part III.

One morning in 1980, while waiting for coffee in a student restaurant at Victoria University, Wellington, my eye caught a notice on the wall. It was headed 'History of Modern Africa' and listed the titles of lectures to be given. At the bottom a note to students giving advice for preparation said simply, 'Read nothing published before 1960' (i.e., just the previous 20 years). I did not attend, and so have no idea whether the lecturer regarded the history of modern Africa to have begun as late as 1960. Certainly it was a good choice of a year to represent the approximate boundary between colonial times and the subsequent era of national sovereignties. Perhaps the lecturer thought the students did not have time for broader reading. Maybe he had his own political agenda, based on a poor view of colonialism, and thought it best to ignore the past – a dangerous idea if he really was a historian. Or perhaps he knew it is hard to understand the past with the mindset of the present: *autres temps – autres moeurs.*

Modern mythology has it that in the late nineteenth century Africa was ruthlessly carved up between imperial powers, regardless of the wishes of its indigenous peoples, for purposes of exploitation. Thereafter exploitative regimes took over for the benefit of the powers rather than the people, and this continued right up to national independences. I find these simplifications troubling, because they leave much out. Perhaps they are merely convenient images produced in the era of nationalism of the past half-century; convenient because 'colonialism' can be used, and often is, to explain enduring ills.[1]

If, on the other hand, one takes the trouble to read historic sources about East and Central Africa, it seems clear that the humanitarian impulse, in terms mainly of anti-slavery sentiments, was a considerable force driving the major European powers concerned with Africa – up to the early 1880s at least. By then exploration was over, but slaving was still rife. Missions were beginning to be established. As well, various other foreign elements were making independent incursions – concession seekers, traders, adventurers, hunters, parties with economic or political incentives, representatives of scientific societies, and so on, attracted by lands unknown to them and in most cases for the sake of gain. Such elements were generally not backed by governments and had no capacity or authority to carry out territorial acquisitions or any systematic policies for the maintenance of peace. Arab and Swahili bandits with former slaves were causing violence over wide areas of East Africa already devastated by slaving, intertribal war and trade in firearms. In short, these independent elements were making an unmoderated advance into an already disordered environment.

Then between 1884 and 1890, a period of intense interventions by foreign governments occurred in Africa that, paradoxically, was much more concerned with affairs in Europe. Foreign politics were suddenly extrapolated to Africa – specifically, national rivalries and the game of maintaining the balance of power in Europe.

East Africa had long been a mostly British 'sphere of influence', but without territorial claims. King Leopold II of Belgium had been the prime mover in establishing an African International Association (AIA) in 1877 that, to begin with, was philanthropic and scientific. He caused Belgian posts and missions to be set up in the early 1880s at Tabora, modern Tanzania, and on Lake Tanganyika at Karema (see Figure 6). Later his interests switched to the Congo. France's concerns lay primarily with its long-existing holdings in island territories off the East African coast (Madagascar, Comoros, etc.). Portugal had for centuries held the east and west possessions of Mozambique and Angola.

However, in the early 1880s Germany's ambitions became a very active factor. Industrialising and increasing in power, it became intent on possessing an overseas empire, as a matter of relative prestige vis-à-vis other European countries. East Africa was seen as a field of opportunity, despite few economic and strategic advantages for Germany there. (It has been said, 'The foundation of the German colonial empire was primarily inspired by Bismarck's desire to obtain an entente with France by picking a quarrel with Britain').[2] After only two years of the realpolitik tactics of Bismarck, Germany had established a claim to wide stretches of East African land. The tactics were for German representatives to make quasi-official treaties with sundry small chiefs – treaties of friendship and protection giving Germany territorial rights. (Similar methods had earlier been followed in German Southwest Africa.)

An AIA meeting in Brussels in 1885 recognised the sovereignty of Leopold over a Congo Free State. Two Anglo–German Agreements (1886,1890) transformed spheres of influence into partitioned protectorates.[3] A commercial venture was set up by Germany covering present-day Tanzania, Rwanda and Burundi, and a British one in Kenya and Uganda. Thereafter, the pace of political change slowed, Germany having made the point and gained territory.

This curious interlude, quite different in nature from the preceding slow-moving revelation of unknown Africa to the outside world, suddenly and completely changed the picture and prospects for the future, particularly for the indigenous people, and it left certain European countries with responsibilities of a new kind. However, a different popular atmosphere was growing in Britain at least. The South African (Boer) war at the turn of the century left strong feelings of disappointment and disillusion, which spelt the end of the British imperial impulse. Imperialism became a music hall joke before the end of the first decade of the twentieth century. The Liberal Party came to power in London in a landslide victory in 1908 on an anti-imperialist platform.

The period from the 1890s to the First World War in 1914 was spent entering into colonial responsibilities, establishing administrations under law and building basic infrastructures. For example, rail lines converged on the heart of Africa: from Mombasa to Lake Victoria (1902), and from Dar-es-Salaam to Lake Tanganyika (1914). Around the same time, settlers and trading companies were pushing north from South Africa, establishing Rhodesia and crossing the Zambezi. A rail link reached Broken Hill (in present-day Zambia) in 1906, and soon after extended to the Katanga province of Congo. Roads (unsurfaced) reached most interior centres by the 1920s.

Until the end of the nineteenth century, missions played an important role as the main source of western ideals and ideas, and over large areas were the most important agent of modernisation.[4] However, in general, missionaries found the process of Christian conversion disappointingly slow and traditional ways difficult to alter – converts were few over time, and schools hard to establish.[5] One is tempted to compare the assumptions of the first missionaries, who thought they had only to bring the good news of the gospel for it to be recognised and adopted, with those of modern apostles of technology. The buzz phrase 'transfer of technology' is based now on the same sort of facile assumption, and in like manner adoption of the latest gospel is slow.

Then the First World War in Europe spread to Africa – active warfare in

German territories in East and Southwest Africa. Premonitory rumbles of conflict had been in the air since big politics and subdivisions into countries commenced in the 1880s. The end of the war in 1918 brought further territorial adjustments and new responsibilities, handed out under the aegis of the League of Nations, forerunner of the United Nations.

In a post-war spirit that was not at all imperial, mandates were laid down in 1922 for governance of the redistributed territories in Africa, the sense of which was that they should be governed primarily for the welfare of the people there. The extent to which these mandates were followed in British, French and Belgian possessions was determined very largely by the extremely poor economic circumstances in Europe between the two world wars. Those were bleak years. During the Great Depression there was little money to spare in Europe to develop overseas colonies. Politically, the various responsible governments remained, on the whole, close to the intentions of the mandates of the League of Nations. To say, as have some critics,[6] that the mandates became thinly disguised extensions of the old colonial empires, did not improve the situation of the peoples of the territories, nor bring about any great improvement in regional stability, is manifestly untrue. On the contrary, significant improvements were made in humanitarian fields and in public utilities, and the territories were governed more stably than before. In the improved economic circumstances of post-World War II times, progress was made towards the building of modern states. Generally, methods of colonial administration were positive and progressive rather than exploitative.

Was there really a scramble for Africa? I believe we need to review the conventional notion of a predatory swoop by imperial powers. There certainly was a scramble to get out of Africa in the mid-twentieth century by European nations who could no longer afford the responsibilities they had taken on. I suggest it would be nearer the truth to see imperialism as short-lived, and the following 'colonial' period of about 70 years as having been necessary to progress; it was slow, but for all its faults benign and constructive rather than exploitative. The reshaping of colonial responsibility, which took place after WWI, produced a clearer vision for the future. Subsequent government, under humane and orderly conditions, deliberately laid the foundations of nations one day to emerge. But despite progress made since WWII, it is still uncertain whether most of these ex-colonial states are yet viable economically and politically.

Notes and references

1. Guest, R. (2005). *The Shackled Continent.* Pan Books, London.
2. Coupland, R. (1939). *The Exploitation of East Africa (1856–1890)*, p.397. Faber & Faber, London.
3. However, various Boundary Commissions had to toil for many years to establish actual borders: e.g., Gore-Brown, S. (1964). The Anglo–Belgian Boundary Commission. *Northern Rhodesia Journal, No.4*(5): 315–329.
4. Rotberg, R.I (1964). The missionary factor in the occupation of Trans-Zambesia. *Northern Rhodesia Journal, No.4*(5): 330–338.
5. Rotberg, R.I. (1965). *Christian Missionaries and the Creation of Northern Rhodesia (1880–1924).* Princetown University Press.
6. Rieff, D. (2003), Liberal Imperialism, pp.10–28; In: *The Imperial Tense. Prospects and problems of American Empire.* Eds. Bacevich, A.; Ivan R. Dee, Chicago.

8

L'idée Fixe

The exploration of the African Great Lakes is a well-known story. Names associated with it, such as Burton and Speke, Livingstone and Stanley, have entered folklore. For several centuries before they came to Africa there had been persistent reports from Arab and Portuguese sources of large lakes in the central interior. Speculation naturally arose about whether these water bodies were linked with the source of the Nile, an enduring fascination of mankind since the ancient civilisation of Egypt. It was thought the upper reaches of the Nile might help to explain the phenomenon of its unfailing pulse of flood that reaches Egypt each September and sustains cultivation and large populations. The upper reaches had long lain mysterious in an interior impenetrable by reason of vast unhealthy swamps, cataracts and dense bush. The explorations that struck inland from the east coast in the mid-nineteenth century were therefore not only looking for the rumoured lakes but also hoping to reveal whether a connection existed with the Nile. Indeed the Nile remained an underlying theme of the exploration of East and Central Africa.

Nowadays, one can see much of the Nile from commercial flights. The usual way from Burundi (see Part I, Chapter 6) to Europe was by the Belgian airline Sabena, the flight beginning virtually at the Nile headstream, the Kagera River in the Burundi mountains, and ending at the delta in Egypt. The river flows though a great variety of landscapes – lakes, swamps, forests and deserts – but to my mind the most striking contrast was where desert changed to the irrigated, vividly green delta.

Almost as complex as the hydrology of Central Africa were the ideas and ambitions driving the first explorers. Along with geographical curiosity there was a growing international interest for humanitarian and commercial reasons. Concurrently, Arab trade was growing inland from the east coast, and not least in impact was the widespread introduction of guns among indigenous peoples. Exploration took place at a time of rapid change and mounting disorder. Here I want to trace how this process was experienced in the region of Lake Tanganyika, bearing in mind most explorers were

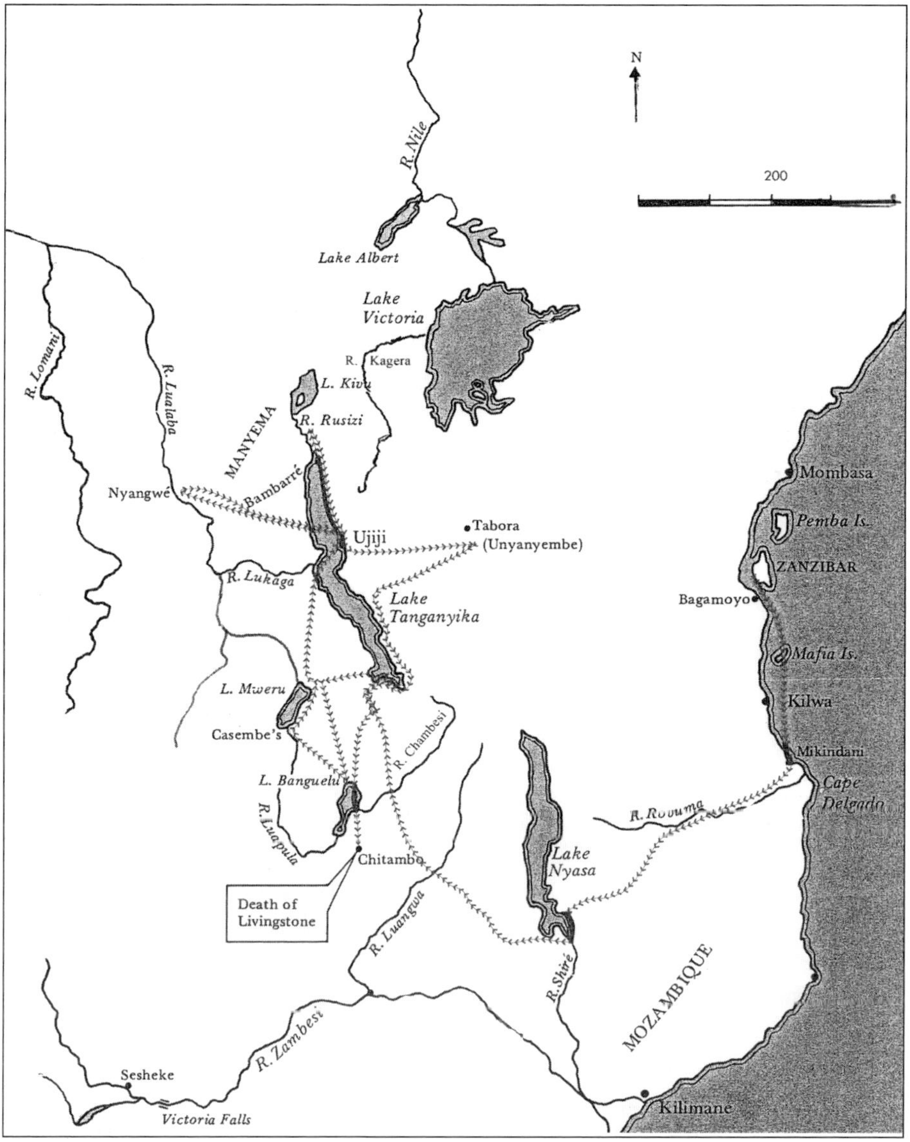

Figure 9. Route of David Livingstone on his last journey (1866–1873). Arrows indicate direction. From Huxley (1974).

obsessed with the Nile sources. It is still easy to get caught up in the drama of this quest. I will avoid use of the word 'discover' (nowadays offensive to some – perhaps 'explore' in the sense of first appraisal by the outside world is acceptable).

As shore and mountain landscapes became familiar (gazing from a slow boat on Tanganyika) I tried to look through the eyes of those finding their way without the benefit of an overall geographic picture. Their terms of reference were not only based on hypotheses but, as is typically human, their theory had also after a while hardened into beliefs or obstinately fixed ideas, which led to many mistakes. The earlier explorers (Burton, Speke, Livingstone) were influenced by myths and legends built on nothing we would call observational evidence. It was difficult for them to banish these ancient tales from mind and deal solely with observations on the ground. For instance, the Greek historian, Herodotus (who ascended the Nile to Aswan around 460 BC), spoke of the Nile arising from fountains in the far interior; and Ptolemy's famous map of the second century AD shows the Nile rising from two lakes fed from high mountains, the so-called 'Mountains of the Moon'. The explorers' accounts demonstrate how these images were worked into partly understood geography. Furthermore, as they presented their findings to audiences at home, observation, myth and theory tended to harden into fixed opinion.

Burton and Speke

The first European visitors to Lake Tanganyika (in 1858) arrived at Ujiji quite ill. Burton and Speke had badly impaired vision, and Burton could not walk. Hiring canoes with crews, they made their way to the north end of the lake where, they had been told, a substantial river flowed out. It was called the Rusizi. Reaching Uvira (see Figures 6 & 8), they stayed nine days on the lakeshore almost at the river mouth, but were unable to go further. Nothing could induce the crews to take them to the river although, according to Speke, they said the remaining distance was only about six hours' paddling. The Warundi tribe at the river were said to be hostile. But Uvira residents were emphatic that the river actually flowed into, not out of, the lake. Speke climbed neighbouring heights and observed, '. . . the mountains increasing in size as they extended away to the northward, and effectually closing in this low lake, which is not quite half the altitude of the surface level of the general interior plateau,'[1] (i.e., more consistent with an inflowing than outflowing river).

Burton had allowed himself to hope that the river was the Nile, and was deeply disappointed ('I felt sick at heart'). So they returned to Ujiji, virtually certain the river flowed into the lake. In his book about the journey, Burton[2] stated that the Rusizi 'is the main drain of the northern countries, and the best authorities, that is to say those nearest the spot, unanimously assert that it is an influent'. Burton found that traders on Tanganyika knew of no outlet, though many inflows were known. However, the fact that the explorers had not actually seen the Rusizi was to give rise to contention and confuse future exploration.

In Bujumbura in the 1970s I was frequently around the Rusizi delta, and wondered about the explorers' accounts. Why was Speke not able to determine the flow direction of the river when he climbed the hills behind Uvira? The lake is only about 22 km wide at the truncated north shore, and the main delta ('Grande Rusizi') enters about halfway across, while a smaller branch ('Petite Rusizi') enters near the northwest corner (see Figure 8). He was quite close; the six hours paddling estimate was an exaggeration. Two explanations seem reasonable: first, the typically muddy water of the Rusizi dives on entering the clear lake, disappearing quickly and leaving little discolouration, the river being denser than the lake because of lower temperature and high sediment load. So although there is a remarkably sharp boundary between brown river water and lake water (it is striking from an aircraft), it occurs fairly close to land and might not have been visible to Speke. Second, the lake in any case was higher in 1858 – of the order of 10 metres higher than today (see Notes 21 and 22 for discussion of the hydrological balance of the lake). Since the Rusizi flows in a very flat plain the lake would then have extended further into it, and so the delta might have looked very different from today.

Short of resources, the expedition had to return. On the way to the coast they paused at Tabora. Speke, the fitter of the two, took the opportunity to make a three-week journey north where, according to Arab traders, lay another lake. On seeing it he was impressed by its size, named it Lake Victoria and was convinced it must give rise to the Nile. Since he had reached only the lake's south end, his conviction was largely inspirational (although some of his reasoning made good sense; for example, his measured altitude of Victoria was considerably higher than the known altitude of the Nile at Gondoroko in the Sudan, about 5 degrees north of his assumed northern boundary of Victoria).

Speke fell out with Burton on abruptly announcing that he had found the source of the Nile. Arriving back in England ahead of Burton he received the glory, and the funds to go back to Victoria to confirm his Nile conviction. Burton, on the other hand, found his Tanganyika expedition overshadowed or hijacked. Soon Speke and James Grant walked around Victoria, found where the Nile flows out, walked on to Gondoroko and sailed down the river to Cairo. The Nile, he pronounced in 1862, was settled. But it wasn't to be so simple. In 1864 Samuel Baker and his wife reached Lake Albert, where the Nile enters and shortly exits again (see Figure 9), but they did not confirm the sources of that large lake, which of course left the Nile sources still in question. Geographers argued. Burton, reversing his previous assurance that the Rusizi flowed south, gave it as his opinion that it flowed north and probably connected Tanganyika with Lake Albert. Unfortunately Speke died in a shooting accident before the matter could be debated.

In short, Lake Victoria as the source of the Nile had become the idée fixe of Speke, and Tanganyika that of Burton. Sides were taken, and the origin of the Nile became a question of huge public interest. Further investigation was needed to settle it once and for all. David Livingstone was given the mission.

Livingstone

The Royal Geographic Society seems to have swung in favour of investigating the great watershed just south of Tanganyika as the likely Nile source (see Figure 9),[3] (a viewpoint Livingstone himself shared). So the Burton–Speke controversy had shifted the focus of the search about 1,000 km south of Lake Victoria. It also encouraged delusions to develop, in the mind of Livingstone at least, that the Nile might spring, not from a lake, but from fountains on a watershed – as Herodotus had said.

Livingstone landed in East Africa early in 1866, for an expedition that in fact lasted until his death in 1873. Much of this peripatetic period was spent around Lake Tanganyika, exploring its place in the hydrographical configuration. He too had fixed ideas – some have said obsessions[4] – centred on the Nile and on the slave trade, which seem to have fluctuated in priority in his mind. Although details of his routes are well known, writers have differed about Livingstone's actual options and driving motives. So it may be worthwhile to look again at probable options at several crucial points on his way, and try to understand why he chose as he did. My only qualification for this is that I know the country Livingstone passed through (except Congo), and also Lakes Malawi/Nyasa, Bangweulu, Mweru and Tanganyika, at different seasons of year.

It was in fact a rather preposterous venture. He took no other European, was poorly financed and expected the journey should not take long. As Moorehead[5] succinctly put it, the expedition was based on misassumptions: the Nile was not in the region he went to, he had no power to put down slavery (in the teeth of great vested interests), and it was almost impossible to go such distances, ill-equipped and unarmed, with a small band of Africans, through disturbed and insecure country. It all ended in apparent disaster yet, paradoxically, succeeded beyond measure within a few years. His two great causes were accomplished most effectively by his martyrdom: influencing public opinion in Europe strongly against slavery, and inspiring Stanley to take up the search and subsequently go down the Congo River.[6]

Starting at the Rovumu River on the mid-East African coast (see Figure 9), Livingstone made his way to Lake Nyasa/Malawi through country disturbed by slaving. He could not get around the lake to the north as intended because of fighting, nor could he get a slave dhow to cross it because of suspicion of him by the Arabs. So he had to walk around the south end. Up the west side the country was troubled by raiding *mazitu*, the Ngoni tribe. Most of his caravan porters deserted (it seems he saw the unwilling ones off with relief). His pack animals died. The rainy season set in, making travel difficult, and there was little or no food to be had. The last straw was the theft of his medicines when a little north of the Luangwa Valley (the wildlife park in present-day Zambia). It was a crucial point.

Mortality among Europeans on cross-country travel was high; they depended on medicines, especially anti-malarial quinine. It was virtually suicidal to go without it (this probably turned out to be the case for Livingstone too, in the long run, for he was continually weakened by subsequent illnesses). His options were to return over at least 1,000 km of foot track, recuperate and refit another caravan – if funds could be found – or to press on into unknown country and continue the exploration. The latter was not reasonable – yet that was the decision he took.

A change in attitude appears in his diaries; it has been called the onset of fatalism.[7] Something of the same sort had occurred under difficult conditions in his earlier expeditions, and was put down to foolhardiness or fearlessness by his European companions. Here, however, was a situation with which no one could sensibly cope otherwise than by quitting, yet he chose to go on, as if 'letting his course be shaped, not by his own deliberate plan, but by the play of circumstance – or by the hand of God'.[8] For the next four and a half years (until, in fact, he and Stanley met at Ujiji in November 1871) this attitude seems to have characterised his behaviour. By it he was enabled to travel and live for long spells closely with Arab slavers, depending on them for protection and often food and care, to wait with them in their irritatingly slow and intermittent journeys, all the time witnessing and in his heart condemning their business. By it, too, he was enabled to endure long spells when illness or inactivity in seasons of bad weather prevented progress. He could be content through setbacks, disappointments and loneliness – content in general, that is, but his journals clearly show it was not without many struggles of self-will. Despite accommodations of principle, and subjugation of his desire to be always active, there remained in him a persistent striving towards his goals which denies the explanation of fatalism.

Burton thought the idée fixe of the Nile eventually cost Livingstone his life. And others have suggested he was essentially obstinate (e.g., Elspeth Huxley's suggestion[9] that his 'refusal to accept defeat was matched by his refusal to admit a fact that denied an entrenched belief or thwarted a fixed purpose'). To my mind, it seems reasonable to believe in the consistency of Livingstone's actions and words, for at another level than his explicit purposes lay an extraordinary conviction that he was guided by Providence and could surrender himself completely to God's design ('it is in Providence and not in me').[10]

Pressing northwards, east of the Bangweulu Swamp (near where he was eventually to die in 1873) and crossing the Chambesi River that feeds it, he at last reached Lake Tanganyika on 2 April 1867. Illness and delay, while waiting to avoid tribal war ahead, made Livingstone stay around the south of Tanganyika for five months. Most of that time he lived in Chitimbwa's village on the high plateau along with an Arab caravan. He made a foray in May down to the Lufubu River and back (see Figure 7).[11] Finally he started west with the Arabs to Casembe's (a main crossroads of the slave trade, visited earlier by the Portuguese Lacerda), then up the east side of Lake Mweru to its exit, the Lualaba River (Figure 9).

Rains had set in and the caravan camped there at Mpweto's village, but Livingstone, perceiving the large river flowing northward that he thought might be the Nile, realised he had to determine its source. Drawn compulsively by the Nile question, his independent self came to life again and he went, with just a few helpers and despite the rainy season, back south and came to Lake Bangweulu. Not much exploration was done there, as canoes were difficult to get, but Livingstone seems to have understood the connections of the upper waterways (Chambesi – Bangweulu – Luapula – Mweru – Upper Lualaba), a region he increasingly came to associate with the source of the Nile (Figure 9).

Returning to the Arabs at Lake Mweru, his options were to follow the Lualaba into Manyema (Upper Congo region) and establish eventually whether it was the Nile, or he might find a caravan crossing Tanganyika to Ujiji where medicine and supplies should be waiting. After long delay because of fighting ahead he chose the latter, and for most of the three months it took to reach Ujiji he was seriously ill. His Arab friend, Mohammed Bogharib, tended him and had him carried when too ill to walk, saving his life. At Ujiji he found his supplies looted. However, strength and optimism surprisingly returned, and after several months he set off to Manyema again, re-crossing Tanganyika and aiming to reach a more northerly point on the Lualaba. He had only (as he wrote to Consul Kirk at Zanzibar) to connect the 'sources' he had found at Bangweulu with the Nile, believing that the Lualaba would eventually flow into Lake Albert. But in case he had been working on the Congo as well as the Nile, he might 'have to go down the eastern line of drainage' to investigate.[12] So it should be only a short expedition; a few months he thought.

In fact he plunged into more than two years of frustration, illness, hostility from Manyema people and lack of canoe transport to go on the river. Enforced halts at the villages of Bambarre and Nyangwe, the latter beside the Lualaba River (see Figure 9), left a great deal of time for introspection. Traders he met from Katanga described four rivers on a watershed to the south rising from fountains. This supported the vision that increasingly dominated his mind. Impotently watching the river – it proved impossible to hire canoes; one suspects the Arabs prevented it – he became persuaded that it was indeed the Nile. According to local information the river swung west but after that continued north. Manifestly, however, a trip downstream would be too difficult and distant with his scanty resources. In passing the time he sketched fishes from the Lualaba, in order to be able eventually to compare them with fish species of the lower Nile. (Ironically, this was an interesting line of enquiry. Had modern zoogeographical data been available to him, it would have shown that the Nile and Congo assemblages of fish species are significantly different.)

So Nyangwe became another crucial crossroads. His desire now focused on going upstream, back to the Mweru–Luapula region visited already. Somewhere on that watershed the fountains awaited, taking ideal shape like a mirage. His intent was therefore to identify the Nile by finding specific source fountains, rather than following the river to the sea. But although he pleaded and offered to pay the Arabs for canoes and men, they were unobtainable. At that point, on 15 July 1871, a massacre occurred of Nyangwe people by the followers of the Arabs (see below). Horror shocked Livingstone into returning at once to Tanganyika. There, at Ujiji, no practical options were open for the time being; he was weak from illness and destitute. Stanley's arrival with supplies and medicine on 10 November 1871 was a godsend.

When Livingstone recovered, he and Stanley went by canoe to the north of Tanganyika (see Figure 9) to confirm once and for all whether the Rusizi ran into the lake (curiously, they were told by residents at Ujiji that it flowed out, just as Burton and Speke had been misinformed thirteen years before).[13] They saw that the Rusizi *flowed in* – Tanganyika certainly did not connect with the Nile that way. Neither, as far as they could ascertain, was any outlet from Tanganyika known. (Yet 'it must find an exit' Livingstone reflected.) In fact there was no outlet in his day.

Livingstone's options were to return home with Stanley (the most reasonable course given his weak health and the months it would take to get more men and supplies up from the coast); to return to Manyema; or to go north to Lake Albert and search further for the Nile. Other options that Stanley suggested were turned down. He decided to wait for fresh men and supplies and, almost predictably at this stage, go south along Lake Tanganyika to Bangweulu and find the Nile fountains. Once again this was the riskiest course, but he was placing himself in God's hands so as to complete 'my work' as he now called it.[14,15] Accompanying Stanley as far as Unyanyembe (modern Tabora), he waited for the supply caravan, which came in very good time – five months.

In that space Livingstone pondered his work. The iniquities of the slave trade came to the fore again, probably because of the impact of the Nyangwe massacre. But he rationalised that, by solving the Nile question, he would be able to speak out against slavery to a wider world audience. Convinced of the target area, he set forth: 'It is all but certain that four full-grown gushing fountains rise on the watershed eight days south of Katanga, each of which

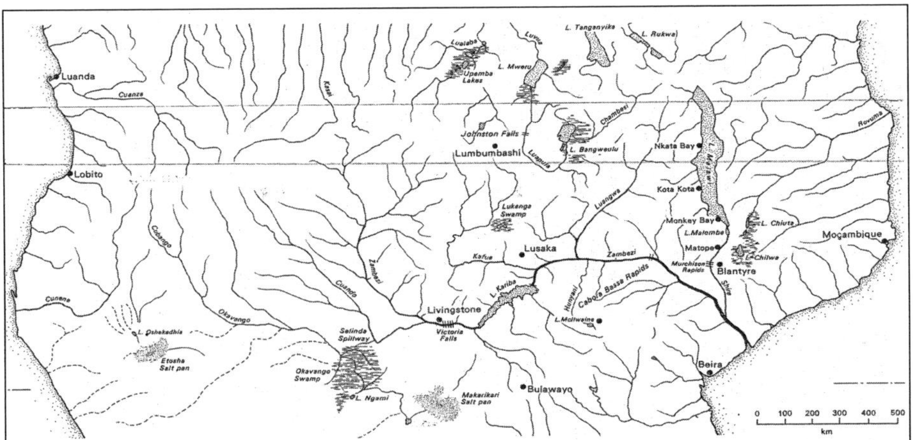

(A)

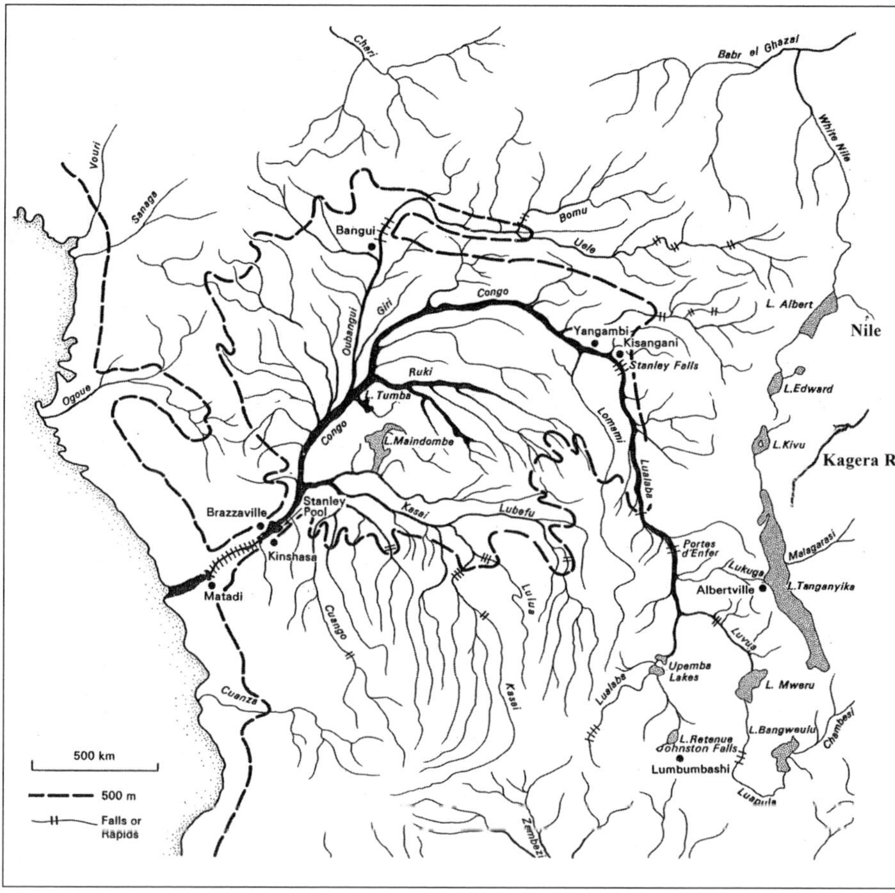

(B)

Figure 10. Hydrological systems of the Zambezi (A) and the Congo (B) Rivers.
Note: The two great river systems are not directly connected with each other or with the two other major river systems of Africa, the Nile and the Niger. Upper tributaries are close in places, however. (B) shows the watershed between tributaries of the Congo, flowing north, and those of the Zambezi flowing south. (B) shows upper reaches of the Chari River, which ultimately leads to Lake Chad and the Niger in the west, and upper reaches of the Nile (Bahr al Ghazel) flowing to the east.
The possibility of past interchanges of aquatic faunas between river systems have excited speculations by zoogeographers (eg. Graham Bell-Cross's studies on the tributaries of the Zambezi; also Max Poll's papers on the fishes of the Congo system and Lake Tanganyika, listed in Coulter, G.W. (1991).
According to Beadle (1974), p.152, 'From the distribution of the present soudanian (nilotic) aquatic fauna it is impossible to doubt the reality of water connections from time to time during the late Pleistocene across the whole region from the Nile to Senegal ... the composition of the fauna of Lake Chad can only be explained on the assumption of recent connections, not only with the Niger and Congo basins whose upper waters share watersheds at the present time, but also and especially with the Nile'. In (B) the area of the fairly flat central basin of the Congo River is indicated by the 500 m contour (interrupted line). (Maps from Beadle 1974.)

at no great distance off becomes a large river.'[16] The last phase followed inevitably, like a Greek tragedy.

At the south end of Tanganyika, ascending the plateau in the southeast arm, familiar ground to him, Livingstone set course for Bangweulu. Whether he intended to go down the west side of that lake (where he'd been in 1868) direct to the Luapula River, or swing around east of the Bangweulu Swamp and then west to pick up any tributaries of the Chambesi and Luapula, appears uncertain. At any rate, he got sadly lost on reaching the swamp[17] and floundered in that dire area during the worst months of the rainy season. At the south side, after great hardship, he died, still asking for directions to 'the four fountains'.

One cannot help speculating what might have happened had he successfully bypassed Lake Bangweulu and its swamp on relatively dry land and survived? It seems almost certain that, on reaching the Luapula River, he would have proceeded west, between about 10 and 12 degrees latitude south (see Figure 10A). Continuing along the watershed he might eventually have reached the west sea coast near Lobito – about 2,000 km direct distance – and on the way found the source streams of a number of rivers. On the north side rise the Congo (Zambian and Kasai branches) and Cuanza rivers; and on the south the Zambezi and its tributary Kafue, the Okavango and Cunene rivers (Figures 10A & B).[18, 19] Livingstone's intuition was correct insofar as the area is one of the great watersheds of Africa, but alas it does not contain the river he sought. The fountains were mythical.

Cameron

The watershed was traversed shortly afterwards (1874–75) by V.L. Cameron, more or less along the route suggested above that Livingstone might have taken. However, one is struck by the different approach of Cameron (and of Stanley who followed him on Tanganyika) from previous explorers of the region. Neither was influenced by ancient writings or fixed ideas – they found their way by indications on the ground and the experiences of contemporary explorers. Furthermore, both were at pains to examine the incipient connection of Tanganyika with the Lukuga outlet leading to the Lualaba; and both were open to the possibility that the Lualaba could be in either the Nile or Congo system.

Cameron, a naval lieutenant, headed the relief expedition for Livingstone in 1873, but it was intercepted by Livingstone's companions bearing his body to the east coast. Cameron went on with a small party to Ujiji to recover some of Livingstone's papers, and there he took the initiative to hire canoes (as a practical sailor, he cut his own sail), and circumnavigated the south basin of Tanganyika. Cameron's book[20] is refreshingly straightforward. He also spotted the most likely location of any outflow from the lake. At the time, this (the Lukuga channel) was blocked with deposited material and weed, but according to local people it led to the Lualaba River. Cameron reached Nyangwe overland, but there found himself in much the same position as Livingstone in 1871, unable to hire canoes to get further. Importantly, however, he realised by calculating river altitude that it was too low to be a tributary of the Nile, and thus was probably part of the Congo system.

The Arab merchant Tippu Tib, of whom more anon, advised him strongly against risking the river, but helped him with guides south to Katanga from where he struck across the great east–west watershed to the Atlantic coast (Figure 10A). On the journey he realised the upper affluents of the Congo and Zambezi rose on either side close to each other (he even conceived an artificial link might be made between them).

Stanley

Better financed than previous explorers, Stanley brought his own boat. It could be disassembled and carried (see Chapter 6, note 3). With this little flagship (the *Lady Alice*), as well as hired canoes, he headed straight for and circumnavigated Lake Victoria (see Figure 11), avoiding the criticism made against Speke who had not checked all its tributaries. He then showed that the influents of Lake Albert connected only with Lake Edward (which otherwise was isolated). Lastly he had to investigate the possible connections of Tanganyika with the Lukuga and Lualaba Rivers, and find where the main stream led – to the Mediterranean or to the Atlantic.[21]

He observed that the level of Tanganyika was higher and its outward flow from the Lukuga greater than Cameron had found. He accurately predicted its intermittent nature, and thus solved the question that had puzzled previous explorers – whether or not Tanganyika has an outflow. It is, in fact, determined in present times by a delicate balance between rainfall and lake evaporation.[22,23] Assembling *Lady Alice*, he managed to get Tippu Tib (the same) to accompany him some way down the Lualaba with a large shore party.

It is interesting to compare the situations of Livingstone, Cameron, and Stanley, at Nyangwe on the Lualaba River (see Figure 11). Livingstone,

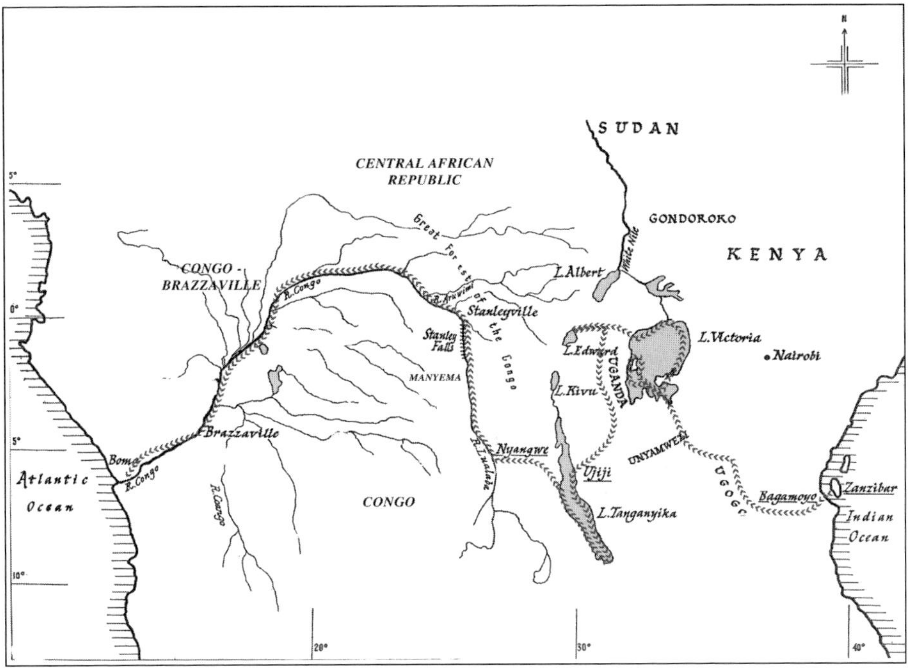

Figure 11. Route of H.M. Stanley across the continent, from the Indian Ocean to the Atlantic (1874–1877). From Hall (1974).

distressed and poor, could not get help, even to cross the river. Cameron, fitter and better supplied, was nevertheless deflected from going downstream. Stanley, confident, determined, with a vessel of his own and wealthy (Tippu was to receive $5,000), got his way. (Tippu in fact went only part of the distance downstream, his contract amended,[24] but it was far enough to prevent desertions from Stanley's own caravan.) They were committed to the river, and finally penetrated to the sea. Wherever they encountered cataracts they carried their little flotilla around them. Near the end, the good ship *Alice* had to be abandoned.

By this great trip on Lakes Victoria, Edward, Tanganyika and the Congo River in 1875–76, the Nile question was indeed settled. At length Burton had to admit that his favourite theory of Tanganyika's connection with the Nile was in error. Pondering the misassumptions and confusions of the search, he concluded, 'the time to leave [Africa] is when the idée fixe begins to develop itself'.[25]

Arguably, the ultimate source of the Nile is the most substantial tributary of Lake Victoria – which is the Kagera River. Its main source is the

Nyawarongo stream in the mountains not far east of Bujumbura (see Figure 8). This was ascertained by the German explorer-surveyor Richard Kandt in 1900.[26] Nothing particular is to be seen there, just a bare mountain where the stream rises.

Looking at it, I thought of the irony that the early explorers, Burton, Speke, Livingstone and Stanley, should have come so close to the Nile's furthest source without knowing it, preoccupied as they were by the notion that the nearby Rusizi might be the source.

Notes and references

1. Speke, J.H. (1864). *What Led to the Discovery of the Source of the Nile*, p.247. Blackwood.
2. Burton, R.F. (1860). *The Lake Regions of Central Africa*, p.146. Sidgwick & Jackson.
3. Roderick Murchison, President of the Royal Geographic Society, proposed that Livingstone, in searching for the upper Nile, was to look at the watersheds of Central Africa and pay particular attention to the area near the south of Lake Tanganyika. To these purely geographic objectives Livingstone added the obligation he felt to do whatever was possible to extinguish the slave trade, and to talk to the people about religion (see Coupland, R., 1945, p.25. *Livingstone's Last Journey.* Collins).
4. For example, Brodie, F. (1967). *The Devil Drives*, p.230. Eyre & Spottiswoode.
5. Moorehead, A. (1960). *The White Nile.* Penguin Books.
6. Coupland, R. (1945). *Livingstone's Last Journey.* Collins.
7. ibid. p.53.
8. ibid. p.56
9. Huxley, E. (1974). *Livingstone and his African Journeys.* Saturday Review Press, New York.
10. Coupland, R. (1945). p.82.
11. *Livingstone's Last Journals.* (1874). p.20. H. Waller (Ed.), London.
12. Coupland, R. (1945). p.75.
13. Stanley, H.M. (1887). *How I found Livingstone*, p.479. New York.
14. *Livingstone's Last Journals* (1874), p.206.
15. ibid. p.169.
16. In a letter to Kirk in Zanzibar (quoted in Coupland, 1947, p.75) Livingstone said, 'The volume of water which flows north from latitude 12 degrees south is so large, I suspect I have been working on the sources of the Congo as well as the Nile.'
17. A previous accident to his chronometers threw out his estimates of longitude; his sextant was also faulty and in any case could not be used on cloudy days (Huxley, 1974; p.208).
18. Bell-Cross, G. (1966). The Distribution of Fishes in Central Africa. *Fish. Res. Bull. Zambia, Vol.4*: 3–20. Lusaka, Zambia.
   Graham Bell-Cross studied the complex distributional relationships between the fishes of the major rivers flowing south from the watershed to Central Africa. He

found the distribution of fishes to be to a large extent characteristic for each river, although all have significant affinities with the Congo.

19. Beadle, L. (1974). *The Inland Waters of Tropical Africa.* Longman.
The Congo Basin to the north is an ancient hydrographic system and its fishes characterise one of the two principal fish zoogeographic regions in Africa – Congolese and Soudanian (or Nilotic). The zoogeography of faunas in African lakes and rivers is a vast subject. Fishes are the best-investigated group, and the evolution of their remarkable diversity has been associated with reproductive isolation both within and between lakes and rivers by physical, ecological and behavioural barriers.
20. Cameron, V.L. (1877). *Across Africa.* London.
21. Stanley, H.M. (1878). *Through the Dark Continent.* Sampson Low, Marsten, Searle & Rivington, London.
Many rivers flow into Lake Tanganyika, but there was no outlet in Livingstone's day. He had seen the Shire River flowing out of Lake Nyasa/Malawi, and he knew about the Nile outlet from Lake Victoria, so it was reasonable to believe Tanganyika overflowed at some place. Although he must have passed close to the Lukuga channel outlet while on the lake, he was never aware of its function as an intermittent overflow. Stanley put it well, in his fulsome style: 'We have also seen in the Lukuga the first symptoms of that overflowing which must come. At present there are only a few inches of mud banks and a frail barrier of papyrus and reeds to interpose between the waters of the lake and its destiny, which is now, year by year, steadily approaching. When the Tanganyika has risen 3 feet higher, there will be no surf at the mouth of the Lukuga, no sill of sand, no oozing mud-banks, no rush-covered old river course, but the accumulated waters of over a hundred rivers will sweep through the ancient gap with the force of cataclysm bearing away on its flood all the deposits of organic debris at present in the Lukuga creek, down the steep incline to swell the tribute due to the mighty Livingstone' (*sic*: Stanley's name for the Lualaba; see pp.51–52.).
22. Coulter, G.W. [Ed.] (1991). *Lake Tanganyika and its Life.* Oxford University Press.
Lake levels have fluctuated in relation to the volume of water in the basin. Tectonic rifting processes deepened the basin over millions of years. Moreover, climate changes have continually altered the balances of rainfall and evaporation. In present climates, rain run-off from the basin catchment is very small in relation to the great volume (great depth) of the lake, and evaporation accounts for by far the greatest water loss. A delicate balance between rainfall and evaporation now exists, which causes slight changes (especially in evaporation) to make lake levels fluctuate. Thus Tanganyika is connected by its Lukuga outlet to the Congo only intermittently. There are evidences of ancient shorelines 500 to 600 metres below the present, and the lake (or lakes) may have lain in isolation at such low levels for possibly six million years (in the Pliocene–Pleistocene periods). Volcanic activity 14,000 and 11,000 years ago formed Lake Kivu, which overflowed southward into Tanganyika via the Rusizi River about 9,500 BP. So in fairly recent time (geologically speaking) Tanganyika acquired the input of the Rusizi River, which caused the lake to rise and overflow at the Lukuga. The Kivu basin was closed between 3,500 to 1,400 BP because of climate change, and without the Rusizi River Tanganyika fell about 75 metres. When the Rusizi flowed again the lake rose and its levels have varied

around the present. It was higher in historic time (Burton and Speke), then fell about 10 metres after the lake broke through at the Lukuga – as Stanley imaginatively depicted it would.

23. McGlue, M.M., Lezzar, K.E., Cohen, A.S., Russell, J.M., Tiercelin, J-J., Felton, A.A., Mbede, E. & Nkotagu H.H. (2008). Seismic records of late Pleistocene aridity in Lake Tanganyika, tropical East Africa. *Paleolimnology, 40*: 635–653.
    This paper concerns recent research on dynamic changes in the level of Lake Tanganyika.
24. Hall, R. (1974). *Stanley: An adventurer explored*, p.67. Collins, London.
    Stanley's own diaries of this great journey only came to light in the mid-twentieth century – see Stanley, R. & Neame, A. (1961). *The Exploration Diaries of H.M. Stanley.* Kimber, London.
25. For source reference of this reflection by Burton, see Brodie (1967), p.231.
26. For Kandt reference, see Louis, W.R. (1963). *Ruanda-Urundi (1884-1919)*, p.106. Clarendon Press, Oxford.

9

An Open Path

In a famous speech in 1857 at Cambridge University, David Livingstone appealed for missionary volunteers for Africa. He said, 'I go back to Africa to try to make an open path for Christianity.' What did he mean by 'an open path'? What were the circumstances?

He had lately returned from making the first west to east crossing of the continent, between Luanda on the Atlantic side and Quelimane at the mouth of the Zambesi at the Indian Ocean. He had walked the footpaths of the indigenous people, and the journey had taken some twenty months. One has to understand Livingstone's words in terms of what he had just experienced, as well the social conditions in Central and East Africa – which in mid-century had started to change quickly.

It was not until Livingstone's next expedition (1859–63), when he chose the Zambezi as a 'path' into the interior ('God's Highway'), that he came in close touch with the slave trade around Lakes Nyasa and Tanganyika. Thereafter it loomed large in his mind. On the way upriver he was baulked by the Kebrabassa Falls, and instead took a tributary, the Shire River, which led him and his party to Lake Nyasa. This lake extends 590 km to the north. With the glimpses of Tanganyika and Victoria gained by Burton and by Speke in 1858, and now this great Lake Nyasa, the vision opened to Livingstone of a possible 'highway' of lakes, running up the backbone of Africa, which might greatly facilitate access to the interior (see Figure 3 in Part I).

It seems curious that so little was known of the heart of the continent until the mid-nineteenth century. Even after the existence of Lakes Victoria, Tanganyika, and Nyasa was realised, their physical configurations were not mapped and possible river connections between them were still only speculative. There was also, of course, the geopolitical question of the source of the Nile. To Livingstone in 1859, the extirpation of the slave trade and the spread of Christianity, commerce and western civilisation, all had as a precondition the creation of open paths or highways to the interior. In making these, the history of inland Africans became entwined with that of European enterprises, which thereafter began to alter African traditional life.

What sort of conditions determined the making of open routes through the lands around Tanganyika and Nyasa in the nineteenth century?

In the first two or three decades, tribal settlement was generally much as it had been for centuries. Within that pattern people were cultivators, hunters, fishermen, and a minority cattle-owners. Material cultures were practically static and movements of population slight. Large areas were sparsely populated, though around the lakes and the most fertile places denser populations lived. By and large they were people of small groups in self-contained villages. Awareness of the outside world was limited.[1] Tribal dispersion was very heterogeneous, most tribes being small. Evidence of this diversity can still be seen despite later population flux, for example in the surprising number of separate tribes identifiable in Tanzania, estimated at over a hundred.[2]

A few tribes specialised in trading, and travelled widely, notably the Nyamwezi to the east of Tanganyika (centred in Unyanyembe/modern Tabora), the Yao tribe east of Lake Nyasa and the Bisa west of that lake. The 'thin network of trade that threaded east central Africa'[3] at that time was the initiative of the inhabitants of the hinterland themselves. Even up to the middle of the nineteenth century, as Arab and Swahili merchants gradually pervaded the country, indigenous caravans bearing salt and copper, slaves and ivory, handled the bulk of trade.[4] Their routes ranged between the great lakes and the coast. It is remarkable how slight in that hinterland was the influence of the coast and Zanzibar, where foreign immigrants had been settled for centuries. Even as contact grew in the first part of the century, it was still 'the interior which came to the coast, rather than the coast which went to the interior'.[5] The lakes restricted traffic westwards, but some trade went across Nyasa handled by the Bisa people. There does not seem to have been much traffic across Tanganyika. However, a major route passed between the two lakes to reach Katanga (Congo) copper, widely desired for personal adornment.

The more or less stable conditions up to 1830 were disturbed by a southward movement of the warlike Masai into central Tanzania, but they did not stay. Of much greater impact was the following irruption of the Ngoni from the south (early 1840s). The Ngoni broke from the Zulu empire and moving northward crossed the Zambezi in 1835. By 1840 they had settled near the southeast end of Lake Tanganyika. However, they divided again in about 1845 into bodies which struck out to lands southwest and east of Lake Nyasa, while others raided up the eastern side of Lake Tanganyika, finally settling in Unyamyembe under the powerful chief Mirambo (who later was a major force with whom the Arabs and missionaries had to contend).

The Ngoni – fierce, disciplined and fast-moving warriors – had drastic effects on the numerous small dispersed tribes eking out local subsistence lives; like a large predator falling upon small prey. Many of the defeated and plundered tribes were incorporated into the Ngoni, whose force thereby grew. The loosing of hordes of raiders and refugees all around any temporary settlement of Ngoni caused widespread disruption. Stronger tribes tended to group into alliances for protection. Thus by direct impact, and indirectly by disturbing nearby tribal polities, the Ngoni destabilised older settled ways of life east of Tanganyika and around Nyasa.[6]

The country to the south of Lake Tanganyika (present-day Zambia) also was riven by tribal warfare. The Bemba people had a large and strongly centralised political system and raided widely, especially after they were strengthened with guns from Arab traders (providing slaves and ivory for guns). To the west the Lozi, and to the south the Matabele people, were powerful and persecuted smaller tribes. The area has been called a cockpit of marauding tribes.[7, also 1,5,8] For example, on Livingstone's last journey around Lake Bangweulu in the few months before he died, he makes frequent mention of the difficulty of obtaining food and hiring guides because of local devastation of the country by tribal raids and suspicion he might be associated with the Arabs.[9]

Into this disturbed scene Arab and Swahili traders penetrated from the coast in response to growing demand for slaves and ivory. The trade intensified in mid-century, as the result of several factors. The Sultan of Muscat and Oman, Seyyid Said, shifted his seat of government to Zanzibar in 1840. He pursued the economic development of his holdings along the East African coast. Slaves were needed for clove plantations, and ivory as a trade commodity. There were also substantial requirements for plantation labour in the French islands of the Indian Ocean. Seyyid sponsored trading caravans to the interior. He also fostered the growth of the Indian community on Zanzibar and the coast, who put up financial credit for inland trading.[10,11] But the trade in guns that came with the Arabs was probably the greatest disruptive factor, as it gave marauding tribes and bandits everywhere the power to tyrannise.

By the mid-1850s pathways over the lake hinterlands to the coast had become essentially a few main routes – the so-called central route via Tabora to Ujiji on Lake Tanganyika, a northern one branching at Tabora to Lake Victoria and Uganda, and a southern route from Kilwa on the coast to Lake Nyasa (see Figure 9). They were still just trails, of course, shifting with the seasons and the attitudes of tribes holding land en route (usually demanding tax for passage). For example, the coast to Ujiji was a 1,300-km march, requiring three to four months and many, sometimes hundreds, of baggage carriers. Getting to Nyasa via the Zambezi and Shire Rivers was a dependable route except at low river levels in the dry season. Goods to Tanganyika were mostly transported by the Nyasa route, with portage over the plateau between the lakes. But no overland path was easy or 'open'. Travellers had to be very cautious and able to protect themselves, as violence between tribes and with slavers was common.

Clearly, these two great lakes would be enormously valuable highways through the interior once boats could be got there. To begin with, vessels were shipped in pieces from Europe and reassembled on site. This was successful on Lake Nyasa, and with better communications missions took root. A commercial company (African Lakes Corp.) saw to transport and trade around the shoreline, and an administrative foot-hold was obtained for what eventually became British Nyasaland. Slaving was thereby suppressed – on the whole an outcome, materially at least, along the lines of Livingstone's vision. But it was different with Tanganyika. Apart from distance and terrain to be covered, there were times when war (e.g., between the Arabs and Nyamwezi) blocked the land routes.

The opportunities offered by Lake Tanganyika were exploited by missionaries, for example E.C. Hore and A.J. Swann, both ex-mariners. In nineteenth-century African history only a few names seem to have lodged in public memory; Hore and Swann are relatively unknown. Missionaries in particular tended to leave little written trace except in their church archives; their obscure lives were spent in service – Bible translating, teaching and building. From Hore, however, we have a revealing account of eleven pioneering years on Lake Tanganyika (1878–88), the first book by a resident;[12] and Swann, a near contemporary, wrote another.[13]

Hore arrived with the London Missionary Society (LMS) five years after Livingstone's death, one of the first waves of missionaries inspired by him. The group left the coast for Ujiji in 1877. As a master mariner, Hore had a special responsibility to make Lake Tanganyika into a mission 'highway'.[14] The LMS directors in London realised a new approach was required. Since the lake had until then been visited only by passing travellers, they directed the missionaries to regard themselves as settled residents with opportunities to get to know the country and people intimately.[15] Hore, as a 'practised observer', was given a roving commission.[16,17] He quickly developed opinions of his own. While paying due respect to customary status and ownership by the peoples of the lakeshore, he determined to try to ensure the lake itself became 'an international high sea ... for free and open use ... for lawful purposes'. One has to see this broad, perhaps presumptuous, desire in the context. There were no expressed intentions of annexation of the lake by overseas powers at that time. In any case LMS policy was strictly non-political. Hore was influenced most by conceptions of future free passage and cooperative use, as the people of the lake interacted and developed trade with the outside world.[18]

Hore made a two-year lake survey to introduce to the people his unfamiliar purpose of carrying the Christian gospel; he was not there for slaves or trade. Voyaging far and wide in a converted slave dhow (an open dug-out with planked bulwarks, sailed and paddled), he produced a map of human geography[21] and a plan for a more effective system of communication, especially a steam-powered ship large enough for all weathers. He went back to England to organise this, returning with the parts of a 30-foot steel 'lifeboat' which he assembled at the lake. The larger vessel (to be called the *Habari Ngema* or *Good News*) was to be shipped in numbered pieces to the Zambesi, thence up Lake Nyasa and then head-loaded to Tanganyika. The saga of transporting the larger vessel,[19] and the prodigious labour it took Hore to get his sections of lifeboat by hand-cart and head-load from the coast,[12] are both remarkable stories.

When Hore returned in the lifeboat (named *Morning Star*) to his chosen mission site at the south of Tanganyika, he found the area had been devastated by tribal raiding. Remnants of the friendly Walungu people had gathered in the valley of the Lovu (or Lufubu) River some distance off, so there Hore and his colleagues decided to build the *Good News.* A slipway and work-shed were made and the 56-foot-long vessel constructed as parts arrived. At one point in the year and a half of boat building and waiting for parts at the Lovu, Hore had to go down to the coast by the Nyasa route to retrieve his materials, blocked by disturbances. From the Zambezi he took the parts by sea to Zanzibar and thence organised a caravan overland again to Ujiji.

The *Good News* was launched in the Lovu in March 1885, and then the boiler and engines were laboriously installed in a dry dock constructed on Kavala Island halfway up the lake. Hore tells of the finish with feeling: 'On the 7th September [1886] steam was got up and with all our party on board we made a short trial-trip out into the straits. It was a time of great and thankful rejoicing with us as after many days we found ourselves steaming out on the waters of Tanganyika at last in our beautiful vessel, now practically complete in all essentials. Every plate and plank of her has a history, and every rivet a story of months and years of labour only known to a few.'

Several colleagues, notably Swann and a marine engineer J. Roxburgh, had worked on the vessel. Along with boat building, they also serviced mission stations on the lakeshore, using converted canoes and Hore's lifeboat. But it

Wreck of the *Good News* in Kituta Bay, circa 1973

The SS *Good News* in dry dock in 1886 (after Swann)

was hard going. By the end of that first decade eleven men of the mission had died ('from difficult conditions of life and work'),[20] twelve had left through sickness, and twelve were established in a few places. Hore speaks of achievements in terms of 'a line of peaceful influence of nearly 1,000 miles [1,800 km] overland, and another line of 1,000 miles around Lake Tanganyika'. Certainly it was progress towards 'an open path', but at high cost.

The experience of continuous contact with people of the lakeshore was crucial.[21] Although often threatened at first, he and other colleagues stayed to establish friendly relations.[22] (Hore's attitudes and experience were similar to those of the explorer Joseph Thompson, who described how the two were together in a threatening instance on Tanganyika which ended amicably.)[23] He was optimistic as to extending permanent mission stations in peace, and stressed simply the need for more missionaries. He handed over his marine department to Swann in 1888.

That first decade of the LMS was a heroic epic by any measure. One can only wonder at the cost in lives, and the rare dedication and hardihood needed to do what they did. Other missions at about the same time went through similar experiences – notably the Catholic White Fathers who set up permanent stations at Karema, Mpala and Rumonge, but only Hore and Swann took the approach of itinerant mission voyaging. This episode, 1877–88, was the first attempt by expatriates to settle at Lake Tanganyika.

But thereafter the *modus vivendi* with Africans, as well as with Arabs and Swahilis, changed as they were threatened by German forces on one side of the lake and Belgians on the other. The Niamkolo mission at the south of Tanganyika found itself cut off among an uneasy population.[24] At Lake Nyasa sporadic warfare between slavers and the new British administration cut routes and caused the missions on Tanganyika to feel even more isolated. In the minds of the population, missionaries began to be lumped with encroaching foreign forces, resulting in the disaffection of hitherto friendly people. In one case of serious aggression by Swahili bandits (so-called *ruga-ruga*), Swann, in self-defence with a few other Europeans, attacked and drove out their tormentors from two neighbouring villages out of which they operated. For more general peace, Swann attempted mediation between Belgian forces on the Congo side and the Arabs, through his Arab friend Rumaliza at Ujiji. But he was also drawn, by H. Johnson, British Consul in the adjacent Nyasa territory, into trying to secure for Britain the Rusizi valley at the north of Tanganyika.

Such activities became too political for the mission directors. Already they were dismayed by the deaths and illness of so many personnel. After much heart-searching, Swann left and joined the Nyasa administration. The *Good News* fell into disuse, there being no sailors to continue its work, and it was sold to the African Lakes Corporation (and eventually sunk by the German navy in 1915 – see Chapter 9 and Chapter 11). In a few years, LMS effort was removed from the lakeshore and replanted on the surrounding plateau from where it successfully spread south.

One has to understand Hore and Swann in their context: believing the Arabs to be powerful, they could not appreciate how soon the latter would be crushed. Nor did they understand that the process of colonial 'pacification', then just beginning, would shortly make the lands round the lake safe. For them the land contained unknown danger, whereas Lake Tanganyika provided secure travel and settlement on its shores. But in any case, the early twentieth century saw the African population around the south shore relocated inland because of tsetse-fly-borne sleeping sickness (see Chapter 4). Thus came to an end, after immense effort, the dream of opening a way around Lake Tanganyika so that a little flotilla of ships might service missions.

A bigger vision followed in the 1890s – of Tanganyika as part of a highway from the Cape to Cairo. This was the imperial vision, or more correctly that of some imperialist dreamers – men of action supported rather grudgingly by the British Foreign Office. The idea conveyed in the words 'Cape to Cairo' is most associated with C.J. Rhodes, capitalist, idealist of empire and philanthropist. In effect it meant driving a railway and telegraph line across the continent from south to north. Rhodes' contribution was his personal inspiration, plus investment by the British South Africa Company of which he was chairman. By 1900 considerable progress had been made. The telegraph[25] had almost reached Lake Tanganyika (it eventually went as far as Ujiji), and the railway was anticipated to get to the lake fairly soon. (It has still not done so.)

Rhodes was persuaded to write an introduction to a book (usually he corresponded only in telegrams) written by two young men who made the journey overland to Cairo in 1898. They travelled up Lake Tanganyika on the *Good News*, by then a commercial vessel. Rhodes wrote to one of them, E.S. Grogan,[26] as follows:

> 'I must say I envy you, for you have done that which has been for centuries the ambition of every explorer, namely, a walk through Africa from South to North. The amusement of the whole thing is that a youth from Cambridge during his vacation should have succeeded in doing that which the ponderous explorers of the world have failed to accomplish. There is a distinct humour in the whole thing. It makes me the more certain that we shall complete the telegraph and railway, for surely I am not going to be beaten by the legs of a Cambridge undergraduate.
>
> As to the commercial aspect, everyone supposes that the railway is being built with the only object that a human being may be able to get in at Cairo and get out at Cape Town. This is, of course, ridiculous. The object is to cut Africa through the centre, and the railway will pick up trade all along the route. The junctions to the East and West coasts, which will occur in the future, will be outlets for the traffic obtained along the route of the line as it passes through the centre of Africa. At any rate, up to Bulawayo, where I am now, it has been a payable undertaking, and I still think it will continue to be so as we advance into the far interior. We propose now to go on and cross the Zambezi just below the Victoria Falls. I should like to have the spray of the water

over the carriages. . . . your success has given me great encouragement in the work that I have still to accomplish.'

Grogan realised that Rhodes' great vision probably arose from the American experience earlier in the century of rail building. So Grogan later visited the USA, Australasia and Argentina looking for lessons to be drawn. In the preface of the next edition of his book, he pointed to

'. . . the object-lesson which the trans-American lines afford. They were pushed ahead of all settlement into the great unknown exactly as the Cape to Cairo line is being pushed ahead today. But there is this difference: in America they penetrated silent wastes tenanted by naught else than the irreconcilable Redskin, the prairie marmot and the bison; while in Africa they pass through lands rich in Nature's products and teeming with peoples who do not recede before the white man's march. . . . when the main railway system of Africa, as sketched out by Mr. Rhodes, is complete, there will be no single point as remote from a port as are some of the districts in America which are today pouring out their foodstuffs along hundreds of miles of rail.'

Well . . . that fabulous dream has long receded into a past when it might have been accomplished. What self-confidence to think they could do it! Over a century later the project is more remote than ever, although its positive logic remains. In the event, the high imperial impulse flagged. Rhodes died in 1902. The railway from Cape Town reached Ndola about 700 km from Lake Tanganyika in 1906 (see Figure 4). A German railway from Dar-es-Salaam reached Ujiji in 1912. Mind-sets altered; the continent fractionated. Instead of long-distance transport and communication, colonial administrations gave priority to improving their own internal systems. On Lake Tanganyika, commercial boat links were developed to serve its lakeshore countries. Otherwise nothing much has changed. Going overland from Cape to Cairo is still pretty laborious.

Notes and references

1. Smith, A. (1963). The Southern Section of the Interior, 1840–1884, pp.253–296. In: *History of East Africa*. Ed. Oliver, R. & Mathew, G. Clarendon Press, Oxford.
2. Gulliver, P.H. (1959). A Tribal Map of Tanganyika. *Tanganyika Notes and Records, No. 52*: 61–74.

3. Smith (1963), p.267.
4. According to Sir Richard Burton (1860) the Nyamwezi 'established trade connexions to the eastward, ... which, throughout the eighteenth century and into the nineteenth formed the chief artery of traffic from the Zanzibar coast to the interior. Yearly they came down in great caravans – it was said in thousands – to the coast, and there settled and cultivated for two or three months before returning to their own shambas in Unyamwezi when the rains fell there in November and December.' (See also Smith, A. 1963, p.266.)
5. Oliver, R. (1963). Discernable Developments in the Interior; c.1500–1840. pp.169–211. In: *History of East Africa.* Ed. Oliver, R. & Mathew, G. Clarendon, Oxford.
6. ibid. pp.208–210.
7. Brelsford, W.V. (1956). *The Tribes of Northern Rhodesia.* Government Printer, Lusaka.
8. Fagan, B.M. (1964). Iron Age Peoples in Northern Rhodesia. p.461. *Northern Rhodesia Journal, 5*:(v).
9. Rawstorne, C.H. (1955). Livingstone in the Luwingu District. *Northern Rhodesia Journal, 2*:(vi); p.59, said: 'He found the natives in a most terrified state. The Bemba under Chitoka, from the east had fiercely attacked the Bisa on the north side of the lake [Bangweulu] a year or two previously, and the trail of deserted country with ruined villages through which he passed bore testimony to the ferocity of the onslaught. Again, Livingstone's necessary but unfortunate association with the slavers of Mweru, awakened every suspicion in the native mind. Wherever he went, the villagers closed their stockades to him and only with the greatest reluctance assisted him.'
   It seems probable these circumstances, causing lack of food and tedious delay, hastened Livingstone's death.
10. Coupland, R. (1939). *The Exploitation of East Africa: 1856–1890*, pp.1–7. Faber & Faber, London.
11. Smith (1963) p.268.
12. Hore, E.C. (1892). *Tanganyika: Eleven Years in Central Africa.* Stanford, London.
13. Swann, A.J. (1910). *Fighting the Slave Hunters in Central Africa.* Frank Cass, London.
14. Hore (1892), p.223.
15. Hore (1892), p.129.
16. Hore (1892), p.223.
17. The critical difference in effectiveness of 'visitors' as opposed to 'residents' is one mentioned elsewhere (e.g., Chapter 5). Time spent with the people of the country, as against accomplishing pre-determined goals on a short visit, is not wasted.
18. Now, 130 years later, cooperation to manage lake resources is needed more than ever. The UN Food & Agriculture Organisation has suggested rationales and legal frameworks whereby the four countries sharing Lake Tanganyika could cooperate in its development.
   (doc. GCP/RAF/271/FIN, FAO, Rome.)
19. Moir, F.L. (1923). *After Livingstone: An African Trade Romance.* Hodder & Stroughton, London.
20. Hore (1892), p.296.
21. Hore, E.C. (1882). On the Twelve Tribes of Tanganyika. *Journal of the Anthropological Institute of Great Britain and Ireland, XII*: 2–21.
22. Hore (1892) wrote: 'I have many times sailed along and visited the tribes living on the 1000 miles of shore of Tanganyika, and three several times have lived for two

years at different places there in the process of making first acquaintance with those natives and building stations in their countries. Over and again I have been surrounded by leveled spears and drawn bows, whence, if I hastily passed on or returned, I should but have to report of the "savage opposition" of those tribes; but waiting to investigate and explain, or trusting to the friendly results of their investigation, I have lived to prove that their action was but courageously defensive, and to report that, in all my voyages and travels in Central Africa, I have slain no man, nor received mark or wound from African weapon or missile.'

23. Thompson, J. (1881). *To the Central African Lakes and Back*, pp.201–202. Sampson Low, London.
24. Swann (1910), p.255.
25. The story of the Cape to Cairo telegraph, which ultimately reached Ujiji, is told by S.R. Denny in the *Northern Rhodesia Journal*, (1962), *5*(1): 39–43.
26. Grogan, E.S. & Sharp, A.H. (1900). *From the Cape to Cairo.* Nelson, London.

10

Heart of Darkness

The bicentenary of the abolition of the West African slave trade was celebrated in 2007. Little mention was made of the fact that the trade continued long afterwards. Following the Abolition Bill came an Emancipation Bill in 1833 to free all slaves still held. But as the Atlantic trade declined, another slave trade expanded in East and Central Africa. It had existed on that coast for centuries, but in the 1850s it grew rapidly. Slaves were exported to Arab countries and as far as Persia. Another slave trade up the Nile drew slaves mainly from the Sudan. Great numbers of Africans were involved and slaving methods devastated populations over vast areas. An abolition agreement was signed by the Sultan of Zanzibar in 1873 under political pressure and a British naval blockade, but more than two decades were to pass before the trade could be said to have died out in East Africa.

It is worth remembering the historic anti-slaving movement in a little detail. Its roots were in the religious revival of the latter eighteenth century which preached personal conscience, Christian conversion and salvation. All men were seen as having individual value. To John Wesley, the Methodist, the slave trade was 'execrable villiany'. In 1787 a Society for the Abolition of Slavery was formed by influential philanthropists, and in it a Christian group, the so-called 'Clapham Sect', were very active; Wilberforce, McCauley, Buxton and others of similar mind, carried through the campaigns for Abolition and Emancipation.

Associated with the same religious ideas, a wave of missionaries went out from the early 1800s, chiefly to India. This movement to bring Christianity was different from all such previous endeavours, because it combined with it strong beliefs in current values of western civilisation – work, clothes and confidence in the modern. Antagonism grew between, on the one hand, missionaries and administrators, and on the other, populations that held to ancient cultures and religious practices. The eventual outcome was the Indian Mutiny of 1857, entailing a savage struggle and terrible reprisals. The project to evangelise and modernise had gone badly wrong, and officials came to believe that direct interference in native customs was unwise and led to strife. Thus, in 1858, Queen Victoria in a proclamation renounced 'right or desire to impose our convictions on any of our subjects'. The East India Company was wound up, and thereafter the Crown ruled through a Viceroy. Officials of the Government of India administered largely with, rather than against, indigenous traditions.

The British had learned a bitter lesson; missionary influence was much diminished. The experience deeply affected British Foreign policy when it came to acquiring land and establishing 'colonies' in Africa. By the 1870s sufficient of the interior of East and Central Africa had been described by explorers to attract a train of missionaries. These held much the same convictions as earlier ones in India, that gospel evangelism should help spread western civilisation and commerce. The agenda of Livingstone's second Zambezi expedition (1858–64) included finding routes along which commerce could flow, and places where Europeans could settle (see the previous chapter). However, experience had been disappointing, and the Foreign Office's attitude against colonising Africa hardened. Livingstone himself came to the view that colonising in the usual sense of the term was not feasible in tropical Africa.[1]

Furthermore, little evidence was produced by other explorers of natural resources to exploit, or productive populations with whom to trade.[2] This only reinforced the reluctance of H.M. Government to acquire land in East Africa, although several opportunities (in the shape of initiatives by the Sultan) arose. But popular pressure by the anti-slavery movement maintained the presence of a consul in Zanzibar. John Kirk was there longest, his great purpose being to negotiate the ending of the slave trade, which he did in 1873. However, slaves were still kept at the Coast and in Zanzibar, and minor subsequent attempts to continue the trade indicated it would erupt again unless foreign opposition stayed firm. Marking the last international effort to end the slave trade was the Brussels Act of 1890. At the suggestion of the British government, King Leopold arranged a meeting the outcome of which was an agreement by seventeen countries (including the USA) to make all efforts to finally extirpate slavery everywhere in Africa. Fittingly, Kirk assisted at the conference.[3]

Conrad's classic book *Heart of Darkness*[4] has provided perhaps the most widespread mental picture of plantation slave labour in Africa. It was based, supposedly, on his own observations in the Congo (he worked on a steamer on the Congo River in the late 1890s). Nevertheless, the book has often figured, perhaps still does, in university literary curricula and its images remain in the popular imagination, suggesting they are still current. (For example, only several years ago a well-known travel writer took the book to read on a trip through Africa.)[5] Another old but formative impression on the public was the scarifying report by Roger Casement, a British Consul to the Congo.[6] His meeting with Conrad is believed to have helped provide inspiration for *Heart of Darkness*.

The important point is that the book was written in 1899, and Casement's report in 1903. They may well have reflected conditions about the turn of the century, but things changed substantially afterwards (the Belgian government took over officially in 1908). Slavery was put down by wars with the Arabs, and law and order with a countrywide administration were set up.[7] This is rarely mentioned now. Ironically, since 1960 the Congo (Democratic Republic) has returned to a state of chaos and cruelty not much different from that portrayed in Conrad's book.

Raiding between tribes and the taking of slaves was an age-old way of life. However slaves were not only the object or by-product of war, nor was taking slaves practised only by aggressive tribes. In times of hardship and famine the practice of selling children was not uncommon. Conversely, the adoption of captured children was carried out by some tribes to recruit their strength.[8] Even relatively weak tribes, like the Walungu at the south of Tanganyika, went in for slaving as opportunity offered.[9] The slave trade, as such, depended on captives being sought as a commodity, an article of exchange, on a large scale. Human beings were indeed one of the few tradeable products from the interior that could be sold at the coast along with portable commodities, like ivory, wax and copper, in exchange for goods like cotton, beads and iron hardware.

Trade in humans grew with a rise in market demand at the coast, encouraging Arab and mixed-race (Swahili) traders to push inland to buy for themselves (see the previous chapter). The trade varied with price fluctuations in other commodities,[10] and it varied territorially in that more slaves went out by the southern (Kilwa) route, and more ivory by the northern routes (Ujiji and Tabora).

Official abolition by the Sultan in 1873, and the forbidding of slave caravans on land in 1875, restricted the flow of slaves overseas. Dhows leaving the East African coast had to run the gauntlet of British naval blockade. For an interim phase of several years, slavers sought desperately to run the blockade or to seek markets along the coast where the holding of slaves was still legal. This period of restriction of export by sea and suppression on land was a time when continuous diplomatic pressure was needed upon the Sultan and his associates. It was applied by the consul at Zanzibar, Sir John Kirk. A strange personal relationship developed between the two men, in which friendship and trust played a large part despite their battle of wills (see Note 3).

Slaving surely represented the chief evil of the times. But the Christian missions of the interior depended to a large extent upon a curious relationship between the Arabs and Europeans, involving a deep misapprehension of principle. To the missionary, the treasure of Africa was the intrinsic value of its humanity, not to be measured in material terms. The Arab, in contrast, viewed indigenous pagan humanity as just a commodity whose value, like ivory and gunpowder, was determined in market terms. The slave trade was part of their business and living; and slave raiding a long-standing custom only promoted and extended by their trade. These were irreconcilable viewpoints.

Paradoxically, however, mutual admiration and friendship between individuals was common on both sides (e.g., 'all the explorers testify to a sympathy and helpfulness which was more than formal').[11] At the top level, friendship between the Sultan and Kirk was maintained over 12 years. Similarly, at Tanganyika, good relations continued between the merchant princes of slaving, such as Tippu Tib and Rumaliza, and the missionaries.[12] In the journals of the latter and of explorers, goodwill with individual Arabs is often mentioned, in terms like 'warm and generous hospitality'. Livingstone was nursed by them in serious illness, and doubtless on several occasions Arab protection saved the lives of Europeans.[13] Such friendly feeling cannot be explained only by the fact that explorers and missions came bearing introductions from the Sultan. There must also have existed genuine sympathy and liking, despite candid recognition of their differences and frequent protests from the Europeans.

Somehow, the utter callousness to life (the price of every living slave was five, even ten deaths)[14] had to be set beside the need, on the part of missionaries, to coexist. The main paths they had to follow were generally slave routes, frequently in company with Arab caravans for the sake of safety. Letters sent to the coast generally depended on being taken by these caravans. Most ironic of all, the security of isolated missions depended on maintaining stable relationships. Looking back on their first decade of work at Tanganyika, Hore said, 'difficulties with the natives and the Arabs have been entirely avoided by a prudent and conciliatory policy'.[15]

Importantly, up to its suppression, slaving had been essentially a trading system between the coast and interior. Enclaves of settled Arabs held on in trade depots around Tanganyika, chiefly Ujiji, but the market for slaves and ivory was being stifled. Stores of ivory were building up in depots on travel routes. Potentially still very profitable, the trade in its last phase moved westwards across Lake Tanganyika to the Congo basin. Ivory was abundant there, and settled African populations vulnerable to the traders who were by now becoming marauders. The concept of the Congo River as a possible alternative export route to the west coast instead of Zanzibar, was growing in the minds of the merchants; while the Sultan for his part vainly sought ways of keeping trade from the interior still orientated eastwards to Zanzibar.[16]

Markets and profits were not the only factors in the rise and nature of the slave trade. The availability of firearms greatly intensified slaving. Guns and powder imports rose alarmingly between 1860 and 1880,[17] displacing all other goods from the outside world as the most desired trade item. It strengthened tribes already given to raiding, and boosted the trade (enabling, for example, the Nyamwezi near Tanganyika and the Yao around Nyasa to become major slavers).

The most brutal decade was the last, 1880–90. Scattered armed bands preying upon settled communities destabilised and ruined wide regions – especially in the Congo. Slaving had changed in nature, from a trading system to predatory pillage. Goods of various kinds and guns still came up from the east coast and across Lake Tanganyika. However, conditions now emerged where slaves were employed to cultivate large plantations in the interior owned by Arabs and native warlords from the slaving tribes. These attracted to themselves irregular armed militias, which lived by destruction and tyranny,[18] causing even more mortality and misery than the trade itself had done.

In summary, the slave trade in East and Central Africa grew from the first decades of the century up to the mid-1870s. Action by Britain then halted it at the coast. In a final phase, ivory trading and slaving, especially the use of slaves on plantations, continued along with subjugation and pillage. It was worst in the Congo. An end came in the 1890s when encroaching Belgian forces from the west and Germans from the east, crushed the Arabs in their main centres. But chaos by armed militias or guerillas continued long after. These are the bare bones of a process observed and detailed by explorers and missionaries entering the region in the same period, who had of course to live with existing conditions.

Some salient accounts emerged. An instance is Livingstone's exploration of Manyema (Upper Congo) in 1869–71 (see Figure 9), accompanying the furthest commercial penetration to the west by the Arabs to that time.[19] Starting on the west shore of Tanganyika, his trip into Manyema took more than two years and was, he thought, a complete waste of time and effort. He had failed to reach his geographic objective, and endured long forced delays and illnesses. As it turned out, his letters about this last phase of slaving and its character were dramatically to influence world opinion; especially his description of the massacre at Nyangwe on 15 July 1871. Although frightful in itself (hundreds shot and villages burned), the Nyangwe event was only one of many such; but Livingstone's impassioned reporting conveyed the scene vividly.[20] He had established friendly relations with local Africans over the months he stayed there, and in particular enjoyed walking around the market, a centre of activity in a populous region. His description of market days, the give and take of bargaining and cheerful chaffing between people, depicted human behaviour of a sort typical in a market-place anywhere in the world. In shocking contrast, therefore, was the inhumanity of the massacre by armed ruffian followers of the Arabs. Livingstone described the helpless panic and sequel of burning and looting. Although he was used to seeing cruelty, the effect of this occasion upon him was deep.

Other travellers recounted similar scenes in the Upper Congo in the 1880s (e.g., Stanley[21] and Von Wissmann[22]), repeating the themes of relentless pillage and the helplessness of settled cultivators faced with mobile bandits bearing guns. Both these travellers found places they had previously known as peaceful villages turned into derelict ruins.

An outstanding Arab personality dominated the Congo through the 1870s and 1880s; Muhammad bin Hamid known generally as Tippu Tib. He came from a family working on the central route through Unyanyembe. Around the time Livingstone was trying to get to the Upper Congo, Tippu was busy establishing himself near the southwest end of Tanganyika. He was bent on obtaining political power as a means of acquiring wealth and ivory. Starting in Katanga he moved north, subjugating tribes with fire and terror. Over time he came to exercise wide authority, levying taxes, dominating trade, and commanding armed militias through subordinates. Characteristically, it was a system of weak control ('the normal Arab situation')[23] depending on unruly mobs of armed raiders – Swahilis, freed slaves, any kind of bandit attracted by plunder – acting at the periphery to extend Tippu's empire. In his time, over 20 years, he came effectively to control large areas of the Congo Basin, largely forested and well populated, which formerly had remained difficult of access to outsiders. The procedure of gradual subjugation would indicate it was a deliberate regime, an effective way to get ivory and, where and when required, slaves from the Congo.

What Livingstone had seen was but the beginning. Tippu sent occasional huge caravans bearing Congo ivory to the Zanzibar coast and became wealthy.[24] His notorious business empire extended far beyond the west shore of Tanganyika and his lines of communication crossed the lake.[25] The marauding activities of Tippu and his contemporaries (the latter continuing well into the 1890s) left the Congo Basin and Katanga ravaged and disturbed. King Leopold II is commonly blamed for the continuance of disorder and exploitation at the turn of the century. (This infamous epoch is summarised in Reference 7.)

In the twentieth century we were more than ever aware of destruction wrought by armed militias in Africa. Here is a quotation from IANSA (International Action Network on Small Arms); September 2007:

> Illegal firearms pose a major threat to public safety throughout Central and East Africa, encouraging crime and fuelling and prolonging conflict. Small arms and light weapons such as assault rifles are especially suited to the irregular warfare that is still widespread in the region because they are cheap, easy to use, widely available and durable. Bladed weapons like machetes have also been widely used in conflicts in Rwanda and Burundi ... Millions of lives have already been lost in the region, and the supply of arms to both governments and rebel groups continues to grow... In [the year] 2000, 10 countries signed the Nairobi Declaration on Small Arms and Light Weapons, and in 2002 the East Africa Police Chiefs Committee was formed. The Committee has set up a programme to register and classify firearms. However, ongoing instability presents major challenges for these and other initiatives.
>
> www.iansa.org/regions/cafrica/cafrica

Disorders from so-called 'rebel' guerilla groups have proliferated in the past half-century. One thinks of the long drawn-out struggles in Mozambique and Angola conducted more by semi-independent bands than by official armies. In the Lake Tanganyika region the Congo is chaotic and Burundi still seriously troubled by 'rebel' groups. Similar problems afflict Somalia, Sudan, Ethiopia, Eritrea, Chad, Cameroon, Central African Republic and Republic of Congo (Congo-Brazzavile) (see Figure 3). Sudan is currently prominent in the media, with over 200,000 citizens killed. International TV portrays gaunt images of the two million refugees in camps. The usual story is of sudden attack by an armed group on an isolated village. Survivors flee their land and need immediate help. Humanitarian relief measures, such as camps with food and facilities, are provided by international organisations until, hopefully, government can function and keep law and order. Meanwhile the militias must somehow be kept in check by UN 'peacekeepers' (of which, according to current media reports, there are 17,000 in the Congo alone).

The muskets and simple rifles of Tippu's time are replaced by AK-47s, but what has not changed is the extreme vulnerability of populations living by subsistence agriculture. This integral part of the problem is not well understood in Western societies. If one walks into a village in countries such as those mentioned above, in parts where people live in a more or less traditional way remote from modern communications and cities, one quickly notices an object which is the container in which grain is stored (and perhaps other food). It may be a mud-plastered framework or basket, thatched and mounted clear of the ground or suspended high in a tree. At any rate, it is some proven way of storing next year's seed against the ravages of insects, rodents and damp. The store is very precious, along with sure tenure of cultivable land and water supply. If a community is suddenly driven off by guerillas, their life quickly becomes precarious. Movement to another place friendly and fertile enough for survival may not be possible. So bandits are very bad news. They can plunder and live off scattered villages virtually at will. Villagers may have to put up with much distress before they finally flee.

In 1994 I encountered such people on the border of Malawi and Mozambique. Their numbers were remarkable. The Malawi side of the road running along the border was densely populated, while the other side was utterly deserted – not a person or habitation visible up to the distant horizon. Various goods were being sold at the roadside. I stopped for vegetables, and also saw cans of kerosene, blankets and clothes for sale. These people were some of the 1.1 million who had fled from Mozambique and were crammed for security just over the border of Malawi (itself highly populated). They were being fed by the UN High Commission for Refugees and probably other agencies. The vegetables were grown for sale, and extra aid items like kerosene and blankets sold off for cash. They had fled from soldiers of the 'Renamo' or 'Frelimo' political parties operating in guerilla style, and now were simply surviving as best they could. What remained in my mind, apart from the sheer numbers of humanity, were their stunted physiques and listless behaviour. Young adults were child-sized. Although such people may eventually get repatriated, the drastic effects of displacement must surely last a generation or more.

The Congo is one of the most regressive countries in Africa today. It is among the richest in natural resources, which, paradoxically, has contributed to its socio-political problems.[26] Of the different provinces, perhaps Kivu in the northeast has been most ruinously ravaged over the past several decades – through eruptions of militias and refugees from Rwanda and Burundi.

Kivu Province is relatively small with a lovely deep clear lake. It was still fairly peaceful in the 1970s when I lived in Bujumbura. At one time, Bukavu

Institute for Scientific Research in Central Africa, Lwiro, Kivu (in 1974)

Captive mountain gorilla at the Lwiro institute

at the south of Lake Kivu and Goma at its north were well-known tourist resorts. The cool climate and beauty attracted visitors. At the north the active Virungu volcanoes tower dramatically. High, forested country, famous for animal and plant diversity, frames the lake magnificently.

I went there occasionally for peace and quietness, staying at a splendidly situated centre for biological research, Lwiro. It was appealing for its contrast to the post-emergency atmosphere existing at the time in Burundi. The institute building was in dazzling contrast to our utility laboratories in the project at Bujumbura, with its solid and graceful masonry and clay-tiled roofs. Within were gleaming stone floors, and dark native hardwoods formed immense ceiling beams and wall panelling. Lwiro had the ambience of old tradition, and might have been a palazzo at Lake Maggiore. Another world.

A little zoo outside held remaining captive animals. Although well tended, they had an air of redundancy. Some unfortunate birds had grown too large for their cages, and the mammals, especially monkeys and chimps, looked dull. The forests nearby are among the last habitats of mountain gorillas, and one old fellow in solitary confinement in a high-walled enclosure looked dispirited.

Similarly, the library felt deserted; empty shelves and no journals. One shelf held Africana, valuable historical works (some first editions) and biological publications – a reminder of the admirable research once done here on Lakes Tanganyika and Kivu. Clearly nothing much was happening now. The neglected institute seemed a metaphor for the country itself, rich in promise but badly in need of government.

Notes and references

1. Coupland, R. (1939). *The Exploitation of East Africa, 1856–1890.* Faber & Faber, London. Page 104 quotes from Livingstone: 'The idea of a colony in Africa, as the term "colony" is usually used, cannot be entertained.'
2. For example, Thompson, J. (1881). *To the Central African Lakes and Back.* Sampson Low, London.
3. Coupland (1939).
4. Conrad, J. (1899). *Heart of Darkness.* Blackwood's Edinburgh Magazine (recently republished in Penguin Classics).
5. Theroux, P. (2003). *Dark Star Safari.* Penguin, London.
6. Casement, R. (1903). *Report on the Congo Free State.* Report to the Foreign Office, London, December 1903.
7. The following is quoted from the review by W.V. Brelsford (in *Northern Rhodesia Journal*, No.2, Vol.5, 1962) of the book *King Leopold's Congo* by Ruth Slade (Oxford University Press 1962): '[Leopold] was stirred by the discoveries of Stanley in the Congo Basin but the Belgian Government made it clear that it would have nothing to do with gaining a colony. So Leopold carried on alone spending his own fortune on the project, sending out emissaries, particularly Stanley, to make treaties with chiefs. He formed the Association Internationale du Congo, and at the Berlin Conference of 1884-85 he managed to persuade the rival powers of Portugal, France and Germany that the Association was "a small, philanthropic, and innocuous non-political organisation which aimed at suppressing the slave trade and introducing legitimate commerce into the Congo Basin, while strongly supporting the principles of free trade". Leopold thus became individual ruler of the Congo, a vast domain in which he never set foot. It is true that he encouraged Christian missions, naturally preferring Catholics, and he stopped slaving. The Arabs were strongly entrenched and at first had to be conciliated, the infamous

Tippu Tib being made State Governor at Stanley Falls. But eventually they were driven out, one group under Chiwala settling close to what is now Ndola [in Zambia]. But the King had to recoup some of the fortune he had lost and the administration he had set up was concerned mainly with forcing labour into development projects in gathering wild rubber and ivory, the poorly paid officials getting a percentage on what they obtained. Scandals were inevitable and Britain took the lead in whipping up public opinion. It was acknowledged that the King had wished nothing more than to recoup his losses and he sincerely believed that he was opening up the Congo for the good of Belgium. He had left the Congo to Belgium in his will. By the 1890s, Leopold was in serious financial difficulties because the administration of the huge colony was costing too much. He borrowed money from the Belgian Government, but in 1894 that government got wind of a scheme under which Leopold was to sell land to a British syndicate. This stirred the Belgian Government far more than had the reports of atrocities committed during the collection of rubber and ivory, and steps were begun to take over the Congo from Leopold. They were completed in 1908.'

(See also Gore-Brown on the Anglo-Belgian Boundary Commission: Note 3 in Chapter 7.)

8. Smith, A. (1963). The Southern Section of the Interior (1840–1884), p.276. In: *History of East Africa.* Eds. Oliver, R. & E.Mathew. Clarendon Press, Oxford.
9. Swann, A.J. (1910). *Fighting the Slave Hunters in Central Africa.* Frank Cass, London.
10. Smith (1963), p.275–276.
11. Coupland (1939).
12. Examples are Livingstone and Mohammad bin Gharib, Burton and Snay bin Amir, Stanley and Tippu Tib, Cameron and Jumah Merikani, Sharpe and Abdullah bin Suleiman.
13. Swann, A.J. (1910), p.172.
14. Coupland (1939), p.140.
15. Hore, E.C. (1892). *Tanganyika: Eleven Years in Central Africa.* Stanford, London.
16. Coupland (1939).
17. Smith (1963), pp. 276–77; 294.
18. Smith (1963), ibid.
19. Coupland (1947), p.78.
20. Coupland (1947), pp. 120–127.
21. Stanley (1885). *The Congo and the Founding of its Free State.* London.
22. Von Wissmann, L. (1891). *My Second Journey Through Equatorial Africa from the Congo to the Zambesi. London* (trans. A. Bergmann), pp.183–210.
23. Bennett, N.R. (1969). *New Introduction,* p.xxviii in Swann (1910), 2nd edition (1969).
24. Smith (1963), p.274.
25. Trade around the shores of Lake Tanganyika itself seems to have been conducted by a relatively small number of Arabs and Swahilis at trading posts or depots, notably Ujiji, headed by Mwinyi Kheri and Rumaliza the friend of Alfred Swann. By Tippu's own account, he held the greatest power among the Arabs and their Swahili and African followers ('All authority was mine ... I was really the Paramount Chief'). See Bennett's New Introduction in the second edition (1969) of Swann (1910).
26. Guest, R. (2004). *The Shackled Continent.* MacMillan, London.

11

If You Fight for Your Country

"If you fight for your country, even if you die, your sons will remember your name"

Rudyard Kipling [Inscription on the Askari Monument, Dar es Salaam]

'The Germans surrendered just over there, about 200 yards to the right of the post-office,' I was told by an elderly inhabitant of Abercorn. It was the place where the official surrender by General von Lettow-Vorbeck brought to an end the first Great War in East Africa (1914–18). It was a dramatic scene on an unmarked historic spot as on 25 November 1918 von Lettow paraded the remnant of his little army, the Schutztruppe, and formally capitulated.[1] Ironically the Germans had attacked Abercorn early in the war, but were driven off. In the following four years they led the British and Belgian forces a merry dance all over East Africa in a classic guerilla war. In fact the Germans did not lose the campaign and remained a fighting force to the end. The armistice signed in Europe on 11 November 1918 left them no choice but to give in.

I encountered an echo of the East Africa Campaign in my own country, Ireland, in 1962. Going with my father-in-law to see his auctioneer in a small country town, I was introduced as 'being on holiday from Lake Tanganyika'. The old man gave me his full attention: 'Did you ever hear tell of the battle for Lake Tanganyika?' he asked. 'Well, I was there and took part in it.' Delighted to have a listener, he swept aside all other business (a good story is valued in a small town) and launched on a yarn almost beyond imagination.

He'd been a member of the 'highly secret naval mission' sent to Africa in 1915 to fight the Germans on Lake Tanganyika. They shipped two 40-foot wooden boats to Cape Town, and from there went by rail to the Congo. Then the boats had to be manhandled over tracks through forests, along rivers and, on a final scrap of railway, reached Tanganyika. Little was said by the old auctioneer of the battle itself, but he went on at length about the Herculean task of transporting the boats over the natural terrain. It involved bush clearing, building bridges, hauling with steam traction engines and oxen and using pulleys and levers. What remained in his mind were these man-handling operations and the overcoming of almost insuperable logistics. 'It was like the building of the pyramids,' he concluded. The story of the naval part of the campaign on Lake Tanganyika has been told in several publications.[2]

A friend of my father had been in the South African brigade, and I questioned him about the war. He would say little but 'foot-slogging – I must have walked everywhere in East Africa; often on short rations'. Then in Burundi, in the 1970s, I questioned an African who had been an *askari* (soldier) on the German side. A genial old man with a fringing white beard and Muslim dress, he lived in the *quartier asiatique* in Bujumbura. His replies were similar – 'much marching' – mentioning places across the region. He took great pleasure in recollection, repeating especially that he had received a pension 'all these years'. His happy glow from former camaraderie was made brighter by the pension. In fact these three survivors had little to say about actual warfare, remembering instead the hard conditions and heavy exertions.

Few people now know much about the 1914–18 campaign in East Africa. It is an obscure episode of history. Even at the time it was remote to people in Europe. In Africa there was no direct cause for fighting and the conflict in Europe was not well understood. The soldiers simply fought for their country, as in all nations. Yet the catastrophe that spilled over from Europe profoundly transformed East Africa, affecting the entire Great Lakes region. Soldiers and carriers came to the war area from as far as Uganda and South Africa, from Congo and Malawi. Casualties from fighting and disease were severe. The countries of Tanzania and Mozambique were ravaged by guerilla warfare, and local inhabitants put to flight.

In Africa the governments (more accurately, civil administrations) directly involved took a regional viewpoint, and when war was declared in Europe they were loath to start hostilities; specifically, German East Africa (Tanzania, Burundi, Rwanda), the Belgian Congo, and British East and Central Africa (Kenya, Uganda and Rhodesia). The Governor of German East Africa (GEA), Heinrich Schnee, ordered neutrality, supported by the Treaty between Germany, France, Belgium and Britain of 1885 (the so-called Congo Act, which set up a free-trade zone between the colonies). It had been agreed that in the event of war elsewhere they would remain neutral.

Schnee was a liberal committed to ongoing programmes of education, health and agriculture, and he desired progress to continue.[3] In establishing central government in GEA there had been two rebellions (the Ambushiri revolt in 1888 and the Maji maji rebellion in 1905), but a reformed administration strongly financed by Germany had, since 1907, provided a model of colonial development. On Lake Tanganyika, for example, a steamship for trade and passengers was brought there as early as 1900 (the *Hedwig von Wissman*), and a rail line over 1,000 km, from Dar-es-Salaam to the lake, was completed by 1914. In Schnee's view there was everything to lose by joining in the war. Similarly in the Congo, the Belgian reformed regime after 1908 was making progress with a new system of government and setting up economic infrastructure. In British East Africa the Governor stated early on that 'Kenya had no interest in the present war.'

Alas, world-scale issues spread to East Africa as the great powers stumbled into war. Friction occurred between civil and military authorities in GEA, but Berlin supported the military because it was realised German forces could harry the British at a sensitive point, the Mombasa–Uganda railway. Also, naval raids could be mounted from the sea coast upon Indian Ocean routes. Germany felt that despite being surrounded by hostile countries, their forces in East Africa had the advantages of being largely self-supporting and having good internal communications, whereas transport and supply would pose great difficulties for opposing armies.

Vitally, Lake Tanganyika was a substantial frontier barrier in the west of GEA (see Figure 3). Troops could be moved rapidly along its shores – provided Germany controlled the lake. While the country could be blockaded along its Indian Ocean coastline, British and Belgian forces could not advance to occupy GEA while Germany dominated Lake Tanganyika. The lake therefore became of major strategic importance. For over a year and a half British and Belgian land forces were effectively stalled. Hence the initiative to put British gunboats on the lake.

Just before the war (31 July 1914), Governor Schnee officially declared his ports to be 'open'. In conformity the warship *Konigsberg* left its base in Dar-es-Salaam. However, soon after (6 August), this cruiser captured a British merchant vessel at sea, and in reprisal British ships bombarded Dar-es-Salaam. Thus the war in Africa began.[4] Two brigades of the British Indian Army attempted to land at Tanga and were disastrously defeated. When the *Konigsberg* went into the Rufigi delta south of Tanga to refit, it was destroyed there by the British navy.

Feeling themselves weak in relation to neighbouring countries, the Germans decided to attack aggressively.[5] Initially, most fighting was located north of Mount Kilimanjaro, focused on the Uganda railway just over the border. On Lake Tanganyika the Belgian shores were shelled by two German gunboats, *Hedwig von Wissmann* and *Kingani*, supplemented by heavy guns

German gunboat *Kingani*, rechristened *Fifi*

The *Gotzen*, rechristened *Liemba*

mounted on a floating platform. Shore parties made sorties. These belligerent activities continued up to the end of 1915. One raid into the British zone at the south shelled and destroyed the mission vessel *Good News* (see Part II, Chapter 9 and 11) and another ship, *Cecil Rhodes*.[6] On the Congo coast the Germans put the Belgian ship *Alexandre Delcommune* out of action.

Such acts decisively ended any question of neutrality by the Congo. While the Belgians prepared to respond (they had imported the parts of a steamer *Baron Dhanis*, but needed respite from German attacks to construct it at the lake) the plan was hatched to bring two small navy boats out from England. It took all of 1915 to get them there. Meanwhile, the Germans added a new big ship (67metres) to their force – the intended passenger and freight steamer *Gotzen* (see also next chapter). It was readied at Kigoma by mid-1915 and given formidable armament.

The two newly arrived British boats had the good fortune to meet the two German gunboats one at a time. On December 26, Boxing Day, they captured the *Kingani*. Mounting a heavy 12-pounder gun on it, they sank the *Wissmann* shortly after. The British then prudently avoided action against the heavily armed *Gotzen*, but their success had given confidence for Allied land advances to proceed.

In February 1916 British forces, mainly South Africans, under the allied commander General Smuts, attacked from Kenya, and in April Belgian armies encircled the north of Lake Tanganyika, sweeping the Germans from Rwanda and Burundi. When Kigoma was captured in July, the trapped *Gotzen* was scuttled at the mouth of the Malagarazi River (see Figure 6). Thereafter, as the Germans retreated to the south, the lake played a lesser part in the war.

A thrust northeastwards from Abercorn by the Kings' African Rifles and Rhodesians aimed to cut off the German retreat.[7] However, von Lettow's companies passed through the thinly spread Allied lines. They carried on the rest of the war guerilla-style, penetrating into Mozambique (although one company dodged back north to the Kenya border causing confusion among the Allies for many months). Eventually the main German force turned west into Northern Rhodesia (Zambia), and their long peregrinations came to an end there.

This outline of events only barely conveys a complex campaign, but something of its nature might be imagined from the following: Unlike the massed forces in Europe, armies were dispersed over wide stretches of country; artillery was not as important, and generals led from the front. At the beginning only small forces existed to cope with ordinary policing and border control. The British had dispersed units of Kings African Rifles in Kenya and Nyasaland; Belgium had units of *askaris* and gendarmerie in Congo and in Rwanda-Urundi around Lake Kivu. The best integrated and trained were the Germans, who had 14 independent field companies, but in fact this force was also small – around 250 Germans and 2,500 African *askaris* in total – plus their aggressive little navy on Lake Tanganyika. After several pitched battles near the Kenya-GEA border, the German commander realised that his role was to conduct a troublesome guerilla war of tip-and-run, avoiding battles that might cause unaffordable casualties. His prime objective must be to attract the largest possible number of allied soldiers and resources to this sphere of the war, diverting them from Europe. He certainly succeeded in this.[8] Logistical problems of transport and supply multiplied for the Allies as their armies increased, whereas the Germans fought a mobile war, launching surprise attacks with independent companies then disappearing into the bush.

At first, the British did not do well (except on Lake Tanganyika), but reinforcements from South Africa in 1916 turned the tide of war. It was a nice irony that the distinguished Afrikaner generals Smuts and Van Deventer, who had given the British such a hard time as guerilla fighters in the Boer War, should have been put in charge against the German force. The hunted had become the hunters. But Von Lettow proved that in the East African bush he was even more skilled in irregular warfare than they. As well as problems of terrain, Allied difficulties were chiefly caused by tropical diseases. In the main advance across GEA, Europeans were shown clearly to be more vulnerable than the African soldiers to heat exhaustion and disease, particularly malaria. (For every European battle casualty about twelve were incapacitated by disease.) Some idea of the scale of the war and of the disparity between the two armies are given by the following: 34,000 allied troops, supported by 71,000 carriers were in the field at the end of the war. On the German side, those who surrendered in November 1918 were: 155 German soldiers, 1,168 *askaris*, 2,000 carriers and 1,101 camp followers.[8]

Success was largely dependent on morale.[9] Among British and South African troops morale was seriously strained by the often futile hunt for an elusive enemy and incessant marching over vast and difficult country (there was little transport). Conditions were made worse by prevalent sickness, danger of ambush, and at times shortage of food supplies. For the Germans, constantly on the run, the circumstances would have been thought particularly hard, and it is a remarkable tribute to their commander, von Lettow, that they fought so well, with loyalty (few deserters) and high morale. The argument has often been made that African soldiers might not have had the motivation of white soldiers, who presumably had some understanding of what it was all about. This misses the point that soldiers of whatever race generally do not fight for lofty ideals, but simply because they are of fighting age and happen to be there. They are driven by excitement, regular food and pay, status, cameraderie and leadership. In Europe, the slogan 'for King and

Country' was used to get men to enlist, but once in uniform other things kept them going. At first, the Allies were reluctant to use African soldiers (the Germans recruited a majority from the start), but after 1916 Africans played the largest role – on the Allied side especially the Kings African Rifles (KAR).

Although fighting was in deadly earnest, it is interesting that traces of old-fashioned chivalry still remained. The 'rules of war' were less ambiguous then. For example, before the British battalions invaded at Tanga, the Royal Navy insisted on warning the enemy of the attack because of a truce the navy had arranged on the coast. Essential surprise was lost; the Germans promptly occupied positions of defence and the attack failed badly. Again, it was the German practice to leave behind prisoners on parole on condition they took no further part in the fighting, or to keep them with the German columns. The commanding officer of the KAR, Colonel Dickinson, was captured and spent a substantial part of the war marching with von Lettow's column. (They became firm friends. On the day of the surrender, von Lettow was invited to dine with British officers but he refused, preferring the company of Dickinson.)

Mutual admiration and respect was common on both sides; for example, when the German commander was awarded a high military decoration by the Kaiser, the news was conveyed to him in a personal letter of congratulation from General Smuts. Years later, after the Second World War, they renewed contact. Smuts visited von Lettow in Hamburg in 1951, and arranged for him to be given an honour parade in East Africa by his former African troops and by officers of the King's African Rifles.[10] It is interesting now to remember this strange mixture of mutual esteem and shared 'civilised' code of honour, existing along with the contingency to make war. At the beginning of the twentieth century many believed wars between civilised nations were a thing of the past. In the end, the cause of civilisation in Africa was not served by the war.

Who won the campaign? The Allies finally occupied the Germans' land, and Belgium secured its chief aim of controlling Lake Tanganyika and Rwanda-Urundi. The German army, never much bigger than it was at the beginning, was not exactly at the end of its tether when it had to give in. In fact, by heading latterly in a westerly direction it raised fears in the Congo for the security of the Katanga mines. Von Lettow had succeeded in his war objective. He could never have hoped to repel his enemies from the country, but his little force tied down great numbers of them. At sea, the Germans claimed 25 British ships in total were involved in the elimination of the *Konigsberg*.

As to the future, it seems von Lettow was encouraged, by his conversations with English officers after his capture, to hope that Germany might be allowed to retain its East African possessions.[11] However, the Treaty of Versailles and subsequent decisions of the League of Nations led to a Mandate being given in 1922 to Britain to govern what is now Tanzania, and Belgium was assigned Rwanda-Urundi. Heinrich Schnee, overruled by his military arm, tagged along with von Lettow and the Schutzruppe to the end, though continuing to insist on his official title of Commander-in-Chief. After the war he vigorously but vainly argued the case for Germany remaining in Africa, but at Versailles the victors denigrated German colonial methods and took away their colonies.[12]

In military terms, with its historic vocabulary of 'splendid victories' and 'strategic withdrawals' (not to mention current idiocies like 'friendly fire'), the struggle in East Africa has been called 'a classic campaign'.[3] It was one of the first guerilla wars using modern weapons but it was, as are all wars, a humanitarian disaster. If Europe had not been preoccupied with its own enormous losses, events in East Africa would have received far more attention. Instead it was just a 'sideshow'. But the costs had indeed been high, in terms of lives lost and social disruption. Columns of soldiers and carriers moving through the country destroyed the food stocks of inhabitants. People were traumatised and displaced. The war touched not only German-held territory, but also much wider regions since carriers had been engaged from peripheral countries. Casualties among the carriers from disease and distress were never fully known. After the war epidemics of disease, especially Spanish flu, spread by returning soldiers and their followers, took an even greater toll.

In Africa the war must have happened like a great calamity. After the fighting, mortality, disease, displacement and changes of government, the returned Africans simply went back to ordinary traditional life. One would have expected an indelible memory among old people, with some echo being passed to the young. But half a century or so later I did not find much trace of abiding memory around Lake Tanganyika. Indeed, it was difficult to get any response to my questions. Occasionally, someone would recall that white men had fought with each other, there had been much death, but otherwise no details seemed to be remembered. A few old individuals recalled some local unimportant incident associated with the war. But the overall picture did not seem to have entered oral tradition or folklore, and its wider significance outside village life was certainly not understood. It appeared to have been just another fortuitous happening, like an epidemic without cause or explanation. Bearing in mind the great effort and loss of life, failure to find traces was disheartening.

Nevertheless, from a broad perspective there was a positive outcome. A new set of attitudes towards colonies evolved from the war and peace settlement. In the process, the purposes of colonialism had been internationally defined, standards were set and distant objectives acknowledged. They were embodied in a set of wide-ranging principles for colonial government in Africa.

Coupland[13] summarised the position:

> 'Germany had staked her colonial possessions on the war and lost them. With violence and bloodshed, that British occupation of all mid-East Africa had come about which could have happened forty years earlier without a quarrel or a shot. But its meaning now was different. By 1922 a more fundamental change had occurred in relations between Europe and East Africa than a change of flags. The future of East Africa had been at last identified with the future of the East Africans. [Before the 1880s] the dominant motive of British policy had been to help those helpless people; but it had been, so to speak, a negative motive – to save them and their country from destruction by the Slave Trade – and in the years of the Scramble it had been overlaid by other motives, economic, political, strategic. Between 1890 and 1914, however, it had become dominant once more, and now it was positive. The occupation of the interior had involved the government of its inhabitants, and it had been recognised that the primary purpose of that government, as of all government in theory, was to promote the welfare of the governed. By 1914 the old school of 'imperialism', which thought in terms of ruling and subject races and regarded tropical colonies as possessions, property, estates to be exploited by their owners, was already out of date; ... They [the League of Nations] were pledged, as the Mandate requires, 'to promote to the utmost the material and moral well-being and the social progress of its inhabitants' and to help them, as the Covenant implies, in course of time 'to stand by themselves in the world'.

Notes and references

1. Gamwell, H. & M. (1961). The History of Abercorn. *Northern Rhodesia Journal, vol.6*, (iv).
2. Tasker, G.H. (1956). Naval Occasions on Lake Tanganyika in the 1914-18 War. *Northern Rhodesia Journal, vol.1*, (iii): 57–68. See also:
   Shankland, P. (1968). *The Phantom Flotilla.* London.

Farwell, B. (1987). *The Great War in Africa.* Viking, London.
Foden, G. (2005). *Mimi and Toutou Go Forth: The bizarre battle of Lake Tanganyika.* Penguin, London.

3. Sibley, J.R. (1973). *Tanganyika Guerrilla.* Pan/Ballantine, London.
4. Paice, E. (2007). *Tip and Run: The Untold Tragedy of the Great War in Africa.* Weidenfield & Nicholson, London.
5. Bishop, D.L. & Dobold, H. (2003). *Tanganjikasee: A gunboat war in Deutsch-Ostafrika, 1914-1916.* By Jingo. www.geocities.com/cdferree
6. The *Cecil Rhodes* was a 27-metre steel vessel. It was discovered in 1996 by divers at 6 metres depth off the village of Kasakalabwe in the southeast arm of Tanganyika; see Paffen, P. (1996). The wreck of 'Cecil Rhodes'. In: Profiles from the past. *Newsletter 20*, UNDP/FAO Project; Lake Tanganyika Research. FAO, Rome.
   On enquiry, the divers were unable to establish its purpose, but it seems likely that the boat was somehow related to work being done early in the century on the proposed Cape to Cairo telegraph line, which had reached the shores of Lake Tanganyika. It was probably sunk by raiding German gunboats in 1915, along with the ex-mission vessel *Good News.*
7. Langham, R.W. (1954). Memoirs; 1914–18 Campaign. *Northern Rhodesia Journal, vol.2*, (iv): 79–92.
8. Paice (2007).
9. Sibley (1973); Farwell (1987).
10. Listowell, J. (1965). *The Making of Tanganyika.* London.
11. Von Lettow-Vorbeck, P. (1922). *My Reminiscences in East Africa.* Hurst & Blackett, London.
12. Schnee, H. (1926). *German Colonisation, Past and Future.* Allen & Unwin, London.
13. Coupland, R. (1939). *The Exploitation of East Africa*, pp.486–7. Faber & Faber, London.

12

Within Living Memory

Sketch of Mbete (*Livingstone's Last Journals*, ed. Waller, 1874, 2.VIII).

Chief Tafuna

In 1960 I met a man who remembered David Livingstone. He was an African of very singular appearance with a long, much-wrinkled face and alert eyes. He was over 100 years old. His family name was Sikazwe, and he was the senior chief or Tafuna of the Balungu people who live in the southeast corner of Lake Tanganyika. I asked the opinion of long-time residents of the nearby town of Abercorn about his age. All thought him over 100 years, probably about 103.

He liked to come aboard the lake steamer *Liemba* on its fortnightly visit to the port of Mpulungu in Zambia, sit under a shade on deck and have a beer. With him were usually some elderly friends. He knew, or had known, English, but in any case I spoke to him through one of his old men as custom seemed to require. I asked whether Tafuna had indeed seen Livingstone. How and when? Tafuna was happy to reply.

As a boy, he had seen Livingstone, the first *mzungu* (i.e., European; and he emphasised *first*). He also mentioned several of the early missionaries he had known in the 1880s. A history of Abercorn[1] tells of him hunting with the town postmaster stationed there in 1907–08. Each time Tafuna spoke of the explorer, he pointed and nodded in the direction of the shore a few kilometres around the bay and some height up the escarpment. Repeating my question in various ways, I got the same simple response, with much nodding towards the place he associated with the first *mzungu*.

In Livingstone's *Last Journals* (2. Ch. VIII),[2] there is a sketched illustration of a view of Lake Tanganyika from the locality Tafuna indicated (reproduced above). The locality giving this view of the southeast corner of the lake is above the village of Mbete (Livingstone called it Pambete). In the far distance are the mountains of the Tanzanian side, and in the middle distance the two islands, Motondo and N'kombola, off a low, ridged shore. In the foreground is a palisaded village (Mbete?). Closer up are men building a temporary camp (which might have been Livingstone's). Livingstone reached there on 2 April 1867. He remained in the vicinity near the south of the lake for an appreciable time (a month at Pambete, and about five months altogether near the south of the lake). On his second visit to the south of Tanganyika on 17–18 November 1872 he did not linger.

I believe the locality of the sketch is certainly that of Mbete. Tafuna indicated the place, and since Livingstone stayed a while there in 1867 it would appear Tafuna's memory probably went back to that year; he would have been 7 to 10 years old (assuming his age in 1960 was between 100 and 103). Alternatively, if it was on Livingstone's second visit in 1872, Tafuna could have been up to 15 years old.

The *Liemba*

Another old-timer, if I may so describe it, is the vessel *Liemba*.[3] Its conception was part of a transportation plan in German East Africa. Noting the British railway from Mombasa to Lake Victoria and the steamers on that lake, German authorities planned to put two steamers, each about 1,000 tons, on Tanganyika. Their home port was to be the railhead, Kigoma. New-style diesel engines were considered,[4] but in the end wood-fired steam engines were decided upon. The steamers were to be named *Gotzen* and *Rechenberg*. The *Gotzen* was built, dismantled and the parts shipped to Africa in 1913; when the railway reached Kigoma in early 1914, the *Gotzen* was reconstructed there.

Note the date: World War I began in 1914. The *Rechenberg* was stillborn, as far as Africa was concerned. It is remarkable that during reconstruction of the *Gotzen* at Tanganyika it was insured by 12 British companies. They had taken care to avoid liability for war risks[5] – which was just as well because on completion the vessel immediately became a unit of the German Navy, fitted with guns and armoured shields. Trials in June 1915 were followed by 'the first great trip to Bismarcksburg' (now Kasanga[3]); as a troopship. It nearly became a great disaster. The vessel ran into strong south winds typical of the time of year, and its mechanical steering failed; also the hand rudder. Engine power being insufficient to steer by, the vessel was driven back up the lake, beam-on and rolling heavily. Avoiding shipwreck but having a rough time (50 hours), the ship eventually got to Bismarcksburg. No doubt the 700 or so men aboard swore never to go to sea again. Only a year later, the *Gotzen* was filled with cement and scuttled (fortunately not in deep water) but for that interval it posed a threat to the Allied side as a warship.

Imagine, if you can, a scene eleven years later, the official reincarnation of the *Gotzen* at Kigoma, on Monday 16 May 1927. It is a dry, fairly cool (less than 25°C) morning. People are hoping no strong southerlies will arise to upset the ceremony and ship trials. His Excellency the acting British Governor, John Scott, is present in full fig, cocked hat and regalia, and Mrs Scott will re-christen the ship *Liemba* (the local name for Lake Tanganyika). The band of 6th Battalion, King's African Rifles, 40 men, have been brought up from Dar-es-Salaam for the ceremony and festivities. Among those present is General Olsen the Belgian Consul at Kigoma. The railway administration, engineers, salvage personnel and newspapers are all represented, and crowds from Ujiji and around gather for the spectacle. Cheers arise as the ship is christened, the band plays, and His Excellency steps forward to give a short speech of thanks. Then come special thanks from lesser fry, and toasts to the success of the *Liemba*. Finally, at a sign from the Commander, his ship moves gracefully out for its official trial run, the band on board playing tunefully. It is not reported if the weather behaved with decorum, but probably it did because an excellent luncheon of seven or eight courses with Champagne Pommery and liqueurs was enjoyed.

But it had been a long and expensive rescue. After the war, when Belgium administered its 'Lake Province', they raised the scuttled *Gotzen* and towed it into Kigoma harbour where unfortunately it sank. With the League of Nations Mandate, the territory (and the ship) passed to Britain. Getting it raised again would require a salvage vessel. The 40-ton *Mwanza*, brought from Lake Victoria, was available for the purpose.[6]

But did the new Territory in fact require the establishment of a Marine Service on Lake Tanganyika (asked a British government minister, Winston Churchill)? That being affirmed and funds found, the work of salvage and a complete refit, together with rebuilding a wharf, slipway and workshops, was put in hand. So the great day in May 1927 celebrated not only the re-born *Liemba*, but also a new lake transport service.

Its intended role was to serve tourism and business traffic (accommodation for 12 first-class passengers). But by the 1960s (as I remember) the tourist cabins were unattractive to passengers other than cockroaches. The *Liemba* became a transport workhorse carrying up to 1,000 people, dried fish and general goods, and often towing barges. Since 1947, when a wharf and a customs station were built at Mpulungu (the Zambian roadhead to the industrial Copperbelt), a regular service has plied from Kigoma up and down the east coast (see Figure 6). The ship heaves to at convenient places (there are no other ports) for villagers to bring out dried fish and trade goods in canoes. In fact the services rendered to remote but well-populated lakeshore communities have probably far exceeded any development schemes introduced around the lake over the years. By simply providing a dependable bulk carrier suited to local needs and informal marketing, the old workhorse has virtually created a large fishery operating along 400 km of coastline.

The *Liemba* fell on hard times in the 1970s, needing comprehensive repairs for which money was short. That these were accomplished was largely due to the efforts and labour-of-love of one Patrick Dougherty.[7] An episode sticks in my mind from July 1975 when repairs were in progress. I saw steel sheets being replaced on part of the ship's side, where the old ones had been corroded through from the inside. On enquiry I learned that these sheets had lined the urinals for nearly 50 years.

An interesting article in the *Financial Times* of London, dated 28 June 1989, entitled 'Two worlds aboard the steamship *Liemba*', tells of considerable smuggling as well as ordinary trade. By reason of its numerous rendezvous, often at night, in isolated places in different countries, it would seem the *Liemba* was ideally suited for illegal activities. The article went on to suggest that on the whole the activities might have beneficial effects by stimulating regional trade.

Nowadays, the *Liemba* still 'moves unimaginably large piles of bags of dagaa [dried lake sardine], and has been used by the UN High Commission for Refugees (UNHCR) as a repatriation vessel to take refugees back to

Congo'.[8] The ship is now well equipped with radar and automatic steering, which made me recall that in the 1960s its distance from land at night was determined by the noise of the frog chorus onshore – or so the captain told me. Its eighty years or so working life on Tanganyika helps confirm an old maxim that 'the material development of Africa can be summed up in the word transport'.[9] It is true of many African river and lake fisheries that whenever a transport system is supplied linking primary producers to a market, an unstoppable flow of products results.

The first half of the twentieth century

I have introduced Chief Tafuna and the *Liemba* to suggest the depth of history to be found around the little town of Abercorn, near the south of Lake Tanganyika (see Figure 7) in the mid-twentieth century. As well, a small group of people lived in Abercorn who possessed a historical perspective of Northern Rhodesia (now Zambia) virtually since its beginning. The following are gleanings from this memory bank, giving a glimpse of their times and viewpoint.

From an ancient DC3 circling Abercorn prior to landing, I ventured to my companion occupying the window seat, 'Nice place to live.' He answered fervently, 'The only place to live.' My friend, Mr Peachey, had been an aviator in the 1920–30s, and said to have taken part in famous races like the Schneider Trophy, and London to Cairo Races. He'd been flying near Abercorn in the early thirties and was forced to crash-land. Quite simply, he liked the place so much he'd just stayed. His eccentric personality fitted well in the diverse company of white inhabitants (some 200 in my time), particularly ones who lived there by choice. Abercorn met all their needs. Peachey himself had a small farm just out of town, and could be seen on Saturday mornings near the post office, dressed in tweeds and a pork pie hat, displaying his vegetables for sale.

It is hard to put a finger on the peculiar character of the town, doubtless a consequence of the diversity of its inhabitants. Situated about as far from main centres of the country as it was possible to be (see Figure 4), the road onwards led only to Lake Tanganyika, or eastwards by a bad track into southern Tanzania. The only spectacles to attract visitors were the lake and the Kalambo Falls, 28 km from town (there is a photograph in Part I, Chapter 5). Basic amenities were several shops, two hotels, airport, occasional cinema, weekly newspaper (the *Abercornucopia*), hospital, church, primary school, garage, post office, police station and prison, golf course and even a local museum; thus a fairly self-sufficient community. The residents could be grouped roughly into *boma* (district officers), departmental officers (public works, agricultural, medical, etc, including myself), business people, farmers from outside town, and 'locust' (the International Red Locust Control Service [IRLCS].

One was aware the town had a significant past; rather strange for a country born virtually at the beginning of the century. Written history was pretty blank in most government stations and settlements of the land away from main towns. Resident officials came and went, and there was little sense of place identity; any written history was in *boma* district notebooks and mission records. Abercorn was different. Its 'founding father', Hugh Marshall, was posted there by Harry Johnson (then H.M. Commissioner for Central Africa) in 1890 as the first official consular officer, magistrate and postmaster. Marshall set up a stockaded wood and wattle *boma* on the Lucheche stream, but in 1896 left this fortified camp for brick houses nearby on the present site of Abercorn. He was there 18 years – the main street is named after him.[1]

In the 1890s there had been a surge of white settlers from South Africa, occupying Mashonaland and Matabeleland, which became Southern Rhodesia (Zimbabwe). But north beyond the Zambezi the land belonged to traditional tribal peoples. The British South African Company (BSA) gained access to the territory that eventually became Northern Rhodesia (Zambia) as a chartered company under the British government. The BSA had secured mining rights but also undertook responsibility for administering the country. As a generalisation it can be said that while missions and commerce first drew the British to the interior, the search for minerals was the prime motive of settlers coming from the south.[10] Diamonds at Kimberley, gold at Witwatersrand in the Transvaal, copper in Northern Rhodesia, and next it would have been the mineral treasures of Katanga, had Belgium not secured the Congo first.

Early in the century, after the Anglo–Boer War, traders, hunters and cattle buyers came north as far as Abercorn, Northern Rhodesia. Companies such as Tanganyika Concessions had a branch there, promoting trade between the Congo and the sea coast via Lake Nyasa. About this time a proposed transcontinental telegraph reached Abercorn. The town grew slowly because of its remoteness, persisting as a collection of expatriate government officers, business people, farmers and Africans employed in the town or on their lands around. Goods needed were trucked up but there could be no viable export business.

In 1902 a meeting of 25 residents decided to commemorate Queen

Victoria by building the Tanganyika Victoria Memorial Institute. As much of the material had to be transported up from Durban, the TVMI was only built in 1904. It functioned as a social centre and latterly a museum, containing many valuable memorabilia. By my time it had long owed its continuity to two distinguished ladies, the Gamwell sisters, who lived on a farm near the town. I first met Hope Gamwell in 1960, as I was occupied in my garden. Aware that someone was advancing over the lawn, I looked up and saw a rather stout, determined-looking lady of late middle age dressed in bushjacket and trousers. 'Young man, I've come to look at your sewage system,' she said. I realised she was one of the famous sisters, and knew they lived in rondavel-like houses they'd designed themselves and that they farmed in a practical way. My house, being new, had the modern system of septic tank with soakaway. She wanted to install such a device and, typically, needed to know exactly how it worked so she could construct one similar. Later, I was invited to their place to tea, and heard something of the history of Abercorn and the country.

It was the first of many insights into the interesting lives and viewpoints of the early white residents. I learned an important fact about Northern Rhodesia. Settlers had never ruled the roost (unlike Southern Rhodesia, Kenya, and other parts of Africa to which European immigrants came in the nineteenth century). The Crown had always kept control, from 1902 to 1923 through the BSA, and later through a governor and a civil service composed largely of graduates recruited from Britain. Historically, influence from British Central Africa (Nyasaland) had been strong. Robert Codrington, administrator of the territory, in particular left his mark; i.e., the position that the country was run by officials who were selected in Britain, and who administered on behalf of Africans and Europeans equally under law.[11] When the BSA gave up its nominal authority in 1923 and the country came directly under the Crown, there was little change in the way things were run. Nevertheless, between the 1920s and 1950s the influence of 'non-official' parties grew, as mentioned below.

One significance of the fact that officials remained in charge was continuity of a sort of government that minimised competition from settler interests. The indigenous people were used to the concept of a distant Crown and detached, even-handed administration by its representatives, especially in outlying areas such as Abercorn. Fortunately, standards of government were kept high. Around Abercorn, retired officials who had settled in the area were respected. I used to think that in the eyes of older Africans, young expats like me lived in their shade.

The group about whose memories I want to speak here were a minor sector. Most did not earn their living from the land as 'settlers', but had long worked in rural Africa as officials, scientists, or in local business or just chose to live there. They had grown away from their original roots and simply wanted to continue in the milieu they knew best. Some, for example, were biologists held by interest in wildlife or plant collecting, others such as medical doctors attached themselves to mission work, others like retired officials found various occupations in and around Abercorn. They were unpolitical, not looking for change, merely wanting the Africa they knew – deeply interested in it and generally happy to talk of their lives. Such transplants occurred elsewhere too – I have met individuals of the same category in Malawi and Tanzania. In the 1960s they began to find themselves rather stranded and separated by the winds of change.

I came to know J.H. Venning when he was in his nineties. He had first crossed the Zambezi at Sesheke in 1904 to work for the BSA. He finally retired in 1930 as a provincial commissioner, administering the Lozi and Makololo people in the northwest of the country. He was therefore one of the earliest Europeans in local government, whose task at first was 'pacification'. From day to day that meant getting to know the indigenous people personally and taking a census of village populations. The independence of native chiefs was then still largely undisputed, and it was necessary to introduce the idea of Crown authority, including acceptance of general law and order. Certain old customs, such as raiding and slaving, were forbidden from the start. Most villages were then stockaded with pole pallisades and earthworks for defence.

Venning had stopped one of the last instances of slaving in the country, in 1908. Suspecting a particular chief to be complicit in the forced removal of some people, he and his local police arrested and held him until all the enslaved individuals were returned.[12] They had been taken over the border into Angola (where, as in Congo, slaving still continued). Venning worked under the first provincial Administrator in the northwest, Robert Coryndon, who had close ties with Cecil Rhodes, and under his successor Robert Codrington, who had worked for Sir Harry Johnston in early Nyasaland. The viewpoints and policies of these men differed significantly. Coryndon was broadly sympathetic to the vision of Rhodes, which saw development being initiated by immigrant Europeans, whereas Codrington looked to direct administration by Crown officials sympathetic to African advancement (however distant that achievement might be). Little changed when the Chartered Company gave up its responsibility in 1923 and the country became a Crown Colony with protectorate status.

Thus Venning's life story virtually covered the country's history (in fact, right up to Zambian independence in 1964). He had worked with men who had taken part in what might be called the last Great Trek northwards, in the Matabele wars, the building of the railway, development of the copper mining industry and European farm settlement extending into Northern Rhodesia.[13] Almost incredibly, one lifetime stretched from conditions of tribal warfare and slavery to a unified country where business and industry flourished, and big progress had been made in education, health and communications. Undoubtedly the most important contribution of men like Venning was in the first two decades of the century, setting up and administering a framework of law in cooperation with traditional structures (later evolved into Native Authorities). He was not a pioneer in the settler sense, rather an official from empire-building times.[14]

The next two decades (1920s and 30s) remained vividly in the minds of the old residents. First the time of promise, when copper mining created prosperity and optimistic immigrants flocked to take advantage of opportunities in this developing territory. Then came the hard lean years of the 1930s – associated with the Great Depression in Europe and America, when copper mining declined, poverty grew bad and many Europeans left or had to be repatriated back to their homelands. The thirties, they agreed, had been a grim time – worst in 1930–33.[15] Nevertheless, in the forty years up to World War II a largely traditional society had moved far along the road to becoming a modern state, although the journey had been uneven.

Two themes were prominent in the oldtimers' recollections: (i) The need for the country to become financially self-supporting. The Depression came as a shock, provoking a re-appraisal of the financial basis of government. When it became clear the Empire could no longer provide grants-in-aid, it was evident the country had to look after itself from its own resources. It was believed it could, because Northern Rhodesia was, 'if not the only British territory in Africa, one of the very few that was able to balance its revenue and expenditure for 1930–31'.[16] But things got worse. Government was 'handicapped rather than helped' by the preceding 'abnormal prosperity'; development plans had to be shelved, work in hand stopped, and very severe measures taken including retrenchment of many government services and repatriation of those out of work.[17] It was not until international copper markets eased upwards that the budget could be balanced (in 1935). The extraordinary thing is that they managed to ride out the storm by austerities, mainly by cutting government services and careful management. They avoided trying to survive by loans from overseas, even from Britain.[18] In 1954 a distinguished politician, Sir Stewart Gore-Browne, said, 'the contrast in what we had to spend 20 years ago and what is available now is a factor which cannot be ignored in any record of what was done or what was left undone in the past . . . finance hampered government and unofficials at every turn'.[15]

With rearmament and the war in 1939 came growth in business, especially mining, and financial stability. After the war, employment opportunities rose again, drawing many Africans to the Copperbelt and boosting European immigration. In the 1950s and 60s, the copper industry boomed. By 1964, when Northern Rhodesia became Zambia, it was the second wealthiest nation in Africa after South Africa.[19]

(ii) The second theme of the oldtimers was the gradual shift in power away from the Crown, with growing representation of 'unofficial' or popular power, first European then African. When the country was first run by the BSA Chartered Company under the Crown, white settlers were not given a voice (although in 1919 an Advisory Council was set up in regard to legislation affecting them). After the BSA, the government was effectively a legislative council ('Legco') under the Governor. In 1938 the Colonial Office gave equality between officials and unofficials in Legco, with the Governor having the casting vote. This constitutional change turned out to be a major milestone on the road to self-government. Amalgamation with Southern Rhodesia with its more prosperous farming sector was advocated by some. It never quite happened.

When the war came, unofficials got senior posts (Directors of Departments), African Provincial Councils and an African Representative Council for the whole country were set up, marking recognition of the right of Africans to play their part in policy and have a say in government. This led almost inevitably to the Constitution of 1948–53, with unofficials as cabinet ministers in all but name, Africans sitting in Legco, and an unofficial majority of 14 unofficials to 9 officials.[15] It was followed in the mid-50s by a further compromise, which had British backing, the Federation of Central Africa (amalgamation with Southern Rhodesia and Nyasaland). But in 1963 Britain retreated from this arrangement and gave national independence on the basis of 'one-man-one-vote'. Thus an African government came to power, and the country was renamed Zambia.

My oldtimer friends had never liked the idea of federation, distrusting the impartiality of federal politicians. They would have preferred independence under the Crown, carrying on as before, but as hindsight shows there had long been a progressive trend for power to move away from the Crown. The fundamental doubt that worried them most was one succinctly expressed by Gore-Browne at the beginning of the federation experiment[15]: 'One may be forgiven for wondering whether the main problem which has dogged all attempts at constitutional change here and elsewhere has yet been solved, the difficulty if not the impossibility of finding a satisfactory half-way house between Crown Colony rule and self-government where a mixed community is concerned.'

This is really the heart of the matter; whether it is possible to find a working power-sharing arrangement between very different cultures and traditions. The concept of federation, where theoretically the races would live together and share power, was perhaps too simplistic an ideal to be realised, at least at that stage in time. The future for racial integration must now depend on the example set in South Africa.

Today the great majority of Zambians have no direct memory of pre-independence days. As for the oldtimers with long memories, the transition from Northern Rhodesia to Zambia was determined by the Monkton Commission sent out from Britain to review the constitution, and make recommendations[20] (which were rather a foregone conclusion). Some expats stayed, but some still retained patriotic ties with Britain (the Gamwell sisters said to me, 'We will leave the day before the flag comes down'). Curiously, on that particular day I was returning from a lake trip passing through other territorial waters and therefore flew the flag on the boat. Coming into harbour I realised as it was lowered that it would never be raised again. In fact, it was the last time the Union Jack would fly on any of the African lakes – the first had been on Tanganyika on 12 April 1858, when Burton and Speke raised it in their canoe setting off from Ujiji.[21]

History should not be forgotten. For the sake of progress in Africa, as in the wider world, a cold eye should be cast over the twentieth century.

Notes and references

1. Gamwell, H. & M. (1961). The History of Abercorn. *Northern Rhodesia Journal, 6*(iv): 515–527. I call it here by its historic name, Abercorn, familiar to me. The modern name is Mbala.
2. *Livingstone's Last Journals* (1874). (Ed.) H. Waller, London.
3. Cane, L.B. (1967). *Liemba. Tanganyika Notes & Records.* Dar-es-Salaam.
4. Diesel engines had recently begun to be manufactured in Germany; for the *Gotzen*, however, its engines were planned to be fuelled by local palm oil or ground nut oil on Tanganyika (anticipating eco-friendly ideas of today!).
5. According to Cane (1967), the policies were 'warranted free of capture, seizure and detention, and the consequences thereof, or any attempt thereat, piracy excepted, and also from all consequences of hostilities or warlike operations whether before or after declaration of war'.

6. The tug *Mwanza* had been transported via Mombasa to Dar-es-Salaam, from where it was railed and put into service on Tanganyika in 1923.
7. Foden, G. (2004). *Mimi and Toutou Go Forth*, p.111. Penguin.
8. Dr Ellinor Michel (personal communication, Oct. 2007).
9. Attributed to Lord Lugard.
10. Gann, L.H. & Duignan, K. (1962). *White Settlers in Tropical Africa.* Penguin Books.
11. Summers, R. & Gann, L.H. (1956). Robert Edward Codrington. *Northern Rhodesia Journal, 3*(1): 44–48.
12. Venning, J.H. (1955). *Northern Rhodesia Journal, 2*(vi): 53–57.
13. Note: European farms in N. Rhodesia were chiefly in its southern region.
14. Gann, L. (1954). Writing History. *Northern Rhodesia Journal, 2*(iii); 73–75.
15. Gore-Browne, Sir S. (1954). Legislative Council, Twenty Years ago. *Northern Rhodesia Journal, 2*(iv): 390–345. The style of government by a legislative council and governor is well described in R.H. Hobson's articles in the *Northern Rhodesia Journal* (1965), Vol.6, pp.135–146 and pp.309–323.
16. Legislative Council, see Hobson, R., *Northern Rhodesia Journal*, 1965, 6, pp.139–141.
17. ibid. pp. 309–322. It was feared that administrative services might have to be cut almost to the to the point of obliteration (a case in point was that 'there was not a single policemen in the whole of the North-East Province'). Unemployed Africans were repatriated to their villages, and unemployed Europeans aided by dole relief or sent back to South Africa and even to Britain. Whites had immigrated to the country with the expectation of at least the same standard of living as they'd formerly had. When instead they became very poor (and many unemployable) they had no means to survive or even to return home. The problem of unskilled whites became acute for the first time – it was clear that low skills support only a poor economy. The Financial Secretary, Mackenzie-Kennedy, made an interesting general statement: 'It is financially impossible, except during periods of extraordinary activity, to continue to administer a tropical dependency in which the population is predominantly native if white officers at comparatively high rates of salary are employed in minor posts which can, providing the necessary training is given, be adequately filled by natives at much lower cost.'
18. ibid. p.318. In 1935 the Governor stated: 'The British taxpayer, his back still against the wall, is unable to assist Northern Rhodesia through its difficulties.'
19. Guest, R. (2004). *The Shackled Continent.* Macmillan, London.
20. Crawley, A. (1988). *Leap Before You Look: A Memoir.* Collins.
21. Burton, R.F. (1860). *The Lake Regions of Central Africa*, p.100. Sidgwick & Jackson.

PART III

Transition: Modern Times

13

Development

African poverty and stagnation is the greatest tragedy of our time.
(Commission for Africa Report, 2005, p.13)

Introduction

The third part of this book looks at change in human circumstances and welfare in Africa during the past half-century, the post-independence era. Essentially it concerns social and economic evolution in the move from 'traditional' to 'modern' lifestyles. Chapter 13 comments on the broad and often vague term 'development', using experience in projects in Ghana, Zambia and Burundi described in Part I. As an example with broad implications, I examine the final phase of the fisheries research and development project in Burundi after the 1972 genocide (see Chapter 6), comparing some aspects with the famous Ujamaa agricultural project in Tanzania. In Chapter 14 ideal types of traditional and modern life are contrasted, drawing on observations of some rural peoples in the above countries when they were still strongly influenced by tradition. Human and economic problems of present-day Africa are outlined, dividing the theme of poverty into rural poor (Chapter 15) and urban poor (Chapter 16). Lastly (Chapter 17), current economic viewpoints and social alternatives are considered.

This is an account derived from personal observation and experience as well as published sources. This admittedly raises questions of interpretation and bias, which cannot be helped. Africa is huge and diverse, and political and economic development policies have differed between countries. I can only hope the limitations of personal viewpoint will not diminish the interest and usefulness of the story.

'Development'

To most aid donors and aid agencies up to the 1970s, the countries of Sub-Saharan Africa (SSA) were in a transition phase where people were still traditional in culture, while assimilating modern influences and being familiarised with technology. Others would have said that people were progressively becoming modern while still holding on to certain old customs and beliefs. In any case, the transition was seen at that time as a gradual passage from one world view to another. What was needed was 'transfer of technology' and training at all levels to help 'institution building'.

However, the countries became deeply in debt through international borrowing, and the International Monetary Fund insisted that further lending would be conditional upon specific economic and fiscal reforms. There ensued a conservative phase (late 1970s through early 1990s) in lending policies among the principal donor nations together with the World Bank, the US Federal Reserve and the International Monetary Fund (the so-called 'Washington Consensus'). Comprehensive 'structural adjustment programmes' (SAPs) were undertaken. They did not lift the SSA countries out of stagnation but instead increased unemployment. Poverty still reigns in a context of ever-rising populations.

The period also coincided with increasing global economic integration, or globalisation (it has been called the neoliberal Great Capitalist Restoration)[1] – a significant title recalling the long history of capitalist growth and reactive protectionist trends stretching back to the nineteenth-century Industrial Revolution.[2]

Despite development efforts, the rural majorities in SSA countries have remained economically almost static in their subsistence lifestyles.[3] As well, a significant proportion of rural people, mostly young men, have migrated to towns and cities. Urbanisation has occurred at a startling 5–7% per year, leading to uncontrolled growth of peripheral city slums.[4] Rural population growth has also continued at high rates, but neither in the cities nor in the countryside has there been much improvement in quality of life. The conservative rural people subsisting by agriculture or fisheries do not produce enough surplus for commerce. They tend to feed only themselves without developing trade with cities or export markets. They are not commercially engaged. The cities, on the other hand, have not produced productive economies that would lead national economic growth. Only small minorities of migrants to cities find jobs and financial security, while the majority of urban dwellers (soon to comprise most Africans in the current demographic explosion) live in deprived conditions in problematic slums (the so-called informal sector). In fact, urban and rural development options have turned out, for the majority, to be economic cul-de-sacs in which standards of living remain poor. Only a few SSA nations have made much general economic progress. Most are little better off materially in the post-independence era (since the 1960s), despite substantial foreign aid.

Furthermore, conflict and prolonged civil chaos in some countries, notably Burundi, Rwanda, Congo, Nigeria, Sudan, Somalia and Sierra Leone, have disrupted traditional cultures and made matters worse.

From the wealth of literature in the past few years (e.g., compendious reports from the UN-HABITAT agency,[4] and the Report of the Commisson for Africa[5]), three salient facts hit the eye: soaring populations, stagnating agriculture, and cities lacking industrial growth. Also there are pervasive health problems, particularly HIV-Aids and tuberculosis. So far, the development prospect is not promising.

Within the above general context, I want to discuss development from a personal perspective, as I experienced it: It began, as described in Part I, in late colonial times (1955) in what became Ghana, West Africa. That was before the anti-apartheid campaign, so I was not preoccupied by its grievances and vicarious feelings of guilt, like many young people coming from Britain. The Europeans I came to know had for the most part worked for many years in West Africa and developed their own particular outlook. They were what their times and the Service had made them. The best were obviously dedicated and closely concerned with the interests of the indigenous people, spoke their language and knew their mind. I imbibed their gradualistic approach to development, which was a step-by-step introduction of western economic thinking and technology to people who still to a large extent followed traditional ways of life. But there was too little time to become shaped in their mould. I had only a short-term perspective, so perhaps not much of their world view rubbed off on me. My own attitudes to the local people grew to a large extent out of observing them and developing working relationships. Although I liked what I was doing in Ghana, it shortly became evident that the outlook for expatriates was short. The colonial epoch there had come to an end.

I was drawn by the ideals of the Federation of Central Africa and a job promising a more extended future. On arriving in Northern Rhodesia in 1959 I encountered European settlers for the first time. Many were second- or third-generation residents, regarding themselves as white Africans. However, although the utopian notion of partnership between the two races was attractive, and the Federation made good economic sense, it turned out that the countries – Northern and Southern Rhodesia and Nyasaland – were too dissimilar culturally and historically to bond. Federation was doomed by deep-rooted suspicions of racial partiality, and above all by the imminent prospect of 'one-man-one-vote' democracy, insisted upon by Britain, which would lead inevitably to separate nations.

When independence arrived (Northern Rhodesia became Zambia in 1964), developmentalism[6] became the philosophy of the day, and indeed the governing paradigm in Africa for decades to come. There had of course been many years of development before independence, in physical structures like roads and buildings, and hands-on advisory work in agriculture and fisheries, and notably in maintaining stable administration under law. However, in the new times development took on a different meaning. It now stood for rapid change; accelerated modernisation. The revolutionary vision was of old things passing away and an imminent new order. Independence in Zambia was seen as part of continent-wide emancipation with benefits for even the humblest. Africans would have new opportunities, especially those with some education. Castles in the air were built by plausible politicians, foreign aid was pledged, and development became the exciting new fashion of modernisation. They were people on the path of development (*en voie de développement* – a common phrase in francophone Africa). As a consequence, indigenous culture and custom became synonymous for many people, black and white, with 'backward' pre-modern ways.

For people like me this led to a shift of emphasis in our concept of development; a subtle change in the way ex-colonial expats saw themselves and their work. Instead of building upon traditional culture, introducing 'appropriate technology' and inculcating the mentality to use and adapt it, the driving fashion was now for speedy change to the modern; i.e., to western ways and values. In a word, *transition* had become *transformation*. This might have been an unfortunately precipitate change of ideology, but it was the paradigm within which one had to work. I accepted it despite lingering reservations about the actual process by which it would come about. Certainly it would demand more than simple physical change. I could not imagine how African traditional world views could be totally translated into a western one; there are deep intrinsic differences. It would probably mean alienating African peasants from their cultural and social realities. The dilemma seemed to have been understood in some degree by the Zambian President, Kenneth Kaunda, in his philosophy of 'Zambian humanism', which was an attempt to hang onto the communalist mindset of traditional life, while at the same time improving living standards along Western lines. But as the problem was far above my head, I got on with my job in biological research for fisheries development.

However, the human face of development could not be dismissed. I found it increasingly hard to connect what I was doing – biology and management planning – with the likelihood of it being adopted and applied in the new dispensation. Put simply, western ways meant turning subsistence life into commercial-type employment. A contradictory factor became clear, certainly by the end of the 1970s: that the Zambian fisheries would be driven by large numbers of small independent operators with very limited money (the way all freshwater fisheries in Africa have in fact developed). Large mechanised boats and sophisticated processing techniques were not for the foreseeable future, rather development would proceed by numerous labour-intensive units. Marketing could be left in the hands of small traders, providing good roads connected fisheries to centres of population such as the Zambian Copperbelt towns. Fishermen's wives would beach-dry fish and sell it to traders. But unless government decided to entrust the exploitation of the Zambian lakes and floodplains to one or two big companies (very unlikely for many reasons), then fishery development meant dealing directly with the local fisherfolk.

Whether they could be induced to participate in some kind of self-managed body, or whether civil servants could act as essentially commercial go-betweens, was unknown. It was possible to conceive of a bottom-up process that, if suitably encouraged and at first subsidised, should certainly produce much more fish. But then the industry would simply grow by the multiplication of small units, until fish stocks declined below the point of worthwhile returns.

The immediate challenge was to work towards a *modus operandi* with the fisherfolk. It would mean getting them to move from a time-honoured way of life, and accept ideas of rational exploitation, commercialism and the creation of wealth. Essentially, therefore, our business was with people. Yet we were employed in science, and expected to introduce the commercial attitudes familiar to us and indeed part of modern culture. We had to make the crucial assumption that the aims of our work were best for the fishing people, and that they would accept and apply our gospel.

Such were my thoughts on leaving Zambia in 1969 for a new UN-FAO fisheries project (so-called 'Projet Pêche') at the north of Lake Tanganyika. It is worth returning to this project (described in Chapter 6), as it more or less typified attitudes and weaknesses of development approaches at the time.

Projet Pêche in Burundi

Science and technology were to be deployed with the ultimate goal that the local people should exploit their resource rationally and sell to wider commercial markets. So the Project Document (plan of operations) came as no surprise. Couched in familiar language – objectives, methods, inputs, timing and expected outcomes – it followed a predictable pattern based on a goal-oriented mindset. Pre-project planning had followed the usual procedures of consultation with the local government.

However, neither FAO nor the Burundi government anticipated the attempted coup in 1972 and subsequent disastrous genocide. In late 1972, when conditions had returned more or less to normal, all expats who remained in the country had to put the genocide out of mind. Pessimistic discussion was avoided. (Inevitably the shadow of a great evil was imprinted on everyone's memory; and we were aware, given the cruelty and hatred that had been revealed, that something similar could very well occur again.) Focusing on the present, it was necessary to rethink and rebuild the project.

While the fishery had been ravaged and de-populated, gradually through 1972 survivors returned to their homes from the hinterland or neighbouring countries where they had fled. Others remained away many years in UN refugee camps in northern Tanzania.[7] The project now had to work with traumatised people coming to terms with losses of family members and livelihoods. Those near the southern border with Tanzania still lived in fear of further invasions. Squabbles over land ownership were common. Despite all this the fishery revived quickly because of the immediate need for food, and while our long-term project aim was to provide a management plan, a priority now was to boost the small boat sector, since most catamarans and canoes had disappeared in the emergency.

I suppose our approach was typical of development attitudes at the time. We were 'improvers' and 'boosters'. The current buzz-phrase was 'transfer of technology'. Implicit was the assumption that if improved technical methods were introduced, they would surely be adopted. In fact we did not have to introduce new means of fishing, but built upon the well-understood and accepted techniques developed by successful Belgian aid projects of the 1950s. These consisted of lamp fishing from steel catamarans with nylon lift-nets.[8]

Albert, a colleague, worked with the fishermen arranging for them to buy boats, nets and lamps through a loan-purchase scheme, as well as offering them training. The dispersed nature of coastal settlement was not conducive to concentrated development, so centres must be established (where assets

A catamaran unit: two metal hulls with four derricks for hauling the net; lamp mounted between the hulls

Kitaza artisanal fishing centre

like schools and health clinics could also be sited by government). If the first centre was successful it could be followed up by others along the coast. A sheltered bay, Kitaza, about 25 km from Bujumbura, was chosen. The Kitaza centre would buy catches and provide a steady market for proximate parts of the fishery.

Since traditional drying of sardine on the beach and selling at opportunity resulted in a poor product (beach-dried fish – so-called *kapenta* – grows mouldy in storage and is prone to beetle infestation),[9] a new method of preservation would have to be devised. In any case the beaches are often unsanitary places; it is not unlikely that occasional outbreaks of cholera around the lake are connected with beach-dried fish. So another colleague, Hans, devised a method of brining and smoking the sardine, finally sun-drying it on raised racks.

Gradually Hans' factory at Kitaza attracted fishermen and went into operation. Processing began at dawn as catches were landed. Factory capacity was up to five tonnes of fresh fish per day (with a small extension it could take ten tonnes). At the beach, fishermen were offered a steady market and fair income. Soon about a dozen catamaran units were coming, and then many more. Training of factory staff, and the building of confidence among the fisherfolk progressed, but we could not count on the same fishermen coming regularly; there were gaps of days, even weeks, when they seemed to have other things to do. We hoped to instil regular work habits by the incentive of a dependable income. Operations were made flexible to cope with irregular landings and seasonal fish fluctuations. Of course, the system had to function economically right through the year, within ordinary constraints of a business.[10]

I remember early mornings at Kitaza bay. The calm coolness of night lingered, and catamarans moved in one by one over the glassy lake to unload their catches. Our factory hands weighed each catch separately and issued receipts. Processing began in a flurry of activity, the voices of fishermen and onlookers rising sociably. Hans checked that each man in the plant had his own set of duties to repeat over and over. In a while we became rather proud of our first centre. It demonstrated that artisanal fishing and factory operations could be integrated profitably.

For example, a loan to pay for a new catamaran and all its equipment could be repaid in about three years, if the recipient fished regularly. Considering the general poverty around, the feasibility of acquiring that much capital value in so short a time marked real progress. Profit could also be made on the marketing side, and there seemed no limit to the market.[10] It was not hard to imagine the replication of other centres along the coast, leading one day to a flourishing industry feeding the country inland.

Albert also found ways of increasing the catching power of a unit. By hitching two catamarans together a larger net could be operated, and along with more powerful lamps catches could be increased fourfold. An experimental fibreglass trimaran of wider span was made, and with a correspondingly bigger net it increased catches a further 50%. In fact, catches could be raised by relatively inexpensive modifications of gear. It was a break-through in cost-efficiency, which the fishermen were not slow to appreciate.

In our euphoria with success after the project's initial setback, we did not realise the trickiest part was still to come – getting the fishermen to adopt the new ideas and implement them in a businesslike way. We expected them to want to make money, or at least climb out of poverty. It is strange we did not recognise more clearly there were two realities, side by side. One was the traditional culture of the fishermen constrained, as we thought, by poverty (actually they lived within self-sufficient subsistence habits); the other was our own market-oriented monetary world. We were aware of this duality in a general way, but did not grasp its crucial significance. We did not understand the magnitude of the change in mindset we were expecting this traditional society to make.

Our thinking emphasised regular production, profitability in the market, accumulation of wealth for reinvestment and subsequent expansion of the industry within the national economy. We anticipated development to proceed along 'rational' lines. In fact, the fishermen went ahead on lines that made sense to them. They were not interested, and never had been, in producing within a market economy for financial gain. They were concerned with increasing consumption and the well-being of their extended families in their own village life. Beyond material necessity, their world view was shaped by social priorities rather than by desire to get rich.

In the next two decades, after the project, the fishermen boosted their catches remarkably, building on Albert's modifications and continuing by themselves to improve gear and techniques. Eventually, the fishing power of the best catamarans came to equal that of a commercial purse-seiner. Now they could afford outboard engines, which allowed them to fish the same offshore waters as the seiners. Catamarans increased greatly in number, averaging about 750 units through the 1980s.[11] Correspondingly greater fishing pressure caused fish stocks to collapse. Consequently purse-seiner catches fell to uneconomic levels, and they quit Burundi waters for other parts of the lake.[12] The improvised, low-cost artisanal rigs had simply outcompeted the more highly capitalised purse-seiners.

Re-visiting Burundi in the 1990s, I saw the Kitaza 'factory' lying disused. A few drying racks were still standing, but fish were being dried everywhere on sandy beaches, as of yore. Constellations of lamps on the lake at night indicated a much larger artisanal fleet than in the 1970s, although the total catch from Burundi waters remained similar (around 20,000 tonnes per year). Obviously, catch per fishing unit had declined drastically. I heard of mosquito netting being used in the bags of nets to catch very small sizes of fish, a retrograde step. Also, the numbers of active units fluctuated a great deal, probably indicating that fishermen retained their desultory subsistence life – satisfying local consumption, not making money.

Certainly, the fishery had not developed into a profitable commercial affair as Projet Pêche had planned. Harvesting was not integrated with processing and fish was not distributed widely. Consumption per head of population was less than before. No overall management was in place to maximise catch by manipulating effort. In hindsight, the project's contribution seemed merely to have been to demonstrate how to fish more effectively. The fishermen had simply continued to improve their gear and multiply in numbers until the stocks were overfished, resulting in a fall in catch per man.[13] This was not the desired outcome. Yet after the project the government authorities had not intervened to manage the fishery, and perhaps even regarded *ad lib* intensification with favour.

It could also be argued, with the benefit of hindsight, that rational planning was not possible in conflict-torn Burundi. People were not living settled lives – far from it. We wanted them to take on a system of steady supply, processing, storage, transport and distribution, as well as overall management; in fact to settle into a routine of commodity production and creation of wealth. They were capable fishermen, but their ideology was conservative and their circumstances hard.

Was Projet Pêche therefore a failure? It had helped restore and enlarge the fishery devastated in 1972, but fishermen ignored commercialisation, preferring instead their hand-to-mouth subsistence style of life. This came as a surprise because we underestimated the power and persistence of traditional culture.[14] Numerous other resource development projects bringing the gospel of the marketplace using technology have had similar experience.

In fact, subsistence-style fishing has everywhere increased on African lakes and rivers, and heavy pressure on fish stocks is a fact of life. Falling market values of catches gradually become irrelevant, as subsistence fishers tend to continue working despite diminishing catches from their effort. They remain poor, and fishing is often an occupation of last resort.

For example, I had a friend working at a heavily exploited lake where access was free and every man acted for himself. Strangers also came to fish. Sitting on the beach the fishermen told my friend how some years ago the lake had produced fine large fish. Now only small fish were left (which with short life cycles could better withstand heavy fishing). But now even these were not yielding much. My friend suggested they cooperate as a community of common interest and manage the resource. Right management, he said, might yield a higher and more sustainable return. To emphasise the alternative he added, 'If you go on like this, one day the last fish in the lake will swim by. Then what will you do?' One man answered, 'I'll catch it', and pointing to his house nearby said, 'my wife and children are waiting there for me to bring them food.' It was hard to think of a rational reply.

Ujamaa

In neighbouring Tanzania a large development project was under way around the same time in the 1970s. It was a pioneering attempt to develop agriculture on a national scale. Although much bigger, its results throw light on the sequel of Projet Pêche.

The famous Ujamaa project originated from the political philosophy espoused by the country's charismatic first president, Julius Nyerere. It aimed to achieve a self-reliant socialist economy based on agricultural collectives. Launched by the Arusha Declaration of 1967 setting out its aims, Ujamaa was essentially an inward-orientated national policy to modernise Tanzania's agriculture and reduce its dependence on international finance for development. The main themes were state control of all business and industry, and national development of agriculture through a process of villagisation and introduction of new more productive farming methods. The Ujamaa villages were planned to be socialist communes, in which the normally scattered peasants would be concentrated.

The word *ujamaa* means approximately 'familyhood', conveying the central idea of a society in which the basic production unit is a group of families in an ujamaa village. Using machinery and fertilisers, the communes would be more productive than scattered peasant subsistence farming with hoes. They would harvest surpluses for supply to towns in Tanzania, and export farm commodities to world markets. Each collective would have a school and health clinic. It was a compromise, designed to modernise while holding onto old social traditions. Nyerere placed great weight on following traditional ways; nevertheless he insisted that farmers separate from their familiar lands into new communes as an essential step towards modernising.

The concept was appealing and foreign finance was generous. About 10 million peasants were moved to new villages in one of the largest planned population shifts of the twentieth century.[3] Yet by 1975 Ujamaa had failed. Nationalised businesses and industries proved inefficient, and peasant farmers did not embrace collectivisation. Even though the army was used to coerce families into the villages, production efforts on the farms were minimal, and people gradually slipped off to resume former ways of subsistence life (which consisted of clearing and cropping a piece of land until it became exhausted, then moving on). There were other practical causes for the failure of Ujamaa; such as overexploitation of land immediately around the new villages, and poor supporting infrastructure especially roads. But the chief constraint was that collectivisation and commercial-style production were out of tune with the social and cultural realities of traditional people. They could not give up time-tested practices of making a living that went with a life centred on social relationships rather than wealth. They were simply not convinced villagisation was in their interests.

The fate of Ujamaa attracted wide attention and provoked a large literature of studies and opinions. For simplicity I cite just two: one concerned with field studies in Tanzania of the transformation of peasant societies to modern ones[3]; coincidentally, many of the people studied were refugees who had fled Burundi in 1972, some from the region where Projet Pêche operated (see Chapter 6); the other study is a theoretical analysis of Ujamaa and its legacy for economic development in Africa.[6] Both provide good bibliographies.

I have interpolated the Ujamaa project here to remark some interesting parallels with Projet Pêche in its rationale and approaches, despite great differences in scale. Both desired to concentrate people into centres of activity (ujamaa villages/fishery centres). Scattered peasantry are invisible to government, producing only for their own needs. From the government's viewpoint, concentration made commodity production for the market and taxation possible. However, as long as free arable land was available in the country the temptation to return to traditional ways was compelling. Similarly, the scattered fishermen on the Burundi shoreline, whom Project Pêche planned to concentrate around centres (by persuasion), preferred to fish near their coastal dwellings where the catch is consumed and little of it traded. Access to Lake Tanganyika is unrestricted, just like free arable land to the farmer.

In both cases, gaps in cultural mindsets seem to have been fundamental barriers to modernisation. Villagisation and fishing centres were the means to move peasants across the divide from traditional to commercial attitudes, getting them accustomed to producing routinely for the market; or, in banal terms, to exchanging their labour on a regular and reliable basis for money. Neither project succeeded in creating a mindset reconciled to modern practices. The shift constitutes a large psychological step, involving reorganisation of social life. (The same step took decades or generations to accomplish in eighteenth- and nineteenth-century Europe and America.) The incentive of the marketplace appeared insufficient to attract the peasant. It has been said the two alternatives are simply contradictory – 'commons and commodity can not coexist, it is a choice'.[15]

Some conclude that government pressure or outright coercion is necessary for peasants to take the step.[16,17] (An extreme case was the harsh methods used in communist collectives in eastern Europe.) The question of incentives or coercion has a long history in East Africa. In German colonial times from the 1890s, labour for public works such as constructing roads was raised by paid conscription (recruits lived in camps) for a certain number of days per year; and similarly under British administration from 1920. The British promoted villagisation schemes of various sorts for the cultivation of exportable crops, such as sisal and coffee, and placed schools and health clinics in settlements.[18] Relocation of populations involving cultural transformation tends to be a painful process. In the turbulent history of Burundi, villagisation was attempted, with only partial success, during the presidency of Bagaza (1976–87). In Rwanda, where the events of 1995 caused 70% of Rwandans to leave their homes, many returning refugees were resettled in new villages, although with some difficulty.[19]

From a humanitarian viewpoint an incentive approach is better than coercion, taking into account the nature and magnitude of cultural changes to be made and the specific circumstances of the people to be 'developed'. Rather than ignoring cultural aspects (as we did in Projet Pêche), social studies of the people and their instruction in market ideology should be components from the start. Moreover, had Projet Pêche continued a further ten years, routines and working relationships might have established a new mindset and got businesses started. Ujamaa too was put in place hastily; its policy 'rather too ambitious and optimistic about what could be done within a short span', and its ideological transformation probably not radical enough.[20] Of course, the costs of long-term projects are formidable, especially on a national scale like Ujamaa. Ironically, the key to effecting change may be continuity, allowing time for the right message to be internalised.[21]

As well, both projects made the classical error of a 'top-down' approach, following a blueprint (project plan of operations), with insufficient operational flexibility. The plans were in 'campaign style', with specific times allocated to reach objectives. Today's critics tend to frown on both approaches. Whatever the choice, the fallacies of developmentalism do indeed begin in the minds of developers, if they picture those to be developed in terms of their own culture ('what works for us will work for them').

Notes and references

1. Stanfield, J.R. & Carroll, M.C. (2009). The social economics of neoliberal globalization. *Association for Social Economics, 38*: 1–18.
2. Polanyi, K. (1945). *Origins of Our Time: The Great Transformation.* Victor Gollancz, London, p. 33.
3. Waters, T. (2006). *The Persistence of Subsistence Agriculture: Life beneath the level of the marketplace.* Lexington Books, USA.
4. United Nations Human Settlements Programme (UN-HABITAT) (2008). *The State of Cities in Africa. A framework for addressing urban challenges in Africa.* UN-HABITAT, Nairobi, Kenya.
5. Blair, A. et al. (eds.) (2005). *Our Common Interest: Report of the Commission for Africa.* Commission for Africa, London.
6. Ibhawoh, B. & Dibua, J.I. (2003). Deconstructing Ujamaa: The legacy of Julius Nyerere in the quest for social and economic development in Africa. *African Journal of Political Science. 8*(1), p.74.
7. Note: According to Refugees International (IRI) in 2008; some 15,000 of the people who fled to Tanzania in 1972 returned to Burundi in 2008, and some 45,000 more were expected to return in 2009. This is against a background of Burundi refugees fleeing to Tanzania (and other nearby countries) from 1972 up to recent times. Those returning from Tanzania between 2002 and 2008 totalled 459,363, according to the United Nations High Commission for Refugees in its UNHCR Burundi Fact Sheet, 31 December 2008.
8. Collart, A. (1958). Pêche artisanale et pêche industrielle au Lac Tanganika. *Bulletin agricole du Congo Belge, 49*(5): 1169–1268.
   The earliest record of fishing for the Tanganyika sardine by attraction to light at night is probably Burton's observations in 1858 (*The Lake Region of Central Africa*, Sidgwick & Jackson, 1961). His mentions (p.67 and p.94) imply that fish were attracted by the light of a small fire on the bow of a canoe. It is interesting that Burton also mentions (p.68) that *dagaa* (swahili for *kapenta*), sundried or salted, 'find their way far east', indicating that the trade in *kapenta* was possibly ancient. Since recent times the light has been provided by a kerosene pressure lamp (the cover of this book depicts a traditional sardine net (*lusenga*) still in use.
9. *Report of the Fishery Research and Development Project* FI:DP/BDI/70/508. (1974). FAO, Rome.
10. Treated sardine from the factory (brined, smoked and sun-dried) were sealed in plastic bags, each 0.7 kg. This is adequate to accompany a 4– 5-person meal of maize or cassava staple, providing taste and nutrition. Importantly, shelf life was at least three months. Tests conducted around the country proved there was high demand at a profitable selling price. Taking all costs and overheads into account on a per annum basis, the factory was a viable business.
11. Petit, P. & Kiyuku, A. (1995). Changes in the pelagic fisheries of Northern Lake Tanganyika during the 1980s. In: Pitcher, T.J. & Hart, P.J. (Eds.) *The Impact of Species Changes in African Lakes.* Chapman & Hall.
12. Mulimbwa, N. (2006). Assessment of the commercial artisanal fishing impact on three pelagic fish stocks at the north of Lake Tanganyika. *Verh. Internat. Verein. Limnol. 29*: 1189–1193. See also:

Roest, F.C, (1992). The pelagic fish resources of Lake Tanganyika. *Mitt. int. Verein. theoret. angew. Limnol. 23*: 11–15.
Roest, F.C. (1987). *The status of the fisheries of Lake Tanganyika.* CIFA Sub-Committee for Lake Tanganyika, Bujumbura, December 1987; FAO, Rome.

13. Sarvala, J., Langenberg, V., Salonen, K., Chitamwebwa, D., Coulter, G., Huttula, T., Kanyaru, R., Kotilainen, R., Makasa, P., Mulimbwa, L. & Molsa, H. (2006). Fish catches from Lake Tanganyika mainly reflects changes in fishery practices, not climate. *Verh. Internat. Verein. Limnol. 29*: 1182–1188 (contains references to biological studies of the fishery).
14. For parallel behaviour in persisting with subsistence agriculture, see Waters, (2006).
15. Agbemabiese, L. & Byrne, J. (2005). Commodification of Ghana's Volta River. *Bulletin of Science and Society, 25*: 17–25.
16. Waters (2006), p.224.
17. Seavoy, R.E. (1989). *Famine in East Africa.* Greenwood Press, UK.
18. Waters (2006), p.170–173
19. International Displacement Monitoring Centre (IDMC), (2000). *Rwanda: National and International Response* http://www.internal-displacement.org/idmc
20. Ibhawoh, B. & Dibua, J.L. (2003), p.69.
21. Later, in the 1990s, another international project based at Bujumbura investigated the biological basis of the fishery, and took the first steps to organise fisheries cooperation between the four nations sharing Lake Tanganyika (see Note 13 for references). Lakewide studies by other scientists were made of environmental threats to the lake. For references see: Allison, E.H., Paley, R.G., Ntakimazi, G., Cowan, V.J. & West, K. (2000). *Biodiversity assessment and conservation in Lake Tanganyika.* Technical Report of the UNDP and the Natural Resources Institute (London) project: Pollution Control and Other Measures to Protect Biodiversity in Lake Tanganyika (RAF/92/G32).

14

Traditional and Modern Cultural Mindsets

To be clear what we mean by 'traditional' and 'modern' cultural mindsets, the terms are defined in tabular form below in two series of characteristics representing 'ideal types'.[1] The traditional series is derived from a wide African literature, and personal observation of the fishing peoples described in Part I in Chapters 1, 2 and 3 – respectively, the Tongu people of the lower Volta River, the Fante of the sea coast (Ghana), and the Unga of the Bangweulu Swamps in Zambia. In the 1950s these people still followed traditional mores. They fitted the general picture given in the Table, despite wide differences between their natural environments and livelihood strategies. I also refer to the Hutu and Tutsi people on Lake Tanganyika in the 1970s.

The series under 'Modern' in the Table describes present western economic and social models, and requires little comment. However, no set of ideal types conforms perfectly with real life which, as Hart said, is always a mixture.[1] With this understanding, we may make a general comparison between the two series. They are listed in order of social, demographic, cultural and economic characteristics.

The primary socio-economic unit in a tribe was the family. Associations of extended families formed village communities, which possessed customary rights of access for farming and fishing. Intricate structures of mutual obligation and reciprocity were usual; e.g., the Tongu, Fante and Unga tribes commonly fished in kin-related groups (see Chapters 1, 2, and 3). Also there were numerous instances of division of labour between men and women; for example, Tongu fishermen seasonally migrated from home villages to fish far upstream, while their wives stayed at home and dived for clams. Similarly, Unga men seasonally worked from fishing camps. Fante women played the predominant role in fish trading, and Tongu women traded clams. In each tribe, women did most of the cultivation of crops, while the men's roles included fishing, net repairing, canoe-building, bush-clearing, house-building, etc.

Alternative Life Histories

Traditional	*Modern*
Kinship links strong; family responsibilities and obligations	Association and cooperation within wide society
Status based on birth and/or seniority	Status within wide society; personal wealth important
Family house in community	Rented or purchased accommodation
Small communities	Towns, cities
Security in community and custom	Security within social system
High fertility (many offspring)	Controlled fertility, few offspring and extended parental care
High mortality	Low mortality
Short life cycle	Increased longevity
Cultural instruction	School/university
Group reliant, cooperative	Competitive, individualistic
'Situation-experiencing'	'Problem-solving'
Conservative, repetitive	Dynamic, inventive
Traditional cures	Modern medicine
Customary law[2]	State law
Local communication	Wide communication
Spiritual (animism/ancestor worship)	Secular (ethical paradigms)
Oral history	Recorded history
Self-sustaining (farming, fishing)	Monetary systems (wage, contract)
Economically self-reliant	Dependent on market system
Reciprocal gift-giving	Price setting, cash, credit
Labour-intensive	Technically assisted
Undifferentiated labour	Highly differentiated
Marked division of labour between sexes	Ideal of equal opportunity between sexes
Subsistence	Commodity purchase
Consumption culturally determined	Consumption wealth-related
Food supply dependent on local climate	Food largely independent of local climate
Few staple foods	Variety of foods, many processed
Few livelihood options	Many options
Traditional work patterns faithfully reproduced	Innovative, opportunist
Community rights to land & water resources	Individual, corporate or state ownership
Rural	Industrial
Low ecological impact	Modifier of environment

Each of the columns of ideal types represents a coherent system ('Cultural coherence extends to all aspects of daily life'). Neither extreme is completely static; one assumes a purposive movement from traditional to modern is taking place over time, through the pervasive process called 'development'. Traditional society tends to repetition, keeping in equilibrium with fluctuations in the natural environment, whereas modern society values innovation, especially in technology, and it changes quickly.

Agricultural communities possessing arable land and growing their own food are said to be embedded in 'economies of affection'.[1] They remain outside the marketplace and are virtually self-sustaining. Mutual obligations between kinship groups and neighbours are expressed in reciprocal gift-giving. The bonds within such relationships can be much stronger than market incentives. While such traditional people may be 'in poverty' by western country standards, they are able to sustain themselves independently of external markets. In short, the ideal type on the left of the Table belongs to a simple economy based on agriculture, fishing, hunting and gathering; labour is largely undifferentiated and the economy unstructured. Conversely, the ideal type on the right epitomises a structurally transformed economy, diversified and productive, dominated by manufacturing and services.

In traditional life, thought was regulated by group belief and motives of group welfare. Individualism was not encouraged, although recognition of an individual's contribution and rights was evidently important – for example, the sharing of catches from collective fishing. Sharing on an agreed basis was part of the traditional ethos, an acknowledgement of participants' rights and obligations that served to bond the group. For example, it was Fante practice in setting gill-nets (*tengas*) for individually owned pieces of net to be fastened together to make a longer and more catch-efficient net. However, each individual received just the catch made in his own portion of net. The Bangweulu Unga did much the same (in their *kutumpula* fishing).

There were systems of structure and status in the Tongu, Fante and Unga tribes (in each case, chief, senior men, head fisherman, and someone with responsibility for customary rites and the occult. Leadership was accepted as a practical requirement (e.g., each Fante sea canoe of 12–18 men had a bosun in charge), but group pressure on the individual was strong. Traditional society could not be called egalitarian, although decisions affecting the community were generally made consensually. Economic activities were oriented to the welfare of the community. Unlike 'modern' societies, surpluses were not accumulated but spent upon occasions such as celebrations or funerals.

Social harmony was seen as very important. An example of a major social issue was the prolonged dispute over the introduction of the Fante *alii* net (see Chapter 2). The chiefs and their supporters took the conservative view that this large net was inimical to custom, because its relatively high cost restricted ownership to a few. The basic concern of the chiefs was that, because of its high catching efficiency, an individual owner could become unduly rich and influential, thereby causing social disharmony. Minor disputes were settled by internal mechanisms in the tribe; and major disputes by overarching national law during and after colonial times. Even today, there may be disharmony between customary law rooted in indigenous culture and the law of the state government.[2]

And so on. One can remark on numerous other ways in which the three tribes conformed to traditional life as outlined in the Table. However, each had distinct strategies to exploit its particular environment. While labour was undifferentiated on the whole, apart from age and gender roles the communities were specialised according to livelihood strategies.

Characteristically, great care was taken to replicate the customary methods and tools of ancestors. Nevertheless, a variety of new fishing gear has been adopted by these traditional societies in the past century. For example, they quickly appreciated the advantages of nylon twine (obtaining it, to begin with, by laboriously extracting cord from old motor tyres). Nylon nets were adopted wholesale. The Fante modified drift nets and purse-seines, and developed cooperative ways of fishing them between canoes. The Unga had 17 different fishing methods. Fishermen at the north of Lake Tanganyika provide a striking example of self-improvement in modifying their catamaran lift-nets (see Chapter 13). These examples challenge the notion of unvarying conservatism.

The Table shows three important demographic contrasts between the ideal type series. First, fertility is still typically high in rural communities in Africa (commonly 5–7 offspring per woman). In western societies on the other hand, fertility is controlled and 2–3 children is the norm, with high parental investment in each (some degree of support over two decades). Second, mortality rates are higher in traditional societies, especially among young children. Third, traditional average lifespan is decidedly lower than in western societies. In brief, modern societies produce half the number of children, while doubling longevity. These remarkable differences are consequences of culture, nutrition and modern medicine (and will change in Africa by famine relief, control of disease and contraception).

There is also the question of time: notions of time cannot readily be summarised in a Table. In traditional perceptions, the past is real and related to the present. Successions of events – births and deaths, famines – are remembered, but life tends to be seen as cyclical. Creation and renewal are the subjects of innumerable myths. Time in equilibrium with nature continues into eternity and is immeasurable. Accordingly, the basic pattern of life appears as unchanging and unending. The western concept, on the other hand, is of cumulative time in successive ages punctuated by historical events, i.e., linear time, from which come the practice of schedules and ideals of efficiency.

To the traditional mind, the present and remembered past is the most meaningful expression of time. Time is to be experienced. To a westerner on the other hand, the world and his own existence is continually changing and evolving. Unfortunately, however, he seems to benefit little from historic experience. A perceptive view was expressed by Kenneth Kaunda: 'If I had to describe the differences between African and Western psychology, I would say that the Westerner has a problem-solving mind whilst the African has a situation-experiencing mind.'[3]

Traditional ideas of the future are vague; it is an extension of the present without taking a long view. Concepts of change from a lower to higher order of things, or 'progress' in a western sense, are not developed. Therefore traditional people tend not to plan for a distant future (which is not to say they do not have practical foresight). This is significantly different from the outlook of the westerner, who typically expends a great deal of effort in the present looking to the future; preparing plans, building up assets, investing and insuring. Secular modern man is convinced that by 'taking thought for the morrow' personal well-being can be improved, and the world can be changed through science. Deriving from this is his economic sense of time. Time is of value, and in a competitive utilitarian world time is money; a commodity to be bought or sold.

To the modern mind, traditional lifestyles are often associated with resource sustainability, on the assumption of equilibrium between a stable society and a long-exploited resource. Natural systems are of course subject to dynamic fluctuations even in the tropics. In my observations, traditional fishing people showed little evidence of possessing a conservation ethic – a deliberate and predictive linking of catches with fish abundance. Instead nature is regarded as a generous giver, and fishermen generally try to catch as much as they need. Exploitative fishing effort has greatly increased in Sub-Saharan Africa in the past century as everywhere human populations have increased and the efficiency of gear and marketing have improved. Nowadays, the usual story is of steadily declining catches. (The apparently stable swamp fishery of the Bangweulu Unga is an exception (see Chapter 3). Unfortunately, western concepts of sustainable resource management have not made much headway in Africa (and have often fallen short in the west too).

Truly traditional societies are now rare. Political independences brought greater exposure to the modern world. Most Africans now live in hybrid societies where strands of traditional and modern cultures are entwined – although behind this simplification exists a wide range of societal and economic differences. In an ideal world one would look for synthesis whereby modern ways are grafted onto traditional roots, improving living standards without great cultural disruption. But if western history is any guide, smooth transition is unlikely.

Transition to the modern was disruptive and painful (one thinks of the terrible social conditions during and after the Industrial Revolution, from the mid-eighteenth to the late nineteenth centuries). In Africa transition must overcome profound cultural difference, and the great majority of people are trapped in poverty. Moreover, it is taking place in a context of rapid demographic growth, still far from reaching its full magnitude (see Chapter 15). These conditions tend to slow the rate of development.

Notes and references

1. For example, in this way a comparison was made of empirical behaviour between the two worlds of Kinship (traditional) and Civil Society (modern) in a slum situation in Accra, Ghana, by J.K. Hart in 'Kinship, Contract and Trust: The economic organization of migrants in an African city slum'. In: Gambetto, Diego (ed.), *Trust, making and breaking cooperative relations.* Dept. of Sociology, University of Oxford (2000); 6: 174–193.
2. Yash Ghai (2000). *In traditional societies, the jury is out on legal reform.* UNESCO Courier 2000.
3. Quoted from Leistner, E. (2005). *African Predicament*, pp.31–33. Mlalo Publishers, Pretoria, South Africa.

15

The Rural Poor

In the mid-1990s I lived for six weeks in a small bungalow beside Lake Malawi. Only a few African people were in the vicinity. Every morning as I was having breakfast, a woman passed. She was slight, barefoot, with a baby slung on her back. On her head was a four-sided twenty-litre can known as a *debe*, sold containing kerosene but very useful for carrying water. As I watched through the open verandah she went down the short beach and into the water to more than knee depth. Then, following an unvarying routine, the baby was secured more tightly to her, she removed the can from her head, and she placed a little pad of banana leaves on her head. She bent her knees, lowering the can until it was full of water – but all the time keeping her head upright and the baby just above the water. Then in a swift movement she swung the can up and settled it on her head, adjusting it briefly on the pad of leaves. Returning up the beach and past my house again she disappeared up a track to her hut, about 100 metres off. She never indicated that she saw me. No doubt the water was for her family's daily needs. The baby was probably her first, since no children were at heel.

The little operation went so smoothly that at first I did not realise what a feat it was. It would have been impossible to me. I could perhaps have managed to lift up the can of water, using her trick of entering the lake to shorten the distance of lift. But I could not have carried the weight on my head or balanced it while walking confidently forward. Had the can of water slipped backwards it would have fallen on the baby. This was only one of her many household tasks, for at other times she was busily chopping firewood logs or cooking or hoeing her cultivated patch, always baby on back. Several times I saw her in a group on the way to market, eight kilometres away, while the searing heat of the day reflected from bare rocky hills on each side of the road. All the group bore head loads of canes or vegetables for sale. Yet they were not starving or apparently malnourished. Simply, life is hard for the poor.

Definitions of poverty

Poverty is difficult to define, and a precise and consistent definition may not be feasible.[1] In Africa many manage to be well fed as long as they have access to land to cultivate. Standards of living vary between countries; for example, a relatively 'poor' citizen of a wealthy country might be regarded as rich by the standards of poorer developing countries. Since authorities need to set nominal levels, United Nations agencies use a criterion, 'the poverty line', which is nominally one US dollar a day average income. The UN-HABITAT organisation recognises a basic definition, a bottom line so to speak, for a slum household in which the poor and very poor live. It is a household that lacks one or more of the five following elements: access to clean water, access to improved sanitation, security of tenure, durability of housing, and sufficient living area. Many of the poor in developing countries lack one or more of these elements (see Note 2 in Chapter 16). The definition is only a rule of thumb, for 'access' might mean water or sanitation facilities a kilometre away, which is often the case. Even if the five definitive elements are assumed to be cost free, one dollar is not a lot to buy a minimum intake of food (understood as 2,200 kilocalories per day, below which an adult human is undernourished).

In real life, two categories of poor usually exist: a majority who manage by struggling to keep themselves and their dependents from physical want; and a minority who have fallen into physical want and are destitute. These two categories have been distinguished in many written records of the past. As well there are the elderly, the infirm and the very young, who in Africa are traditionally taken care of by their extended family.

Poverty in Europe has been distinguished as two generalised types, structural and conjunctural. Structural poverty is long-term want in individuals due to their personal or social circumstances. In land-rich societies it comprises able-bodied men and women who work for subsistence, whereas in land-poor societies it contains some able-bodied people who lack employment or are landless. The elderly, incapacitated and young are included in structural poverty. Conjunctural poverty, on the other hand, is a condition into which ordinarily self-sufficient men and women may be thrown by crises. For example, severe drought might culminate in mass famine; or catastrophic events such as disease epidemics may cause the deaths of many, or war may produce displaced people and refugees.

Where land is scarce

In most African countries land does not limit agricultural expansion and, until recently at least, there has been plenty to spare; but climatic conditions are crucial, especially the amount and timing of rainfall. In certain parts of Subsaharan Africa (SSA), such as the small highly populated countries of Burundi, Rwanda and Malawi, land is presently limiting. Moreover, intensive cultivation has caused severe soil nutrient depletion and erosion. I shall focus here on these three countries as extreme examples of land shortage and over-intensive agriculture. Such conditions will spread widely in SSA if population numbers continue to rise.[2]

Once I had a memorable insight into land shortage and weather dependence from a peasant farmer's perspective. It was on the road from Lake Malawi up to the capital, Lilongwe. Surmounting the steep rift escarpment, one approaches Lilongwe over gently undulating land. On each side as far as the eye could see were small cultivated plots jammed together, with few unworked spaces between. Occasional large mango trees stood out and huts were dotted here and there. It was a late October afternoon in the mid-1990s. Towards the north horizon the blue sky darkened, and in the heavy clouds bunched there lightning flashed and faint rumbles of thunder came. It was time for the first rains. Such hints of rain may come and go quite a while before the real rains break. Drought years are not infrequent, or years when only sufficient rain falls to make the crops sprout before they wither. The farmers' labour then is wasted and a shortage of food directly follows. So here was the land laid out expectantly. Waiting eyes watched every distant gathering of clouds. The air seemed charged and tense with anticipation. It was oppressively hot, and in Lilongwe the streets teemed with people, many no doubt depending on the harvest from the land I'd seen near town. My sense of foreboding grew. What if the rains didn't come this year?

The same evening I was invited to a party, the occasion for which I forget, and to which I was not particularly looking forward. But by chance I found myself talking to a UN Food & Agriculture (FAO) man, and felt compelled to tell him of my apprehensions. He understood well: 'If the rains don't come this year we'll manage,' he said, 'as long as drought areas are not too extensive. The big silos on your right as you entered Lilongwe are full of grain for famine relief.' Only partly reassured, I thought: If this life-or-death circumstance can occur fortuitously, and calamity averted only by foreign aid from year to year, life must be fraught with anxiety and uncertainty. In fact, Malawi is self-sufficient only in good harvest years; in poor ones an emergency arises. In the long term, rain-fed agriculture that is subject to critical small climate variations cannot sustain a large population.

Later I shared my thoughts with a Malawian man. He agreed, 'Food security is a country-wide problem,' and as an example he mentioned a village we both knew. 'This year the people of the village realised the land around them was exhausted. Crop yields have declined, there is not enough land to leave some fallow for several years to recover, and the population is always growing bigger. So some of the young men have gone to another village, about a day's walk away. They intend to ask the chief there who has some forested land, whether they could come and cultivate some of it [on the usufruct principle – right of temporary use without ownership]. In return, the chief will expect a proportion of the crops grown. If they can reach agreement, more men and women will come from the home village, cut down and burn an area of trees and prepare the ground for planting and build houses. Their families will join them and settle, expecting better harvests from that vicinity. A minority will stay in the old village, depending upon the tired land to sustain smaller numbers. There is nothing remarkable about this story for it is happening everywhere in Malawi. Pressure is increasing on the land.'

While flying over forested Central Africa one frequently sees evidence of this kind of agriculture ('slash-and-burn' or *chitamene*), visible as groups of circular clearings. One clearing in a group will have crops growing for the farmer's household; the others nearby are left fallow in various stages of forest re-growth. It is a suitable enough method of small farming provided plenty of land is available to permit fallowing for several years. On approaching more populated parts, the forest becomes scanty and groups of cleared circles are closer. Around towns and cities the land tends to be intensively cultivated in individual plots. Land use is accelerating. I know wide areas that only several decades ago were virtually unpopulated except for wildlife; now they contain numerous villages.

The Table below shows land and population data on Burundi, Rwanda and Malawi, drawn from recent Internet reports of aid agencies active in famine relief, health initiatives and refugee resettlement.[3] The reports are numerous and often updated.

Burundi and Rwanda are adjacent and fairly similar in area, topography and population size. Their terraced hillsides and wetland valley floors look similar (see photographs in Chapter 6). Malawi's topography is quite different. Dominated by the slopes of the western side of the rift valley, it has highlands and in the south an extensive marsh. The proportions of land under agriculture given in the Table are probably underestimates, for

	Burundi	*Rwanda*	*Malawi*
Area (sq. km.)*	25,650	26,790	94,487
Agricultural area (% cultivated)	40 to 60	>50	>50
Subsistence farmers (% of total population)	91	>90	86
Population (million)	>8	10.4(2008)	14(2008)
Population growth (%/year)	<3	2.6	2.6
Population density/sq.km.	273	343	118
Children per woman	6.0	5.9	5.3
Life expectancy (years)	43	44	40
Below poverty line (%)	60	60	60
GDP (US$/capita/year)	149	60	160

*Lake area not included.

cultivation is continually being extended into marginal land, and forests cut down. Significant areas are unsuitable for cultivation or pasture. The great majority of people in each country depend on what they can grow, but population increase is causing the average size of cultivated holdings to shrink. Three million households in Rwanda have on average less than a quarter of a hectare to farm. As land is split among large families it becomes harder to make a subsistence living. Fluctuations of annual rainfall can rapidly bring about emergencies.

Land tenure is a contentious issue and disputes frequent – hardly surprising given the direct relation of land with food security. Indeed, the very high density of populations on arable land in Rwanda and Burundi is probably one of the underlying causes of the terrible violence of the past four decades ('land management is the single most important factor in conflicts of the region').[4]

In Burundi and Rwanda one is struck by the densely inhabited lower slopes of hills and intensively cultivated terraces, contrasting with the usually abundant space of Africa. Settlement is crowded except on barren high ground. Yet four million inhabitants in Burundi in 1980 became eight million by the end of the twentieth century, and the population is predicted to reach ten million by 2015. Rwanda and Burundi have the highest and second highest population densities, respectively, in Africa. The Table gives only approximate population numbers because settlement has fluctuated drastically in the past few decades as multitudes have died or fled from war or returned as refugees. HIV-AIDS has also taken a heavy toll. Despite all this, populations keep rising inexorably by natural increase.

As to Malawi, records show growing population increase: from 737,000 in the first census in 1901 to 14 million in 2008. More than half the present population is under 15 years old, so increase is bound to continue. The country has the worst AIDS epidemic on the continent (currently about 12% of adults), and there are an estimated 500,000 AIDS orphans. On the other hand, fertility rates are high, averaging five to six children born per woman. That of course is not the same as actual population growth, which is between two and three per cent per year (representing a doubling time of about two and a half decades). Mortality rates of young children are high, and average life expectancy not much over 40 years.[5]

By the aid agencies' criteria for poverty, more than 60% of people in each of the three countries are impoverished. Actual numbers vary with time of year and harvest success. Poverty, food availability and health are worst between harvests. The countries are structurally food-deficient because of the small size of farm plots, declining fertility of soil and low productivity. Food security requires there to be adequate national buffer stocks to cover lean years.

The past few years have seen successive droughts threatening food security, a virus disease affecting cassava – one of the main staple foods – and a significant increase in imported food prices (in places as much as 60%). Deforestation (to collect firewood for cooking) has been severe: 9% of the Burundi land area between 1996 and 2000 and similar rates for Rwanda and Malawi.

The bad news continues: Food production in Burundi has actually decreased by 24% since 1993, due to soil nutrient exhaustion and population flux caused by wars in Rwanda and Burundi, which destabilised food production for years. Annual food deficits are in the range 300,000 to 400,000 tonnes of cereals. Presently, 69% of the population suffer malnutrition, and 44% of children under five are chronically malnourished.

In Rwanda 45% of infants are stunted, and 10–12% of inhabitants are food-insecure. The World Food Program has provided annual relief rations to 640,000 people in Rwanda and the north of Burundi, and in areas of severe drought in 2008–2009, WFP assistance reached a monthly average of 717,000 people.

In Malawi food security does not exist, except in very good harvests. As a broad estimate, 34% of the population is malnourished, and 22% chronically food-insecure. Maize is the staple crop there, but recurring droughts, erratic rainfall and poor resource management cause wide annual fluctuations in harvests. This has always been so, of course, and particularly bad famines remain in farmers' minds (e.g., the 1949 famine, 1991–92 drought, 2001 crop flooding, and drought in 2002, 2003, 2005. In the latter year more than a third of the population needed food aid to survive).

Health problems in Burundi seem to relate closely to food shortage. Emaciation is common in adults. Among children, both clinical forms of acute malnutrition occur: marasmus (very thin) and kwashiorkor (swollen). Health stabilisation centres are being set up by Médécins sans Frontières to rescue critically malnourished children. Average per capita production from agriculture in the country stands at 1,400 kilocalories per day (recommended minimum intake 2,200 kcal/d). Anaemia affects 40% of children under five and 30% of pregnant women. HIV/AIDS prevalence is up to 18% in the capital, Bujumbura.

Overall, as populations continue to climb in these countries so does dependency on famine relief from abroad. As long as that is available, the chief problem from year to year is forecasting the next shortfall in crops in time, before famine develops. One source[5] calls it 'a juggling act in the search for food security'. Such juggling is recurrent where populations have grown beyond the carrying capacity of the land. In bigger countries, e.g., Tanzania, local famine relief might be supplied from internal sources.[1]

These brief data suffice to indicate the meagre nature of life in the three countries. But even such desolate facts about settled populations do not convey the intense misery of refugees struggling to live in unstable conditions. Wars in Rwanda and Burundi have added a catastrophic dimension to land shortage and pervasive poverty, and generated huge refugee and repatriation problems. In the year 2000, Burundians were the largest refugee population in the world, except for Afghans. Since 2002 the UN High Commission for Refugees has assisted 473,000 Burundi nationals to return from refugee camps in northern Tanzania. The 1994 massacre in Rwanda was immediately followed by an exodus of two million people into northeast Congo. As refugees return home in numbers, they pose intractable problems of resettlement, since in their absence other farmers have often occupied their land. In Burundi, as well as return flows of refugees, there are presently 100,000 internally displaced persons whose land rights remain to be determined. Formal adjudication processes are frustratingly slow (thousands of claims go back to the 1972 refugee flight); meanwhile those awaiting a decision need food and shelter. Their problems are worsened by a deeply established culture of violence and impunity acquired during the long war years in Burundi.

On a more positive note, political positions in Rwanda and Burundi are improving. Rwanda has been under stable government since 1995 and is making good progress towards recovery. A reviving tourist industry signals growing confidence in that country's stability. Interestingly, in light of the above discussion on Ujamaa villagisation in Tanzania (see Chapter 13), one of the early post-war schemes in Rwanda was trial resettlement in new villages, taking advantage of the flux in population. Over 600,000 displaced persons were regrouped into villages in the north of the country. (Objections were raised by human rights organisations on the grounds of government coercion.)

In Burundi a peace and reconciliation accord took place in 2000 between the recalcitrant ethnic groups, and a transitional government carried on until free elections in 2005. Aid agencies were able to shift from targeted relief to recovery activities, still including wide food supply. The gradual return of refugees from camps in Tanzania was speeded up in 2005. International donors pledged $665 million for poverty reduction in the years 2007 to 2010, and Burundi's very high international debt was substantially cut by $833 million in a debt-relief process.

Obviously, massive foreign assistance has been flowing in. Foreign aid accounts for 40% of Malawi and of Rwanda government budgets, while in Burundi it may be more. Aid to Rwanda, Burundi and Congo has been regionally coordinated, acknowledging linkages between the successive internal wars and spillovers of refugees. These countries demonstrate that war adds immensely to the cost of aid, in money, time and misery, and aid agencies still have a huge task ahead.

Malawi, however, has a history of peace over at least a century. The tribes – Chewa, Ngozi and Yao, and several minor ones – manage to co-exist peacefully. They mix well abroad in other countries. For many decades it has become almost customary for young men to seek work outside Malawi, particularly in the Rand mines of South Africa. Savings and remittances from this source are economically important to the country.

Demography and poverty type

When drastic events, such as famine, sickness epidemics or war, hit subsistence societies, structural poverty turns into conjunctural poverty. Death rates mount and populations fall to low levels until conditions improve; or until people migrate to more productive places and numbers rise again.[6]

Human populations were in a reduced phase in the 1870s to 1890s in Central and East Africa. Conjunctural poverty then resulted from cattle plague (almost universal in tropical Africa in the 1890s), locust outbreaks, and epidemics of introduced diseases. For example, the Unga people of the

Bangweulu Swamps were almost wiped out by a smallpox epidemic.[7] Not least, widespread slave raiding and trade in firearms still went on, causing fear and flight (see Chapter 10). Early European travellers in East Africa around this time often encountered abandoned villages and deserted country.

Populations seem to have stabilised, and poverty become structural early in the twentieth century. A major setback occurred at the end of the 1914–18 World War (see Chapter 11), a time of drought, famine and disease, but thereafter famines were better controlled and localised.[8] With roads and the motor car, incipient food shortages could be countered by rapid transport of food relief. Medical help was mobilised. A steady population increase became evident from the mid-1920s, and subsequently, around the period of national independences in the early 1960s, there were instances of poverty through over-population.[1] The poor had become poorer by structural poverty. Large families became a cause of poverty rather than of wealth, as farm plots were subdivided.

Demographic pressure rose with overall average growth of 3% per annum, outpacing food production. One consequence was a rise in migration to towns and cities where, at that time, there was likelihood of finding paid employment. The demographic upswing has continued to the present unprecedented high point. In some countries populations are close to the agricultural carrying capacity of the land or have exceeded it. Poverty is still structural, but crowding beyond ecological sustainability risks catastrophe.

One is tempted to compare the rise in African populations with those of Europe and North America during the industrial revolution, fostered by science and modern medicine. That comparison is not valid, for industry and market economies in Africa have a long way to go to produce conditions for absorbing population increase and creating wealth. According to one view,[2] the basic problem is neither technical nor climate-induced, but linked to socio-economic issues and the inadequacy of traditional structures. In particular, there is no tradition of producing for large-scale market economies.

As a result of poverty, heavy dependence on foreign aid has built up in the poorest countries, especially the small, densely populated countries we have been talking about. Note that, whereas the population of Africa south of the Sahara has quadrupled since 1950, imports of cereals increased ten-fold between 1961 and 2001.[9] Perhaps 'degree of aid-dependency' should be distinguished as another category of poverty?

Food crisis: Agricultural involution

Rural economies are mostly subsistence ones, but this does not mean they are necessarily in serious want, except in a monetary sense. In such societies, social obligations tend to have higher priority than earning money, and needs for goods or labour are often met by reciprocal arrangements. However, Africa produces too little food; overall production per capita has steadily diminished since 1965. Imported food has become very expensive (global food prices roughly doubling in three years).[10] Consequent over-intensive farming leads to soil nutrient depletion and diminishing yields, a process known as 'agricultural involution'.[11]

An interesting analysis of food production was made in twenty poor African countries where the majority of labour is agricultural.[12] These economies are still in very early stages of structural transformation (change to a productive and diversified economy based on manufacturing and services). All the countries had high population growth rates (close to 3%), low farm productivity and very limited non-farm employment. Analysis focused on four factors fostering structural transformation: agricultural productivity, demographic growth, expansion of agricultural markets, and the development of rural industry. The model predicts, for example, that if population growth stays at 3% and agricultural labour is over 80% of the population, then the structural transformation turning point will not be reached within 50 years.

The analysis also examined the relevance of East Asian experience, particularly of Taiwan, in order to suggest development priorities for small-scale, labour-intensive farming in Africa. While Taiwan used the seed–fertiliser combinations of the Asian 'green revolution' in the 1970s, it had also to overcome negative factors similar to the African countries – 3% population growth and a human fertility rate as high as 6.3%. Notably, the country's remarkable success in agriculture was accompanied by family planning, reduction of child mortality and the spread of education – integral parts of the economic development programme. Irrigation played a large part in Taiwan's progress, but is unfortunately unlikely to be significant in Sub-Saharan Africa.[13] However, improved seed and fertiliser should give substantial crop increases even on rain-fed farms (see below).

Taiwan reached its 'structural transformation turning point' when the size of the farm labour force began to decline at an accelerating rate. The study[12] concluded that: (i) transformation of an agrarian subsistence economy depends on substantial increase in productivity, (ii) it relies on marketed agricultural output, (iii) relative growth in non-farm employment accelerates transformation.

A recent comparison of the African food crisis with the Asian green revolution[9] found that in all cases of the latter, three conditions facilitated it: active leadership of the state, market mediation, and orientation to the small farmer. These conclusions are important. African small farmers achieve crop yields only one third of those obtained by farmers in the developing countries of Asia.

The 'green revolution' ***did not reach Africa***. No large-scale advances have happened through seed-selection, inorganic fertilisers, pesticides and organised marketing, although various schemes have produced spurts of smallholder production. For example, the Malawi government subsidised farmers to purchase synthetic fertiliser and improved maize seed in 2006. Helped by the World Bank, 1.3 million poor farming families each got 3 kg of hybrid corn seed and 100 kg of fertiliser at a third of the market price. The 2007 harvest was called the Malawi Miracle; it doubled normal production. The next year there was a 50% surplus over national needs, and maize was exported.[14] Crucially, the rains were good in those years. The results showed that improved seed and fertiliser can make a big difference, even a 'green revolution' based on small land plots, provided there is enough water. The snag is that loans for seed and fertiliser lead the small farmer into serious debt in years of poor rainfall. In another village in Malawi, nitrogen-fixing legume plants such as soybeans, pigeon peas and peanuts were substituted for fertiliser. It seems Malawi farmers need not be dependent on fossil fuel-based nitrogen fertilisers and pesticides. Moreover, adding legumes improves diets.

Another programme, the 'Sasakawa global 2000', brought high-input technical packages to a number of African countries, and indeed raised yields of cereals wherever it was applied. But the programme gave insufficient weight to marketing, so the increased production merely led to disappointing price collapses.[15]

Another factor is 'land grabs': Anticipated food shortage in wealthy countries elsewhere in the world has recently led to a rush to procure agricultural land in Africa. Adesina[15] lists nine selected cases. Already large areas are involved, totalling 15 to 20 million hectares valued at between $15 and $30 billion dollars. Underlying reasons are rising land prices in developed countries, demand for land to produce bio-fuels, land to produce high-value food for rapidly developing countries with increasing incomes (e.g., China, India) and land to secure food supplies for oil-rich countries (e.g., Quatar, United Arab Emirates, Saudi Arabia). Some are private-sector transactions and some government to government. The acquired land will presumably be farmed by large-scale, mechanised methods. Food produced will probably be exported back to the investor countries from African countries themselves short of food – an uncomfortable thought.

Obviously in these 'land grabs' there are considerations of equity (suitable compensation for people who may be displaced from their lands), and of the transparency of the transactions. Positive spin-offs could be local employment opportunities, and demonstration and training benefits. But the history of large-scale commercial agriculture in tropical Africa has not always been marked by success, especially on land that is marginal in soil type or average rainfall. Clearly this new development trend is worth watching.

The Millennium Development Project

From the 1980s, world opinion swung from prioritising 'development' in poor countries to 'poverty reduction'. Reflecting the new mood, member countries of the United Nations committed themselves, at the Millennium summit in September 2000, to the goal of halving the proportion of the global population that survives on less than $1 a day by the year 2015. Many people in poorer countries work all their lives without being able to lift themselves from this level of poverty. So the focus of international attention in recent times is to reach Millennium Development Goals (MDGs).[16]

For over fifty years international aid has attempted to conquer rural poverty by increasing output from smallholder farms. A new initiative of 'Millennium Development Villages' (MDV) was launched in 2006, devised by the Earth Institute of the University of Columbia, USA. It is part of a large multi-national project, the UN Millennium Development Project (MDP). The millennium villages are a joint activity between the University of Columbia, UNDP, UNICEF and other funding partners. Across Africa, in ten relatively peaceful and stable countries, 80 villages are starting to operate at 14 sites, each site representing different agro-ecological conditions. It has been called 'a bottom-up approach to lifting developing country villages out of the poverty trap'.[17] For its ultimate success the project depends on 'scaling up' these initial villages.

The central idea[18] is simple: taking technology and training directly to widespread villages selected for modernisation. The first ones (called Millennium Research Villages) are each located close to a cluster of other villages (e.g., the one in southern Malawi is in a cluster of seven, adding up to 35,000 people). Cooperating communities are assured of ownership by being involved in management. Integrated packages, costing $120 per village person per year, include improvements in agriculture, health, education, clean water, efficient sanitation, women's status, communication, roads and electricity.

The rationale is that, by applying all these improvements simultaneously, agricultural growth in a village, as distinct from subsistence cultivation, will be strongly stimulated. Implementation comes about as a combined effort entailing community mobilisation, project inputs, and national government support in personnel and infrastructure. The expected proving period of an MRV project is five to ten years, after which it is hoped the model village cluster will be self-supporting and can be scaled up to cover wider regions in each country. Notably, the project does not envisage coercion but relies on example, encouragement and financial support.

One gets the impression the plan is being vigorously implemented. Initial reports speak of successes in boosting crops with fertiliser, reducing malaria through distributing mosquito nets and improving health generally. Better nutrition of children seems to improve their school performance. Funding is sufficient for multiple objectives to be attacked simultaneously; thus agricultural improvement goes forward along with granaries, new clinics, schools, roads and whatever is relevant to the needs of the programme. Neighbourhood villages have access to facilities in a millennium village, broadening its scope of activity. Clinics treat not only malnutrition and common illnesses like malaria and parasitic diseases, but also HIV/AIDS and give advice on family planning and contraception.

Strategies for scaling-up are being planned. For example, in a first step to reach 'district level', work will expand to village clusters containing up to 55,000 people.[19] The vision is ambitious, nothing less than – 'to end rural poverty in Africa'.[18] An independent review of MVP concepts in 2006[17] thought the village project might renew attention of large donors to rural development after decades of neglect. The following paragraph summarises main points of the review (in development jargon):

> There are striking similarities with past African agricultural development projects, particularly the IRD (Integrated Rural Development) projects of the 1970s and 1980s. These are now seen as ineffective. Advances gained were rarely sustained. A common criticism, which hopefully may not apply to MVP, was their excessively top-down and supply-driven nature, relying heavily on outside technical assistance. Consequently, they did not leave behind competent management structures. The MVP does have features of the 'blueprint' approach (quantified goals), which leaves the beneficiaries little scope for devising local solutions to their peculiar problems. Also it shares with

> previous projects a 'campaign' attitude, which leaves insufficient time for consolidation of project gains. Dangers are foreseen that links with local governance will be weak, and the rhetoric of 'participation' will not be translated into practice. Misuse of capital assets (like vehicles and equipment) is another latent worry. Ensuring that marketing arrangements are in phase with crop production is emphasised.

(Note: Another organisation entitled Alliance for a Green Revolution in Africa [AGRA] is currently entering the field. It aims to help smallholders by improving seeds, soil fertility and market access. Importantly, AGRA will study past experience to beat the stubborn problems of rural poverty.)[20]

Getting results with MVP

To anyone acquainted with the conservative, slow-paced life-style of remote villages (fishing villages in my own case), the speed and scale of the villages project are breathtaking. Even with abundant donor funds and numerous staff (short-term expats and permanent locals), the sheer scale of work over a number of countries – concurrently getting village clusters running productively, organising market outlets, coordinating activities with local participation at all levels – must be unprecedented among rural projects in Africa.

One recognises poignant snapshots of traditional life in MVP reports, familiar from past development projects. For example, when first distributing seed and fertiliser at one village the amount given to each farmer was estimated on the area of land he was cultivating. But the village committee insisted that each farmer should get just the same amount regardless of land – probably to avoid jealousy. This highlights a difference between expat understanding, based on rational considerations, and traditional social rules of conformity and harmony. Again, when a man was congratulated on his good crops of maize he sighed and explained that his harvests had to be divided with numerous poor relatives who, according to traditional practice, had turned up to share his good fortune. Another tale mentions the difficulty committee members had in keeping up with innovations. These members had special status in their community – hence their place on the committee – not upon grounds of education and technical know-how but rather on social wisdom and experience.

My personal reaction is that MVP, despite its breadth of scope, is designed from a typically western cultural viewpoint, with its quantitative materialist approach and expectations. That is: improvements will be demonstrated, harvests will rise dramatically and local people will be expected to adapt their lives accordingly. When the right material conditions and arrangements are in place and working, the project will be expected to run more or less on its own, despite abundant evidence that transition from traditional to modern attitudes is slow and pregnant with difficulty.[21] If this logic dominates in the MVP it will mean, I believe, that ***development agencies have learned practically nothing in the past fifty years***. New attitudes must accompany technology – this has been the sticking point in the past.

Given that many resource projects have achieved only limited success, or failed, one is bound to ask what is different about this one? If the promised large funds materialise, this project may expand far beyond any previous ones. But are size, scope and finance the keys to success? Is it just a matter of money and effort? I must admit to being dubious about the 'big push' philosophy, which lends itself so easily to political polemic. Dynamic big pushes are not new in Africa – beginning with Nkrumah's big push to industrialise Ghana in 1960s (see Chapter 1); most recently the term was used in the report of the Commission for Africa (2005).[22] Unfortunately, big pushes seldom come off, although the notion is doubtless attractive to donors who on the whole are not keen to commit themselves to long-term projects with prospects of only incremental gains.[23]

Initial bigger harvests or improved health should not be seen as anything but demonstrations of what is possible. It is no surprise that fertiliser and improved seeds give bigger crops, or that people will be healthier if they sleep under mosquito nets. But peasants tend to resist rather than welcome innovations that separate them from their traditions. As described above, the largest agricultural project in SSA so far (Ujamaa, see Chapter 13) failed because the peasantry strongly preferred traditional ways. But whether by steady progress or big push, it is certain that long-term commitment by external agencies will be necessary. In addition to supplying and demonstrating, it is a far greater job to persuade people who have cultivated or fished only for their families or small community to switch to a commercial mindset, giving marketing as much attention as production. Principles of profit and gain, at individual or community levels, have to replace former ethics of sharing and self-sufficiency. People long habituated to tradition must overcome barriers to conform to a different social and economic model. For them it is a big step to enter a market economy and adopt the customs and assumptions of a developed country.

> 'The powerful hold of traditional world views, values and practices on thinking and doing ... differs fundamentally from the technical-scientific mindset that rules and shapes the modern world.'[24]

> 'Economic development, its initiation if not its maintenance, is a function not of impersonal economic forces, but of the nature and nurture of human beings and the society which they constitute in collectivity.'[25]

> 'The crisis in Africa is not only material, but mainly philosophical and psychological, that is, non-material.'[26]

In this context, MVP is a frontal attack. It will rely on exact coordination within and between comprehensive inputs (production) and outputs (marketing and transport). But modernisation is also a matter of social transformation, so plenty of time must be allowed for new ideas to catch on and spread.

Lessons from fishery development

Parallels exist between subsistence agriculture and subsistence fisheries. In both cases, numerous small operators use simple labour-intensive methods. Capital is not accumulated. Production is chiefly population-driven. A resource is exploited in the sense of making do with what is available rather than going for higher production. However, in both cases improvement in living standards must come about by higher productivity, connection with markets, commercial motivation – all within the constraints of cultural resistance to change, rural isolation, demographic pressure and lack of private investment.

Experience supported by a large literature[27] has shown that:

1. Fishermen are adaptable as regards simple upgrades in methodology.
2. Improved techniques (artisanal fishing) can be used cooperatively.
3. Commercial fisheries can grow from component small-scale units.
4. Exploitation rates can increase dramatically when a working mix of production and marketing is found.

To quote an FAO report,[28] 'It has been shown that for many fisheries in the world where satisfactory transport links are established, and a market is available, the thrust to develop the fishery is almost unstoppable.' Indeed, marketing tends to develop spontaneously in flexible and opportunistic ways when roads, transport and market infrastructure become available. Independent traders often play a vital role. Thus a village may 'market' its produce through visiting traders without much effort or change in normal life; it is important only that the traders call reliably and fit in with the needs and habits of villagers. Such ways may seem 'imperfect' to a western-style developer but, whatever the solution, reliable access to markets from an early stage of development is *crucial* to growth. Lake Victoria is a prime example: when large-scale processing and marketing facilities were established there it quickly became the largest fishery in Africa. Similar conclusions might apply to development of subsistence agriculture.

Notes and references

1. Iliffe, J. (1987). *The African Poor.* Cambridge University Press.
2. Verheye, W.H. (2000). Food production or food aid? An African challenge. *Journal of Finance and Development, International Monetary Fund, Vol.37, No.4.*
3. For example, journals produced by the World Food Programme (WFP), UN High Commission for Refugees (UNHCR), UN Food and Agriculture Organisation (FAO), Médécins sans Frontières (MSF) and Refugees International (RI); these organisations often work in partnership with other relief agencies and non-governmental organisations (NGOs).
4. Wikipedia (2009), Rwanda, pp.13–14.
5. http://uk.oneworld.net/guides/malawi/development
6. Waters, T. (2006). *The Persistence of Subsistence Agriculture: Life beneath the level of the marketplace,* p.38. Lexington Books, USA.
7. Brelsford, W.V. (1946). *Fishermen of the Bangweulu Swamps.* Rhodes-Livingstone Papers, 12, Rhodes-Livingstone Institute, Zambia.
8. There were exceptions where severe famines did occur, in Rwanda and Burundi in 1927–28, and repeatedly in Ethiopia (Iliffe, J. 1987).
9. Djurfeldt, D., Holmen, H., Jirstrom, M. & Larsson, R. (2005). *The African Food Crisis: Lessons from the Asian green revolution.* CABI Publishing, Oxfordshire, UK. For review, see Pandey, S. (2007). *Asian Journal of Agriculture and Development, Vol. 2, Nos. 1 & 2.*
10. *Scientific American*, 2008, August issue.
11. Geertz, C. (1963). *Agricultural Involution: The process of ecological change in Indonesia.* Berkeley, University of California Press.
12. Gabre-Madhin, E.Z. & Johnson, B.F. (1999). *Accelerating Africa's Structural Transformation: Lessons from East Asia.* Market and Structural Studies Division, International Food Policy Research Institute, Washington.
13. Rosegrant, M.W. & Perez, N.D. (1997). *Water resources development in Africa.* EPTD Discussion Papers 28, International Food Policy Research Institute, Washington, USA.
14. Bourne, J.K., *National Geographic Magazine*, June 2009, 215(6): 26–59.
15. Adesina, A.A. *Africa's Food Crisis: Conditioning trends and global development policy.* Paper presented at the International Association of Agricultural Economists Conference, Beijing, China. August 16, 2009.

16. At a Millennium Summit meeting in 2000 world leaders set quantified and time-bound Millennium Development Goals (MDGs) to cut extreme poverty, hunger, disease, gender inequality, environmental degradation, lack of access to safe drinking water and sanitation by the year 2015.
17. Cabral, L., Farrington, J. & Ludi, E. (2006). *The Millennium villages project: A new approach to ending rural poverty in Africa?* Overseas Development Institute, London.
18. Sanchez, P. & 23 other authors. (2007). *The African Millennium Villages.* The Earth Institute, Columbia University, New York.
19. Buse, K., Ludi, E. & Vigneri, M. (2008). *Can project-funded investments in rural development be scaled up? Lessons from the Millennium Villages Project.* Overseas Development Institute, London.
20. The AGRA organisation was created by the Rockefeller Foundation and the Bill and Melinda Gates Foundation, with initial funding of $400 million. As well as helping provide farm inputs, AGRA has a very important role in studying policy, and will hopefully take account of experience in many projects and studies over the past half-century to improve the lot of the African small farmer and fisherman. A common thread through this mass of evidence is the reluctance of peasants to leave subsistence life, with its strong traditional associations, for a market economy. See for example:
    Hyden, G. (1980). *Beyond Ujamaa in Tanzania; underdevelopment and an uncaptured peasantry.* Berkeley, University of California Press.
    Hyden, G. (1986). African social structure and economic development. In Borg, R. & Whitacre, J. (eds.), *Strategies for African Development*, pp. 52–80. Berkeley, University of California Press.
    Seavoy, R.E. (1989). *Famine in East Africa: Food production and food policies.* Greenwood Press, England.
    Waters, T. (2006). (Note 6 above.)
21. According to Waters (2006), 'change from a subsistence to a modern economy is a complex ecological transformation which takes decades and sometimes centuries' (p.6); this is because the two viewpoints are believed 'inherently incompatible' (p.2).
22. Commission for Africa, *Final Report.* (2005). (Introduced at the meeting of the G8 countries, Gleneagles, Scotland). http://www.commissionforafrica.org
23. As regards financing, one review of the MVP (Note 19) remarks, 'this renaissance ... has coincided with the apparent inability of many countries to make much progress on their Millennium Development Goals.' Perhaps such countries might be glad to grasp the opportunity given by the multi-national Millennium Village Project?
24. Leistner, E.(2005). *African Predicament.* Mlalo Publishers, South Africa.
25. Sadie, J.L. (1987). Economic Development: Fons et Origo. *Development Southern Africa; 4*(4), p.607. In: Leistner, E. (2005), p.25.
26. Mireku, E. (1988). Weltanschauung and Development: Basic elements of a general theory of development: An African perspective on the restoration of Africa. Dissertation 1070, *Hocheschule St.Gallen für Wirtschafts-und-Socialwissenschaften*, Bamberg, p.17. In: Leistner, E. (2005), p.1.
27. Jul-Larsen, E., Kolding, J., Overa, R., Raakjer Nielsen, J. & Zwieten, P. (eds.). (2003). *Management, co-management or no management? Major dilemmas in southern African freshwater fisheries.* FAO Fisheries Technical Paper 426/2, FAO, Rome.

This publication examines five lake fisheries in Congo (Democratic Republic), Malawi, Zambia and Zimbabwe, and shows they have undergone developmental changes transforming the lives of the fishing peoples.

28. Everett, G. (1995). *Sudan fisheries: An assessment of the situation.* FAO Circular 901. FAO, Rome.

16

The Urban Poor

'Some emerging African city regions are prospective gateway cities and could enhance the continent's integration into the global economy. But they have an even greater potential of becoming cores of intense inequity, corruption and deep human suffering if poorly governed and left to the voracity of unregulated market forces.'

State of the World's Cities UN-Habitat Report (2008)

'During the next two decades, Africa will have to find ways of facilitating urban housing, services and livelihoods for more than twice as many urban dwellers than today. Urban conditions will crucially determine transition to modern.'

(ibid)

'The great transition that has dominated the history of the poor in every continent is taking place in Africa.'

The African Poor, Iliffe (1987)

First, an anecdote: It was a hot afternoon in 1995, traffic was dense and the air thick with exhaust fumes and dust. I was travelling by taxi with an African colleague from the centre of Dar es Salaam, Tanzania, to the outskirts. In the city centre close to the sea stood the formal government buildings I remembered from 1961, when Dar was unchanged from colonial times and its population still small (< 300,000). Now there were over two million inhabitants. The taxi had not gone far before the buildings on either side became dilapidated. Very slow traffic allowed many opportunities to look into the side streets and alleyways, which were narrow and dingy. Shafts of light from the low sun cut across them. They were crowded, some people walking while others sat leaning against the walls of dwellings, and children played around. Goats and chickens investigated rubbish. The impression was of teeming squalor, which extended for miles. This had not been there, or was far less extensive, in the 1960s.

I'd seen similar scenes. Fresh in mind were some in Kampala, Uganda.

There I'd been on foot, and with time to spare walked through streets of closely built slums. It had been raining, all surfaces were still wet, and an uncomfortable chilly draught blew around the narrow ways between houses. Smelly drains were still running with rainwater. Some children played about, but their elders remained in the shelter of corrugated roofs. Despite exchanges of friendly greetings, I felt exposed to many gazes and after a while went back to a main road. I was depressed, partly because it was a dreary day but mostly because the slum had left me feeling desolate. Beneath the depression was outrage.

This sense of desolation came back again in the taxi in Dar. 'Why,' I asked my friend in some agitation, 'do they come to live like that? Would they not have better stayed in their home villages?'

He replied, 'Have you ever lived in an African village?'

'I've been in many villages,' I responded.

'That's not what I meant,' he returned. 'Have you ever lived in a village?' When I replied that I hadn't, he went on to say that only then would I understand why migrants came to town despite its poverty and squalor. He then spoke of his own experience and the liberation he had felt on quitting village life, and gave me the impression he regarded slums as a more or less inevitable phase on the road to modern development.

It was an important conversation. I saw that his viewpoint just reflected personal experience, and was not an objective answer. His relief at quitting village life, and sense of independence and freedom of choice, were understandable. In the village strong social pressure to conform to traditional ways smothers ambition and individuality; everyone's personal affairs are known. He had gone on to high school and university because he was bright and lucky enough to get a scholarship. Now with a professional qualification he had skipped the slum option. In fact, his position was almost as detached as mine.

So my question still stood. Why did people living in traditional homes, with extended family around, land to produce food and in a healthier environment without problems of water and sanitation, leave it all for poverty and squalor in the city? Despite the optimism of intending migrants, especially young ones, the bad conditions in slums are bound to be known to them; and they must also know that relatively few succeed in attaining the level of city elites.

Growth of African cities

African cities have utterly changed in the past half-century. This came about by rapid urban immigration from rural areas, and increasingly by natural growth in the city populations. Comprehensive reports on city growth and slum conditions have been published by the UN Agency UN-HABITAT,[1,2] and in shorter factual accounts by Rakodi[3] and Auclair.[4] The International Development Research Centre (IDRC) Handbooks provide broad perspectives (a particularly relevant title is their 'Informal Employment, Gender and Poverty').[5] Iliffe's excellent book *The African Poor*[6] contains a chapter on the urban poor. Davis's *Planet of Slums*[7] is a readable, well-researched study of worldwide slum growth, which leaves one more than a little apprehensive. Potts[8,9] summarises recent migration trends between town and country in SSA. These selected references are part of a large literature on African cities, migration and slum growth. Here I outline only general aspects; a country-by-country description would take volumes.

I watched urbanisation beginning to take off in Accra (Ghana) and Lusaka (Zambia) in the late 1950s and early 1960s, and also encountered the process at early stages in Dar es Salaam (Tanzania), Nairobi (Kenya) and Kampala (Uganda). Like most people I paid little attention; few then anticipated the deluge to come. By the 1970s unstoppable large-scale growth of cities was a fact of life throughout the continent, especially in the capital cities

Selected data on cities in SSA

UN-HABITAT (2008) estimate that by the mid-point of this century the population of the developing world will have more than doubled to 5 billion people.[2] Africa south of the Sahara is presently the least populated and urbanised region of the world.[1] Only about 12% of the population is urban,[2] but average urban growth is currently 4% to 5% per annum. The West African sub-region will reach the so-called urban transition point (>50% city dwellers) before 2020, while Central Africa may reach it by 2025. The East African region is predicted to double its 2007 urban population around 2025 – in merely 17 years.[2]

Some examples of city growth from 1950 to 2007 are: Lagos 300,000 to 9.67 million; Kinshasa 200,000 to 8.9 million; Dar es salaam 76,000 to 2.9 million; Addis Ababa 392,000 to 3.3 million; Nairobi 94,000 to 3.4 million.[1,2] The growth of a number of cities has been of the order of ten times, but Lagos and Kinshasa have become mega-cities. Most urban growth is now taking place in intermediate-size towns (<500,000 people).

The so-called 'urban informal sector', in which housing, access to sanitation and supply of clean water are very inadequate, averages 72% overall. Slums absorb about three quarters of cities' growth (190,000 newborn babies and immigrants per week[4]). The slum population in SSA will double every 15 years (reaching 332 million in 2015), in the context of a total population doubling time of 26 years. Urban growth has been too rapid for local authorities to provide the housing and services needed. Gigantic slums thus coexist with relatively small formal sectors, the richer communities living in guarded enclaves.

Informal settlements are now accepted to be a permanent part of the urban fabric, but it is still 'unclear ... whether the informal sector has the potential for accumulation and economic growth, or it is merely a subsistence sector of last resort'.[3] Employment is usually in small-scale businesses, mostly services, and productivity is very low on the whole. In Ghana and Nigeria there appears some evidence of dynamic linkages between the formal sector and the informal with its low-cost labour supply. Lagos is the biggest node of a projected corridor in West Africa, which will have at least 25 million people (another estimate is 60 million[7]) and a length of 600 km, stretching from Accra to Ibadan.[2] It could be the biggest continuous footprint of poverty on earth.

In general, appalling poverty extends in SSA to more than 50 % of national populations.[2] The rate of poverty is in fact much higher than the rate of unemployment, as most of the poor continue to work no matter how low or irregular their earnings. Slums have been associated by governments with illegality and social ills – breeding grounds for crime, prostitution, drug trafficking and disease – while regressive changes in income distribution have been occurring for decades; the poor getting poorer with a majority below the poverty line. Housing and services for them have become a market commodity, with people's ability to pay market prices determining access. Extreme health differentials occur between urban rich and poor – more than between city and country.

Family and kinship structures persist, as do indigenous cultural organisations. Despite their resilience, social networks characterised by cultural obligation and reciprocity come under stress in slum conditions. There are indications that urban households no longer rely exclusively on urban food supply lines, but family-produced rural food is taking on an increasing role. Where possible, maintaining a rural socio-economic base provides a safety-net for the urban poor in times of particular hardship. Conversely, some are able to send remittances to rural homes. Since the 1960s an exodus of young males (in the majority) from country to town has taken place, leaving more agricultural work to be done by women. One effect of this is weaker and poorer households.[10] While numbers of food producers have not changed much, urban consumer numbers have risen.

In short, crucial problems are (i) bad slum conditions, (ii) population growth without commerce or industry to give employment, and (iii) lack of financial resources and decisive planning in a context of poor governance hampered in places by conflict.

There were no large towns in pre-colonial Africa, and the great urban populations of today only began to grow with the era of national independences around the early 1960s. Colonial authorities in general did not encourage unemployed or 'vagrants' to settle in or around towns, nevertheless there were often numerous informal settlements (for example, near Lusaka). Iliffe[6] wrote of Africa in the 1950s that, 'Fearing unrest and nationalism, and animated by the reforming zeal of the post-war world, colonial governments encouraged "responsible" trade unions, instituted minimum wages, and sought to create skilled, settled, better-paid labour forces.' But jobs were far short of the numbers seeking them and there occurred 'a rapid increase in unemployment, both structural and conjunctural. Mechanisation, a recession in the late 1950s, rapid growth in the number of young adults, an expansion of primary schooling, and in some cases land shortage in the countryside all contributed.'

As new national administrations encouraged city growth, country people flocked into them seeking jobs, and urban populations rapidly increased. Failing to find accommodation in crowded centres, informal near-town migrant settlements expanded everywhere. Shanty housing was constructed from mud or cement bricks and any materials available, without overall planning and often without formal tenure of land. Such growth outpaced planned urbanisation by far. Similarly, slum-upgrading projects by the World Bank and NGOs could not keep pace and left vast majorities of poor behind.

In early years of the independence era the most important reason for urban poverty derived, ironically, from the increase in urban wages and food subsidies favoured by governments: the so-called 'urban bias', which attracted people into towns. It also encouraged employers to replace workers by machinery, leading to the unemployment, overcrowding, and ancillary problems which the authorities had intended to prevent. Initial cultural dislocation on arrival in the city was accompanied by difficulty in making a living. In these ways, towns produced new forms of poverty; in the words of Iliffe,[6] 'proletarianisation, unemployment, prostitution, and delinquency supplemented older forms of incapacitation, servitude, and hunger, so towns pioneered the transition in the nature of poverty'.

Demographic factors played a substantial part. The period coincided with a phase of high fertility and declining infant mortality over many SSA countries. Population structure was thereby shifted between 1965 and 1980 towards age groups most likely to migrate. Immigrant flows continued in some cities even after economic conditions worsened in the 1980s. This was, at least in part, because rural agriculture was depressed.[11]

After an era when 'modernisation' had been the dominant paradigm (see Chapter 13), African economies in the 1980s and 90s came under the hammer of structural adjustment polices (SAP) advocated by the IMF and World Bank (Chapter 15). These policies reduced urban bias incentives and brought in a package of measures such as privatisation of state enterprises, reduction of public sector ownership and spending, devaluation of the currency and removal of food subsidies and import controls. The economic outcomes of these measures were not good – cutbacks in urban services, soaring prices and decline in real wages, collapse of in-country manufacturing, capital flight, and a steep fall in numbers of state employees and the better-off, salaried class. In effect, SAP resulted in sharply diminished control of an indebted state over its own economy, and it led to deeper poverty and inequality in African cities throughout the 1980s and 1990s.[1] The effects have continued in places well after this period, which unfortunately coincided with protracted drought, rising oil prices, soaring interest rates, falling commodity prices and rising international debt.[7]

In general, one can say that since the colonial era the cities of SSA have undergone three broad economic phases: (i) the 1960s–70s when newly independent governments led development and encouraged migration to cities, (ii) the SAP era, characterised by mainly negative outcomes of the neo-liberal economic programme, and (iii) post-structural adjustment, when cities have grown chiefly by reproduction within them, and also by in-migration and aggregation with nearby towns; leadership by the state was muted relative to pre-SAP times. There has been little economic growth. Urbanisation was a phenomenon of modern times, a social process deeply affecting the people of SSA countries. It was largely poverty-driven as the rural poor sought a better life in cities.

As well, the process has been widely conflict-driven, as refugees seek the relative safety of a city. One out of three countries in Africa has experienced or is still experiencing armed conflict, resulting in massive dislocations of populations. Angola, for example, was forcibly urbanised by a quarter of a century of war (1975–2002), and now a majority live in cities.[7] Just as devastating in human terms have been the activities of uncontrolled bands of armed militia or ex-soldiers terrorising vast areas of country not under effective government, for example in the Democratic Republic of Congo (DRC), Dafur in the Sudan, Angola, Mozambique and Somalia (Chapter 10). Kinshasa, the capital of the DRC, is an extreme example; after decades of disorder the city has grown hugely and chaotically. In general, reintegration of refugee influxes has proved difficult despite massive international aid, e.g., Burundi (Chapter 6).

Dislocations of population have also occurred through expulsions of aliens, most usually connected with political awareness of national identity after independence. Notable was the massive expulsion at short notice of some three million people from Nigeria in 1983. The migrants included a million Ghanaians, many of whom, on returning to Accra, caused considerable congestion leading to relocation of many out of that city.[12]

Adding to distress was the great drought in Africa in the period 1968–85. Fluctuating across the area from the Western Sahel countries to Somalia, and from the Democratic Republic of Congo to Tanzania, it was certainly the worst drought of the twentieth century. Not since the 1830s or possibly the 1740s had the region experienced such a natural catastrophe. Wars, of course, exacerbated famine conditions that had arisen from drought, and created flows of refugees running into millions. Iliffe[6] (pp.251–253) mentions numbers of refugee or 'mass distress migrants' in Sub-Saharan Africa reaching twelve million over the two decades 1964–84.

More recently, prime cities have grown chiefly by natural increase in them. While birth rates remain high the cities keep on growing substantially (about 3% p.a.), even as smaller towns have begun to absorb most immigration. A new urban form, the mega-city, is developing in several places by coalescence of one or more major cities with satellite towns; for example, the growing urban conurbation or 'corridor' along the Guinea Coast of West Africa, incorporating Accra and Lagos.[2] (Incidentally this will envelop the lower Volta region, which was remotely rural when my wife and I lived there in 1955–56; see Chapter 1). Nairobi has added vast peripheral slums by accretion. These extensive regions of population ('centres' would be misleading) differ from the massive urban proliferation around Johannesburg (Gauteng Province), in that the latter is centred on substantial commerce and industry (mining).

Slums have presented enormous logistic and economic problems, larger than city authorities could cope with at the rate they grew. Yet demographers say Africa is still at an early stage of urbanisation, with the bulk of growth yet to come; population curves are predicted to climb steeply for several decades more.

Analogies with rural–urban migration in the industrial revolution of nineteenth-century Europe are inappropriate, because in SSA industry has not developed to provide employment (except in the mining industries of Witwatersrand and the Zambian Copperbelt). Cities have not developed through opportunity for employment; they have not turned out to be the hoped-for 'engines of economic growth'. Migrants from farming backgrounds are, economically speaking, undifferentiated labour. The majority must work for veritable subsistence in casual jobs or in petty buying and selling or work of a service or repair nature.

Employment

Given the circumstances, it almost goes without saying that training for employment in artisan trades or blue-collar skills should figure high on the list of government educational priorities in order to build work forces. Yet it appears not. In the international globalisation–growth–poverty debate in universities and development research bodies, the subject of employment is relatively neglected. The pro-globalisation lobby, on one side, takes the standard neo-liberal approach, regarding labour as an economic factor like capital or land. Informal sectors in cities have become dumping grounds for surplus populations in low-wage services and trade. The rise of the informal sector is in accord with liberalisation. On the other side, anti-globalists have focused on international labour standards more relevant to the formal sector of developing cities. It is unfortunate that more attention has not been given to training in a range of trades and to drawing trainees from the informal sector which, by evidence of its multitude of small livelihoods, must contain many with practical aptitudes.

I have mentioned here and there employing men in fisheries work (e.g., Chapters 1 and 3), and from this experience I was struck by the truth of the observations of Ishumi[13] on education, especially regarding the way villagers see the potential of cities to provide jobs and advancement. His case may be put as follows: Most city migrants are men predominately between 16 and 20 years old, many of whom have passed through primary school. Their mindset typically carries the following misconceptions:

- Employment is something that can be accorded as a gift or present.

- Jobs are naturally there. Those who get them are lucky and privileged.
- Good, well-paid jobs are obtained in the city, where big employers live.
- The 'good life' is to be found and lived only in the city.
- Getting a job is associated with classroom learning and passing examinations.
- A regular salaried job is the most desirable.

Traditional attitudes are reflected here in the expectation of acceptance accorded within a client–patron relationship. The other assumptions seem to village youth quite logically connected. They also assume that an ability to speak and write basic English qualifies them for jobs. Of economic life and wage earning they are largely ignorant. Government and mission schools have turned out millions of such underqualified youngsters for many decades. An additional two years in some line of technical training would widen their chances and choice of employment.

Migrants usually first head to a relative, or one with even distant kinship, who by custom would be obliged to try and provide initial help – lodging, food, advice. Frustration and disappointment follow in the search for jobs and, over a perhaps prolonged period, the migrants become 'de-villagised' and 'de-ruralised'. They learn to survive in a very competitive environment, commonly working for a percentage of the earnings of some petty trading business. Many fall into crime-related activity.[14]

Employers are accustomed to an excess of applicants for jobs. In the informal sector jobs are usually casual and lowly paid manual ones. Except for those with special skills, newcomers are on the market simply as undifferentiated labour. Primary education, which had made them dissatisfied with village farming or fishing life in the first place and susceptible to the allure of cities, has not given them the means for survival in cities. Even where commercial and industrial job opportunities exist, immigrants without some skills may not be employable.

The informal sector increases less by real productivity than by sub-division of already occupied livelihood niches, in what have been called 'ubiquitous and vicious networks of micro-exploitation ... the poor exploiting the very poor'.[7] Remarkably, in many cities the informal sector has continued to grow at 4% to 5% (e.g., Nairobi and Dar es Salaam) despite low employment opportunity.[8]

Clearly, in the passage from traditional to modern, sub-Saharan cities have gone through very difficult times. Neither personal income nor GNP per capita has changed much in most countries since independence in the 1960s (even in resource-rich states, such as Nigeria).[15] Recent debt relief agreements on international loans have lightened economic burdens, but the needs for employment and for improvement in slum conditions remain acute. Hopes for a rational future were placed, at an earlier stage (1960s and 1970s), in developing productive links between the formal and informal sectors. But after formal sectors were reduced by 'structural adjustment', and since industry did not develop, cities simply reproduced spatial patterns of inequality and social fragmentation. Urban spaces tend to be abandoned to the homeless, and the poor subsist as best they can; among the very poor epidemic malnutrition is common. The better-off share protected enclaves. With mushrooming slums and dire poverty, the future of such cities is speculative.

Futures

At a press conference held by officials of UN-HABITAT in New York in October 2008,[16] it was stated, with particular reference to Africa, that 'the least developed countries had premature urbanisation, meaning that moving to the cities was accompanied neither by rising agricultural productivity nor rural development, thus making those countries dependent on international trade and food aid, without which they would not be able to feed their cities'.

One sees in these places converging intractable difficulties and intensifying problems; relentlessly building population pressure, looming food crisis,[17,18] stagnant agriculture, growing dependency on international aid, widespread capacity for violence with imported weapons and, not least, HIV AIDS. To cover all this by the word 'crisis' is a derisive understatement. Global concern needs to focus more sharply, and more urgently find new ways to assist. Supplying parcels of money and technical advice have obviously not been enough. Material assistance in the form of supplying city infrastructure – water, sanitation, roads, houses – would be tangible help.

It is difficult to imagine actual situations if and when the demographic predictions come to pass. One cannot connect population numbers with economic prospects. To extrapolate population trends in terms of slum equivalents is *reductio ad absurdum*. For example, what economic miracle will sustain slum populations when, in two decades, they have doubled and half of sub-Saharan Africa lives in slums?

If cities are still economically unproductive, and if national agriculture cannot provide enough food, the aid bill will obviously grow immense. In the context of human life, more miserable conditions in slums will mean tragic increases in deprivation. We do not know what factors limit slum size or the theoretical maximum slum cities could reach. (Davis[7] suggests that 'growth rates of specific cities may brake abruptly as they encounter the frictions of size and congestion', citing as a possible example the decline, as against predictions, of Mexico City.) Already conditions in the mega-cities Lagos (c.10 million) and Kinshasa (c.9 million) are almost unbelievably bad. Consider that Kinshasa has no water-borne sanitation at all, and two-thirds of its population is malnourished.[19]

There is a more optimistic scenario; the argument that in recent times patterns of migration have changed in response to urban economic declines. The urbanisation process has consequently slowed, and circular migration between town and country is becoming the preferred survival strategy. The main points outlined below are from Potts,[8] (who cites numerous other authors).

Some SSA countries are presently not becoming more urban, or only slowly so. In these it seems population growth has slowed. Almost a third of the cities have grown more slowly than the respective national populations. This seems related to reduced rural–urban migration; indeed return migration to villages has increased. In some cases predicted levels of urban growth have been revised downwards. For example, the projected size of the largest SSA city, Lagos, was reduced from 14.5 million in 1994 to 8.7 million in 2001; it now continues to grow at 3% per year from internal natural increase. (On the other hand, Nairobi and Dar es Salaam have not declined and continue to grow at 4–5%.) But current general trends imply that future urbanisation will be less than usually assumed, and it will be largely through natural increase not migration. In some cities de-urbanisation is indicated by demographic and economic indices, and it seems populations may stabilise below the 50% transition point (urban–rural ratio).

Fertility remains high in the cities. Urban women in Africa have been thought to have lower fertility rates than rural women, but in many cases urban fertility has proved to be higher. However, it should be borne in mind that, up to and into the 90s, high urban fertility was probably due to youthful and fertile age profiles. By the same token average death rates were less.

Being sensitive to economic change, migrations are important indicators of crises in urban poverty. Strong migration shifts were associated with poorer economic conditions between 1960 and 2000, particularly the decline around 1980. In Africa as a whole, the net contribution of in-migration to urban growth was 40% in the 1960s, and 25% in the 1980s. From the 80s, city in-migration kept declining, and circulation to rural villages increased.

Circular migration probably results mostly from negative livelihood changes among the poorest who have no economic safety net. Some farmers migrate to small peri-urban settlements to have better access to services, markets and transport, while households that can straddle urban and rural economies improve their welfare. Assessments of population movement generally assume political stability, but in fact conflicts have strongly influenced migration patterns and still do in many parts of SSA.

In sum, in this scenario future cities may not simply grow by continuous accretion of slums, but would develop closer sustaining links with rural hinterlands. The informal circular migration presently being driven by desperate urban poverty could be made more efficient by foreign aid directed towards improving road and rail systems. There is a strong case for developing industrial farming near cities as a state undertaking.

Notes and references

1. United Nations Human Settlements Programme (UN HABITAT) (2003). *The Challenge of Slums: Global Report on Human Settlements.* Nairobi, Kenya.
2. UN-HABITAT Report (2008). *State of the World's Cities: Regional Update, Nairobi, Kenya.*
3. Rakodi, C. (2004). *African towns and cities: Powerhouses of economic development or slums of despair?* 'City Futures' Conference, University of Illinois, Chicago, July 2004.)
4. Auclair. C. (2005). Charting a framework for sustainable urban centres in Africa. *UN Chronicle Online.* http://www.un.org/Pubs/chronicle/2005/issue2/O2O5
5. International Development Research Center (IDRC) (2008). Informal employment, gender and poverty: The informal economy. http://www.idrc.ca/en/ev-83643-201-1-DO_TOPIC.html
6. Iliffe, J. (1987). *The African Poor.* Cambridge University Press.
7. Davis, M. (2006). *Planet of Slums.* Verso, London.
8. Potts, D. (2008). *Recent trends in rural-urban and urban-rural migration in sub-Saharan Africa.* Department of Geography, King's College, London. http://www.kcl.ac.uk/schools/sspp/geography/research/epd/working.html
9. Potts, D. (2006). Urban growth and urban economies in Eastern and Southern Africa: trends and prospects. In: D. Bryceson and D. Potts (eds). *African Urban Economies: Viability, Vitality or Vitiation of Major Cities in East and Southern Africa?* Palgrave/Macmillan, pp.67–104.
10. Disproportionate numbers of males departing as migrants to cities had serious socio-economic effects in the villages they left. To quote Iliffe (1987), 'The weak household, bereft of able-bodied male labour, has probably been the most common source of poverty throughout Africa's recoverable history.'
11. Verheye, W.H. (2000). Food Production or Food Aid? *Journal of Finance and Development, International Monetary Fund.* Dec. 2000.

12. International Institute for Labour Studies (2006). *Social exclusion and Africa south of the Sahara.* Ch. 4, p.12. International Labour Organisation.
13. Ishumi, A.G. (2008). Pitfalls and successes towards creating self-employment opportunities for youth: The story and experiences in Eastern and Southern Africa: 1960-2000. *Transactions Internationale Zeitschrift für Kulturwissenschaften,* 17/2008.
14. Hart, K. (2000). Kinship, contract, and trust: The economic organisation of migrants in an African slum. In: Gambetta, D. (ed.) *Trust: Making and Breaking Cooperative Relations.* Ch.6, pp.176–193. Department of Sociology, University of Oxford.
15. World Bank, *Nigeria Country Brief.* September 2003.
16. http://www.un.org/News/briefings/docs/2008/081027_Habitat.doc.htm
17. Djurfeldt, G., Holmen, H., Jirstrom, M. & Larsson, R. (2005). *African Food Crisis.* CABI Publishing Co., Oxford, UK.
18. Adesina, A.A. (2009). *Africa's Food Crisis: Conditioning trends and global development policy.* International Association of Agricultural Economists Conference, Beijing, China (August 2000).
19. Davis (2006), p.2 & p.192.

17

Viewpoints

> Development is a process, which in the West took several hundred years, involving changes in ideology and a re-organisation of social life. It also resulted in horrible dislocations which led to the deaths of millions in famines, disease epidemics, wars and revolts. It is a process frustrated by the fertility of a subsistence rural population embedded in ethics of loyalty and status which have their roots in the agrarian revolution of the Neolithic Age some 10,000 years ago.
>
> Waters, p.232.

> Successful development and the introduction of new techniques ... demand cultural change and the adoption of an outlook on life much like the outlook that created these techniques in the first place.
>
> Leistner, p.80.

Economic windows

It is time to reflect on the dynamics of the present situation. We have looked at human circumstances in SSA changing from traditional towards modern conditions over the past half-century. Economic development is slow and there is deep poverty. Populations are exploding. Until the early 1980s development was generally taken to mean turning traditional rural societies into industrial modern ones and, as I have described, the poor were to be advanced to higher productivity and better living standards. But from the 1980s the emphasis of foreign aid shifted to relieving extreme poverty in the poorest countries. This change in motivation no doubt reflected in some degree the fact that certain countries were simply not growing (58 countries in the world, 70% of them in SSA). They now constitute about one billion people, the so-called 'bottom billion' of the world's current six and a half, living on less than one US dollar a day.[1]

We have alluded to the 'structural adjustment' epoch, starting in the late

1970s, in which the International Monetary Fund was the main practitioner of market liberalisation. From that time, conditionality was imposed on loans to countries, which strongly influenced their development policies. The IMF was one of several financial institutions together known as the Washington Consensus (the US Treasury, the Federal Reserve Board and the World Bank). They identified with policies of market fundamentalism, emphasis on trade (more than science-led growth), and reduction in the leadership role of the national state in development.[2] The 'Consensus' held that bad governance was the underlying cause of slow development in Africa.

It is now apparent that before market-led economic growth can flourish in Africa, great expansion in infrastructure and increase in human skills would be necessary. The Washington Consensus policies were in many ways inimical to African circumstances. A more comprehensive framework for the process of growth is needed. Millennium Development Goals (MDGs) set up in 2000 with international commitment (e.g., halving world poverty by 2015) seemed to represent a milestone of progress.[3] But at time of writing (2010), opinion differs as to whether the concept of scheduled poverty alleviation goals is the best way to assist Africa in achieving its 'Great Transformation'. Will the MDGs ultimately promote endogenous development?

Economists presently stress the importance of poverty traps in preventing economic progress in the bottom billion countries. There is little doubt also that civil insecurity in many places deters vital foreign investment.[1] But individual economists differ widely on the specifics of the traps,[4] and on whether and how much financial aid is needed to break out of them. Opinions also differ on the best ways to reach Millennium Development Goals. One set of views advocates much more financial aid (average annual assistance equivalent to at least 20% to 30% of country GDP through to 2015[3]), while another believes financial aid alone cannot rescue countries from certain of the traps.[1]

Yet another opinion is that Africa does not suffer so much from financial shortage as from chronic inadequacy of human societal and institutional capital (HSIC).[5] The argument runs that aid to Africa has not worked because HSIC poses a binding constraint, and the deficiency has been of deep consequence. Again and again in the past half-century, attempts to exploit natural resources and develop industry in SSA have failed because progressive ideas and demonstrated techniques did not take root and spread as it was assumed they would. Right now, progress in the Millennium Development Project (see Chapter 15) depends on the successful scaling-up of modern improvements brought to selected villages, which means in fact takeover by villagers. If this does not happen, MDP will go the way of numerous rural development projects of the past.

It has been suggested that HSIC in the forms of managers, technocrats and skilled labour should be imported from outside the continent, to constitute a permanent international civil service for Africa. In particular, skills are needed to make industrial organisation work properly. While institutional 'capacity building' is a familiar component of development projects, this suggestion to boost human capital by systematic international recruitment goes much further. Without more human skills Africa cannot develop, regardless of how much financial aid is supplied. Capacity building as an attempt from outside to build institutions operated by a local educated elite may not be feasible at anything like the required rate. To quote Leistner,[6] 'Half a century has demonstrated that outsiders cannot "develop" another people.'

In the long run, change in village livelihoods, and employment of skills in industry, are brought about when the bulk of a population adopt new ways of thinking and doing. Development really only happens when that threshold is crossed.

Another major obstacle to progress in many parts of SSA is civil security. Stability must be maintained reliably for private investment to flourish. Outbreaks of violence in past decades have been devastatingly bad for business. So it has been proposed that in cases where security is threatened and governance is bad there should be a means of deploying short-term military intervention from outside. The concept is of an international rapid reaction force, which could, for example, guarantee against armed coups and insurrections.

These proposals for a permanent international service and a stand-by military force might seem extreme, contradicting ideals of national sovereignty. However, convincing rationales can be made that they are necessary for progress in countries that have long been economically stagnant and prone to government malpractice or to outbreaks of violence.

Another proposal is to persuade governments in a region to commit to a system of inter-country legal agreements or charters, containing 'norms enshrined in international standards and codes'.[1] The power of such protocols can be great, as shown for example in countries of the EU in recent decades.

It is useful to recognise that nowadays there is not merely a 'Third World' lagging behind the rest, but a distinct category, the countries containing the bottom billion, defined not only by extreme poverty but also by having made no progress in the past three or more decades. In these cases, foreign aid has perhaps passed the point of diminishing returns and become just a holding operation.[1] The future cleavage of humanity may be between this 'left behind' category and the rest. Of course, many poor remain in countries that are making economic progress (e.g., 30% of India's population are very poor). But narrowing the target of foreign assistance upon the bottom billion and shifting the focus of assistance from direct aid to other strategies offers more hope of improvement: specific strategies recommended are easing trade access by the poorest countries to developed countries, bringing about better civil security, and inducing more foreign investment.

In brief, economic opinions have swung away from the Washington Consensus, yet disagree substantially as to best ways forward for promoting development. There is danger of poverty alleviation being confused with development, which of course should aim at self-sufficiency. It has been said development agencies should stop acting like aid agencies (MDGs are really poverty alleviation goals[5]) and should instead fulfil their task of spurring development. There is widespread disillusionment among donor nations and lending institutions about low achievements from the many hundreds of billions of dollars donated or loaned to SSA countries in the past four or five decades. Wastage by capital flight from Africa ($50 billion/year[5]), and corruption are real issues, despite the fact that all agree in principle that finance must be made to serve the people. Correct macro-decisions are important at this moment, especially on priority in aid allocation – whether it should be given chiefly to rural development or to generating urban productivity, bearing in mind that city-dwellers will be in the majority within two decades

Here, of course, we are not speaking about humanitarian emergency relief operations (although these figure largest of all in public perceptions and media; for example, there is currently a lively international debate about corrupt large-scale diversion of food and finance in recipient countries). Humanitarian aid by richer countries to relieve acute poverty, hunger and disease is a moral imperative. But it is also imperative to ensure supplies effectively reach those intended.

Another part of the development problem is that aid agencies still seem to persist in believing that only technology and economic science matter. For long, the development discourse in Africa has been conducted practically exclusively in econometric terms, although development of the poorest might also be said to be the world's biggest moral dilemma, and moreover social and cultural aspects have been relatively neglected. Yet 'it is man who is ultimately responsible for progress or decline in the economic, political and general circumstances of a people'.[6] The point was made by Pope John-Paul II in a Papal Encyclical in 1987 (para.15),[7] which said: 'Modern underdevelopment is not only economic, but also cultural, political and simply human ... at this point we have to ask ourselves if the sad reality of today might not be, at least in part, the result of a too narrow idea of development, that is, a mainly economic one.' He added (para.17), 'it should be obvious that development either becomes shared in common by every part of the world or it undergoes a process of regression even in zones marked by constant progress. This tells us a great deal about the nature of authentic development: either all the nations of the world participate, or it will not be true development.'

Will African transition follow the western model?

May I return, for an example, to the story of the fishery project on Lake Tanganyika, Projet Pêche (see Chapters 6 and 13). Early in the life of the project the UNDP Representative in Burundi called to make a routine check on progress. Just at that point, international and local staff had all been recruited, equipment was on site, the new project vessel lay in Bujumbura harbour – we were all ready to go. After the inspection and my explanations, his last comment seemed curious, though delivered kindly. He said, 'You know, you will never move faster than the country lets you.'

It seemed he might be hinting that I was unrealistic in my description of what we planned to do. Perhaps I'd sounded over-ambitious about our operations? Or was he perhaps indicating we might be held back by quirky government policies? Later I understood his words: I should have known his meaning from previous disappointing experience in developing country situations; obviously, similar general restraints were likely here too. But I had been seduced by the purposive bureaucracy of my new employer – FAO in Rome. Having been at that big organisation for a couple of months, I'd probably started to believe the new project would indeed function like clockwork, as set out in the scheduled steps of the plan of operations. But the veteran Representative knew very well that success depended less on the technical and management know-how the project could bring, than on the extent to which our messages would be understood and adopted by the local society; that is, whether what we demonstrated would be absorbed and would spread among the bulk of the populace. He was right, of course. Development in such situations means a general mind-shift.

If progress in Africa can be compared with European and American experience in the nineteenth and early twentieth centuries,[8] then a 'Great Transformation' is currently happening that will similarly be accompanied by prolonged difficulty and distress – poverty, slums and loss of cultural certainties.[9] The future will be shaped by the power of the international marketplace. The following conclusions and implications arise from this viewpoint (I follow Waters' work in Tanzania,[8] and his deductions from classical social studies, notably by Polanyi,[9] and Weber[10]).

The subsistence world – production for family and kin – is inherently incompatible with the modern world, where production of all kinds is for an impersonal marketplace. In the new society, social life no longer orders economic livelihoods but economics comes to order social life. The future lies in differentiated production and market-organised distribution and not in agrarian subsistence – it involves turning peasants into industrial workers. The key to development is the differentiation of labour (which can sometimes be helped by education), plus acquisition of an 'unteachable spirit of capitalism' (in which investment and saving is held to be of status value for its own sake). Development of commerce and industry must take place in cities, well connected to each other and the outside world. To build the city, older scattered forms of settlement must shrink and virtually disappear.

This journey from subsistence to modern economy entails social and ecological transformation, which takes place across decades and sometimes centuries. Abandoning old ways is an irrevocable step. The way forward is to 'facilitate the transition of industrious peasants'[8] into consumers and producers in the general marketplace. This must be done by encouraging young people to enter the differentiated labour market which is usually only found in the city.

Development projects have not been primarily directed at transforming agrarian societies into new ones, but mainly with alleviating rural poverty, health and education deficiencies (making the assumption that modernisation with new attitudes will somehow take place in the process). However, although agricultural stimulation policies help to increase production (by fertiliser, seed stock, irrigation, transport, etc.) and to feed the population, possibly reaching national self-sufficiency, they do not provide an entry point into capital markets. Agrarian villages cannot be transformed into a new society simply by making them richer and healthier. Neither can the gulf between life in modern and in African states be bridged until the undifferentiated labour of the countryside becomes urban differentiated labour. In the meantime, 'the continually growing subsistence world cannot exist without the largesse of the broader world market which every few years stops an epidemic with the provision of modern drugs, or blocks a famine with relief food'.[8] The task of adequately feeding populations in need is frustrated by the fertility of rural populations embedded in ethics of loyalty and status.

Transformation has everywhere occurred in the context of coercive pressures from social and political forces, which move rural peasantry from subsistence to market organisation and industry. Development implicitly seeks to create a populace disciplined to the marketplace for both production and consumption. Foreign aid cannot continue indefinitely to support national budgets. The notion that relief programmes are part of a relief-development continuum is a mistake.

In short, this vision predicts that economic development in SSA countries must take place within the wider, regional or world, marketplace. It holds out little hope for smallholder farming. Great cultural change is inevitable, and on the way the process will be disruptive with much suffering. Relief and poverty alleviation are just that and not permanent solutions. The key to development will lie in the differentiation of labour. The Great Transformation must take place in Africa in ways similar to what happened on other continents.

Social alternatives

One hesitates to use the word 'alternative' in a social context because of its common association with eccentric lifestyles. Here I use it simply to question whether a market-orientated industrial way of economic life is the only model for Africa, or even an ideal one. Europe and America had to find their own ways from the early Industrial Revolution to the norms of modern life. In contrast, African countries started more lately from their own traditional bases, and are trying to follow an abstract economic model derived in already industrialised places. Moreover, the African development process has already shown important differences from western experience. Notably, population numbers have risen more dramatically by natural increase (immigration played a relatively larger role in America) to the point where the danger of outreaching food resources is approaching. Second, rampant urban concentration is not based on industry. These features, population pressure and unproductive urbanisation, would not have been predicted sixty years ago to become major problems. They simply happened without much planning or control soon after the continent fractionated into many sovereign states. The question arises whether other major aspects of the transformation process will be significantly different from the Western one? For example, one might foresee uneven development between African countries accentuated even further, or inter-country conflict persisting with areas given over to chaos.

In actual circumstances of poor living standards, aid dependence, unequal distribution of wealth, low levels of education and in many places poor governance, the basic question arises whether conventional, market-orientated industrial models are appropriate? To put the problem in very simple terms, should development in Africa be directed at entering modernity through the economic marketplace? Or should effort primarily be directed to building competent civil administration at district and village level, and boosting agriculture by improved methods towards self-sufficiency?

There are considerable hindrances in the way of Africa exporting itself out of its agricultural crisis and diversifying into manufactured exports. These include barriers created by rich-country protectionism in the case of many potential exports; e.g., artificially low prices in the world cereals market due to US and European subsidies to their own farmers. Further, rich-country dumping of their own surpluses diminishes incentives for African producers and manufacturers. The rapid rise in Asian exporting power, from India and China particularly, now makes it more difficult for African would-be exporters to gain entry into competitive world markets. Solutions to these difficult external constraints must depend to a large extent on political strategies and leadership by institutions outside Africa.[11]

Obstacles are not only external and economic. The reality of how politics is actually practised in Africa is a major binding constraint. Typical of many SSA countries are clientelistic politics and patrimonialism, which operate to safeguard the advantaged positions of elite groups; consequently efficiency is reduced and employment of resources limited so that development remains trapped.[12] Such crude political regimes prefer to continue a status quo that keeps them in power. In such circumstances, government at district or regional level is often weak and under-financed, as it is commonly perceived by central government as a base for opposing opinions and thus a potential political threat.[13] Foreign aid in such conditions may in fact be nugatory, except for humanitarian purposes.

Despite the difficulties, ***building viable local economies in a rural background*** may be the most feasible model for those countries whose economies are stagnant or declining (the 'bottom billion'). Among positive considerations are the following.

There appears to be scope in Africa for a state-driven, market-mediated and small-farmer-based Green Revolution (according to an international study *The African Food Crisis*).[14] Aid agencies can assist multiple local developments directly and tangibly (the MDP approach). Social structures in small communities are more compatible with the traditional mind than the chaotic competitive life existing in new cities. If the things people strive to attain in cities – food security and variety, education, and particularly jobs – could be provided in rural communities, the drive to urbanise would lose some of its deceptive appeal. Compared to present relatively unchanging rural conditions, and the dismal prospects of slum life in cities, a slower synthesis of the traditional and modern in improved small communities holds out hope of better living conditions. Progressive local government at district level along with agrarian improvement are the keys to developing viable small communities.

On the other hand, it is difficult to see what remedies can realistically be applied to the vast awful slums of new African cities (see Chapter 16) in foreseeable circumstances of government. Masses of slum-dwellers, desperate to make a living, do not fall easily into categories that can be helped by foreign aid. Aid dependency is not a permanent solution, and in any case major international lending institutions have not, in the past few decades, shown much understanding of the nature of African urban poverty.[2] Urban labour pools desperate for jobs are extremely vulnerable to exploitation. Theoretically, capitalism in the form of unregulated growth of global markets is inherently unstable, and is unlikely to help these societies become rationally organised with decent living standards.[15,16] Can we really recommend global capitalism to bottom billion countries? And can we do so at a time when it is becoming very evident that environmental depletion and pollution are changing the way the rest of the world must think and live?

Socially aware economists, like Herman Daly, point out that the developed world must cease to pursue growth – that is, quantitative expansion – and seek instead qualitative improvement.

There has of course been much ideological support in the past for the concept of small-scale non-industrial economies on grounds of social justice and self-sufficiency. The Victorian thinker Ruskin is still read, even after the rises and falls of various kinds and extremes of socialism in the twentieth century. In heavily populated India, Gandhi formulated an ethical social system based on village economies virtually independent of the market economy and big industry. His humane people-centred views were entirely different from contemporary mainstream economics, in that they stressed community welfare and self-sufficiency. These ideas left a pervasive legacy. Ireland's long-time premier, de Valera, had a similar vision of a society of village communities, served by efficient local government and linked by a common religious culture.

Such prophets have understood that economic mechanisms cover only part of the development process; human welfare should surely be the central consideration in applying the science of economics.[17] Humanity itself cannot be regarded merely as 'human capital' within an impersonal economic system. Nor can the customs and viewpoints of peasantry bound to conservative cultures by strong ties be dismissed as irrelevant, because these issues invariably crop up in practical ways and slow down reform. In the past half-century development planning in Africa has been deficient in human aspects of the process, despite the fact that in subsistence societies development is chiefly about social and cultural change. *Social* economics[18] have an important role to play in Africa where traditional culture has centred around survival and community welfare.

Assimilating modern understanding and changing cultural foundations are clearly the most essential and difficult elements in development. SSA countries trying to make the leap into modernity need, above all, a comprehensive shift of mindset; either into the competitive individualistic materialism of the market world of the west, or into some hybrid system closer to the human-centred character of traditional Africa with its concern for harmony and community.[19]

Important questions now are: How can foreign aid help the expanding cities, where most Africans will live within two decades, to become economically productive? Or should foreign aid concentrate on helping build national economies based on viable rural communities?

Summary and conclusions

The many countries of Sub-Saharan Africa reached political independence in the 1960s, but they have remained dependent on foreign aid. Development failure and build-up of aid-dependence has been accompanied by wide poverty.

Concepts of 'development' have changed over the past half-century. Gradual change from traditional rural societies into modern industrial ones was overtaken by the notion of direct modernisation. Neoliberal policies (SAPs) applied in the 1980s and 90s were generally not successful. Premature urbanisation took place on a large scale. Today, emphasis has shifted to relieving extreme poverty in the most destitute countries.

Millennium Development Goals were set in 2000, but despite some progress most of these seem unlikely to be reached – in particular, world poverty will not be halved by 2015. Financial aid for the Millennium Project has not reached the levels pledged. In any case, expert opinions differ on ways forward, and current development strategies may not be on the right track. For instance, the link that has long been assumed between financial aid and economic growth is dubious. Despite foreign aid over half a century, Africa has been getting poorer not richer. Apart from finance, the efficiency with which aid is transferred to the poor needs to be improved.

More fundamentally, foreign finance and technology are not by themselves enough to change traditional subsistence societies to modern states. Cultural mores and customary ways of life, and typically slow rates of adjustment to modern ways are important but underrated factors. Subsistence traditions tend to persist. Changing cultural foundations is the most difficult element in the process of development. Society and culture, whether by default or policy, set the pace of change. Perhaps for this reason, foreign development assistance has been only a holding operation in the very poor African countries. Aid there is subject to diminishing returns at a low level ('when aid reaches about 16% of GDP it more or less ceases to be effective').[1]

The quality of state and local government is an important variable, although this also depends to a large extent on the existing level of development. In other words, an upward causality influences quality of governance. Capacity building is a good concept in broad terms, but restricted to institution building, the benefit is very limited. In 2010 we are still learning the old lesson that capital spending (and investment policies) must be tightly regulated for money to serve the people.

The ideal of western-style development has lured people once protected by self-sufficient survival systems into unviable conditions of life. During the transition period they are vulnerable to extreme poverty, especially in new cities where they have less support from social networks than formerly. Break-up of old social systems makes the passage to a modern lifestyle difficult. Transition requires cultural adaptation. Under present conditions, poverty and immiseration increase with urbanisation. Continuing growth in human numbers is part of the poverty problem.

It is conventional to think of development in terms of employment, better living conditions, improvement in basic civil infrastructures, efficient governance and so forth. The poverty trap concept dominating present economic thinking lends itself to the 'poverty relief solution' of simply supplying more material aid. Poverty relief and economic development are not a continuum; moreover, the problem of development is more profound than can be solved by aid money and technology. The Great Transformation[9] in Africa should be regarded as primarily a cultural transition, restoring the position of people as the point of the economic system.

Notes and references

1. Collier, P. (2008). *The Bottom Billion.* Oxford University Press.
2. Woo, W.T. (2004). Some fundamental inadequacies of The Washington Consensus: misunderstanding the poor by the brightest. In: *Stability, Growth and the Search for a New Development Agenda.* FONDAD Conference, Santiago, Chile. March 2004.
3. McCord, G., Sachs, J.D. & Woo, W.T. (2005). Understanding African Poverty: Beyond the Washington Consensus to the Millennium Development Goals (MDG) Approach. In: *Africa in the Global Economy: External Constraints, Regional Integration, and the Role of the State in Development and Finance.* FONDAD, Pretoria, South Africa. June 2005.
4. 'Poverty traps': In the words of McCord et al. (2005), 'tropical Africa, even in well-governed parts, is stuck in a poverty trap, too poor to achieve robust, high levels of economic growth (and in many places, simply too poor to grow at all). More policy or governance reform, by itself, is not sufficient to overcome this trap'. Specifically they cite:
   - High transport costs and small markets.
   - Low-productivity agriculture.
   - High disease burden.
   - Legacy of adverse geopolitics.
   - Slow diffusion of technology from abroad.

   Using the same general concept, Collier (2008) identifies four principal traps in which the 'bottom billion' nations are stuck: conflict, natural resources, land-locked with bad neighbours, and bad governance.
5. Mistry, P.S. (2005). Reasons for sub-Saharan Africa's development deficit that the Commission for Africa did not consider. *African Affairs, 104*(417) pp.665-678, September, 2005.

   Along the same lines as Mistry regarding the prime importance of human capital, Woo (2004, p.35) surmised that 'physical capital formation for overcoming geographical and health barriers is ... unlikely to be the final nail into the coffin in which poverty would be laid to rest. We believe that only human capital formation can come up with better solutions to the centuries-old problem of poverty and the looming challenge of global ecological Armageddon because there is still a lot about the complexities of science-led growth that we have yet to understand.'
6. Leistner, E. (2005). *African Predicament.* Mlalo Publishers, South Africa.
7. Pope John-Paul II's encyclical of 30 December 1987 was entitled *Sollicitudo rei socialis,* and addresses 'the development of peoples'.
8. Waters, T. (2006). *The Persistence of Subsistence Agriculture: Life beneath the level of the marketplace.* Lexington Books, USA.
9. Polanyi, K. (1945). *Origins of our Time: The Great Transformation.* Victor Gollancz, London.
10. Weber, M. [1904–06] (2002). *The Protestant Ethic and the Spirit of Capitalism.* Roxbury, Los Angeles, USA.
11. Djurfeldt, G., Holmen, H., Jirstrom, M. & Larsson, R. (2005). *The African Food Crisis.* CABI Publishing, Oxfordshire, UK.
12. Taylor, I. (2006). *Challenges facing the Commonwealth and the Millennium Development*

Goals in Africa. Paper prepared for Commonwealth Round Table meeting, Cumberland Lodge, Windsor, England, Jan. 5–6, 2006.

13. UN-HABITAT Report (2008). *State of the World's Cities. Regional Update: Nairobi, Kenya.*
14. Djurfeldt et al. (2005) p.258 state, 'For it [the small-farmer Green Revolution] to progress from a one-legged limp to a two-legged stride requires African governments to get up walking.'
15. Stanfield, J.R. & Carroll, M.C. (2009). The social economics of neoliberal globalization. *Forum for Social Economics, 38*: 1–18.
16. Again, Pope John-Paul II's 1987 *Encyclical* [see Note 7] puts the case well (para 16): '. . . one must denounce the existence of economic, financial and social mechanisms which, although they are manipulated by people, often function almost automatically, thus accentuating the situation of wealth for some and poverty for the rest. These mechanisms, which are maneuvered directly or indirectly by the more developed countries, by their very functioning favour the interests of the people manipulating them and in the end they suffocate or condition the economies of less-developed countries.'
17. Lutz, M. (1999). *Economics for the Common Good.* Routledge.
18. Social economics is generally represented as multidisciplinary. It touches on political economy, sociology, ethics and philosophy. It is concerned with the individual and social aspects of economic problems, with values of the person and a humane community. It sees economics in terms of human rather than material welfare.
19. Brown, L.R. (2009). *Our economic world needs a Copernican shift.* http://www.solveclimate.com

    See also: Brown, L.R. (2001). *Eco-economy: Building an Economy for the Earth.* W.W. Norton, New York.

    Brown has used the word 'Copernican' to describe a fundamental mindshift; he is referring to the revolution needed to understand stressed relationships between the world economy and the earth's ecosystem. 'Copernican' is appropriate because, perhaps more than any other figure in the early Renaissance, Nicolaus Copernicus represented the departure to fundamentally new perceptions of the world. (His thought became part of a wider revolution about the freedom of the human spirit to enquire.) Brown argues that the world economy is outgrowing its natural base, and has to be seen as part of the total environmental system rather than vice versa. Economists and ecologists differ on the relative importance, but Brown's main point is that we need a dramatic change in mind-set to transform unsustainable economies in the developed world into 'eco-economies'. I am suggesting a mindshift of comparable magnitude for African development, even if it does not closely follow the western model.

Index